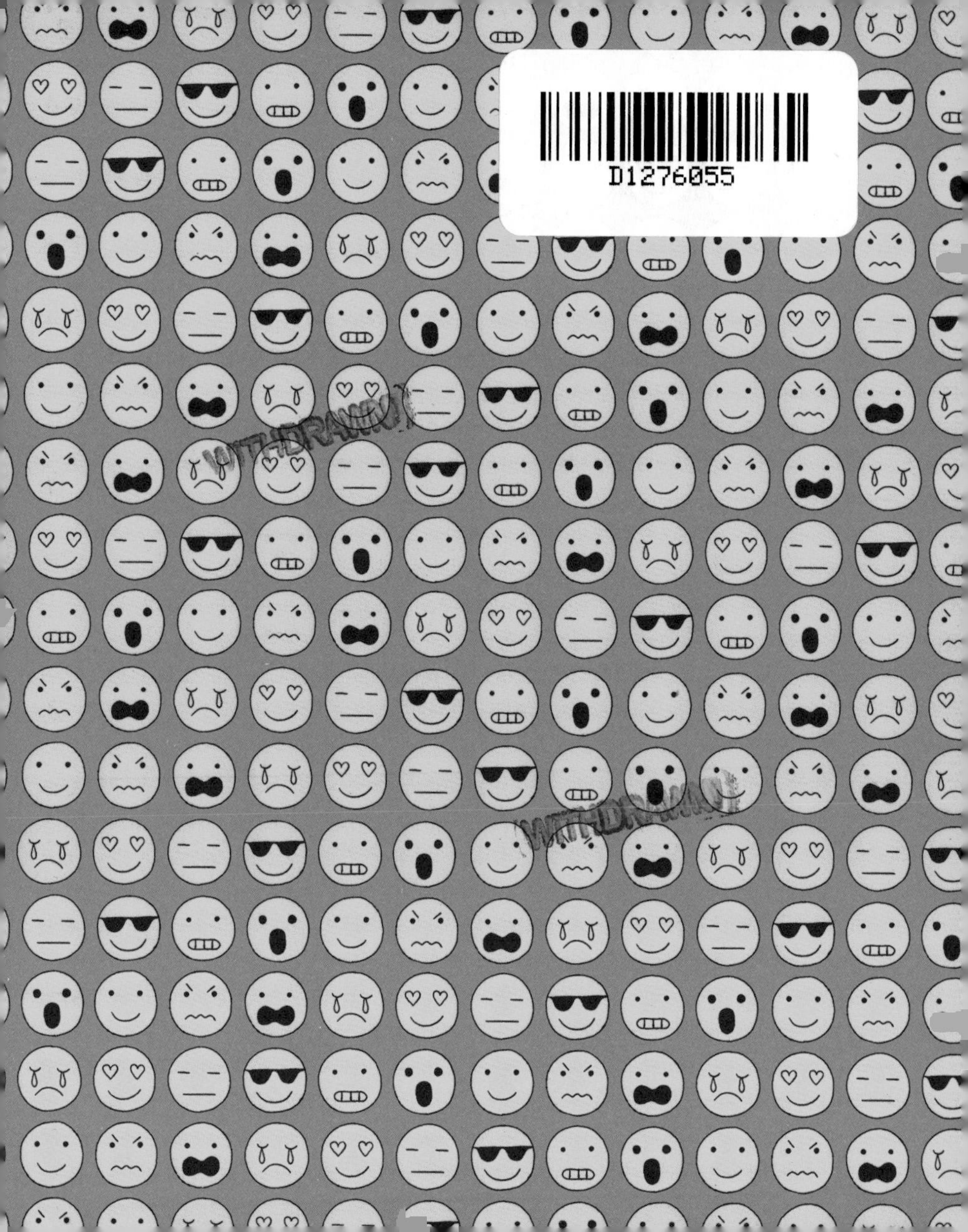

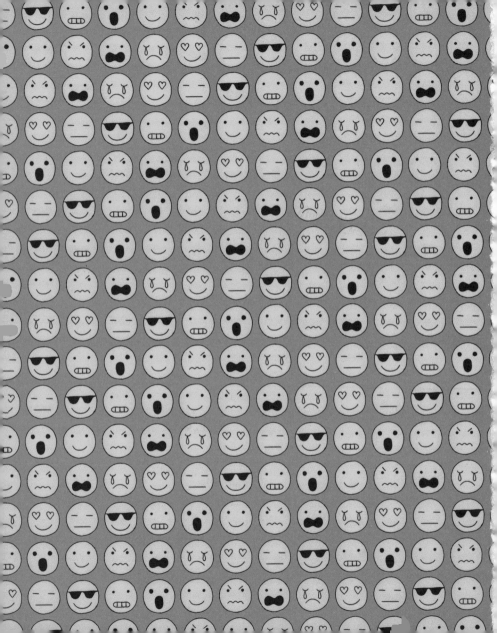

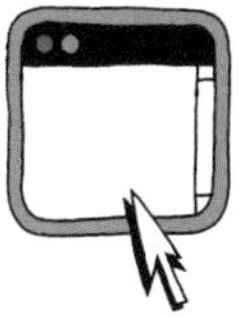

DRAWNANDQUARTERLY.COM

ISBN 978-1-77046-387-5
FIRST EDITION: MARCH 2020
PRINTED IN BOSNIA
10 9 8 7 6 5 4 3 2 1

CATALOGUING DATA AVAILABLE FROM LIBRARY AND ARCHIVES CANADA

PUBLISHED IN THE USA BY DRAWN & QUARTERLY, A CLIENT OF FARRAR, STRAUS AND GIROUX

PUBLISHED IN CANADA BY DRAWN & QUARTERLY, A CLIENT OF RAINCOAST BOOKS

PUBLISHED IN THE UNITED KINGDOM BY DRAWN & QUARTERLY, A CLIENT OF PUBLISHERS GROUP UK

DRAWN & QUARTERLY ACKNOWLEDGES THE SUPPORT OF THE GOVERNMENT OF CANADA AND THE CANADA COUNCIL FOR THE ARTS FOR OUR PUBLISHING PROGRAM.

PRODUCED WITH THE SUPPORT OF THE ONTARIO ARTS COUNCIL

ONTARIO ARTS COUNCIL
CONSEIL DES ARTS DE L'ONTARIO
an Ontario government agency
un organisme du gouvernement de l'Ontario

Canada

FAMILIAR FACE

MICHAEL DEFORGE
DRAWN&QUARTERLY

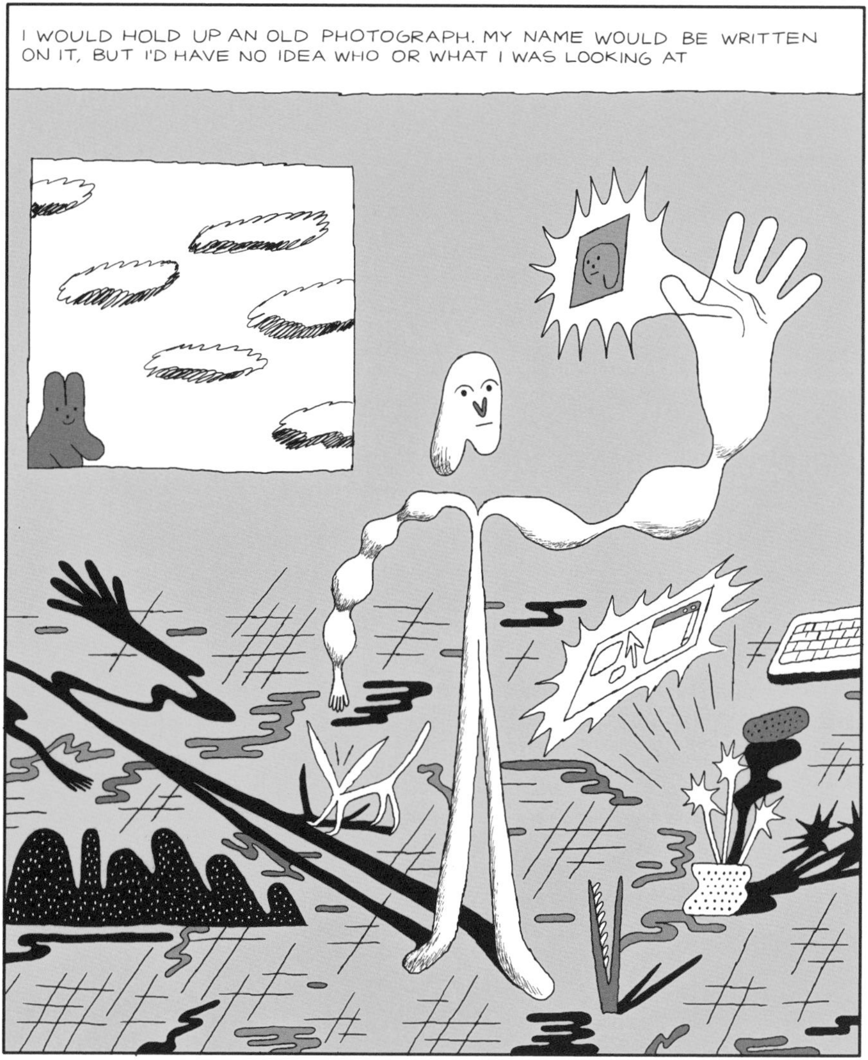
I WOULD HOLD UP AN OLD PHOTOGRAPH. MY NAME WOULD BE WRITTEN ON IT, BUT I'D HAVE NO IDEA WHO OR WHAT I WAS LOOKING AT

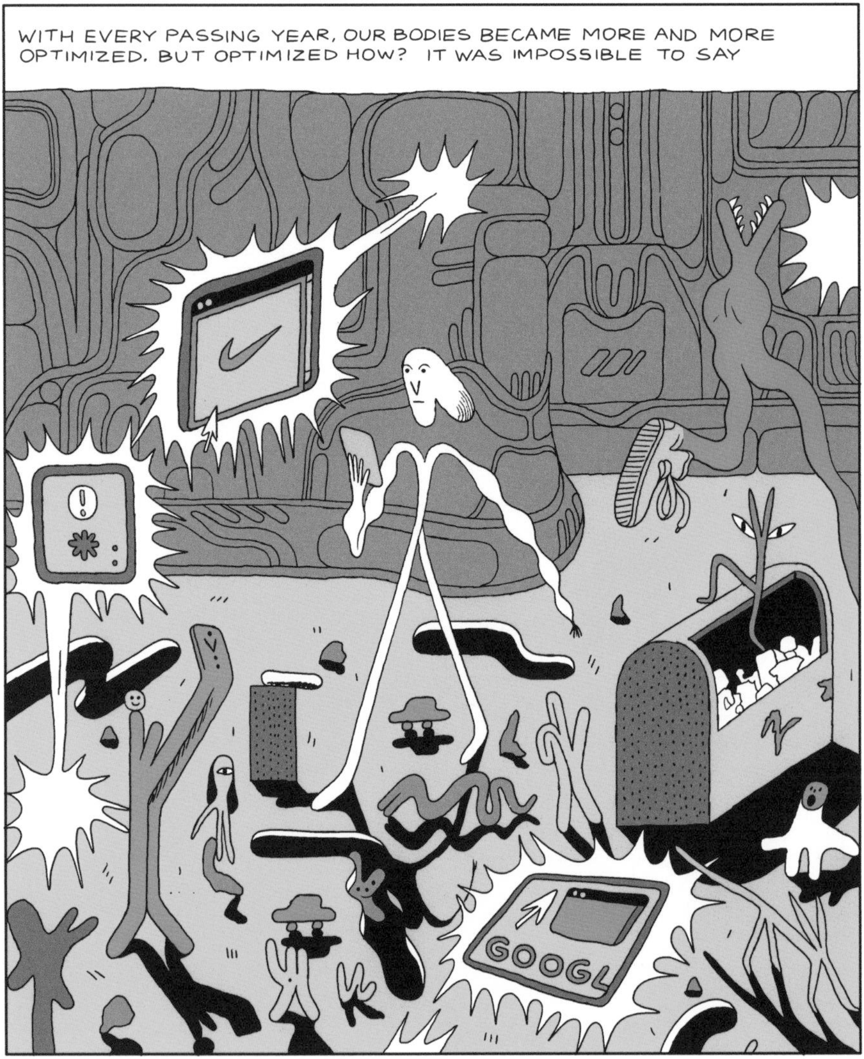
WITH EVERY PASSING YEAR, OUR BODIES BECAME MORE AND MORE OPTIMIZED. BUT OPTIMIZED HOW? IT WAS IMPOSSIBLE TO SAY
GOOGL

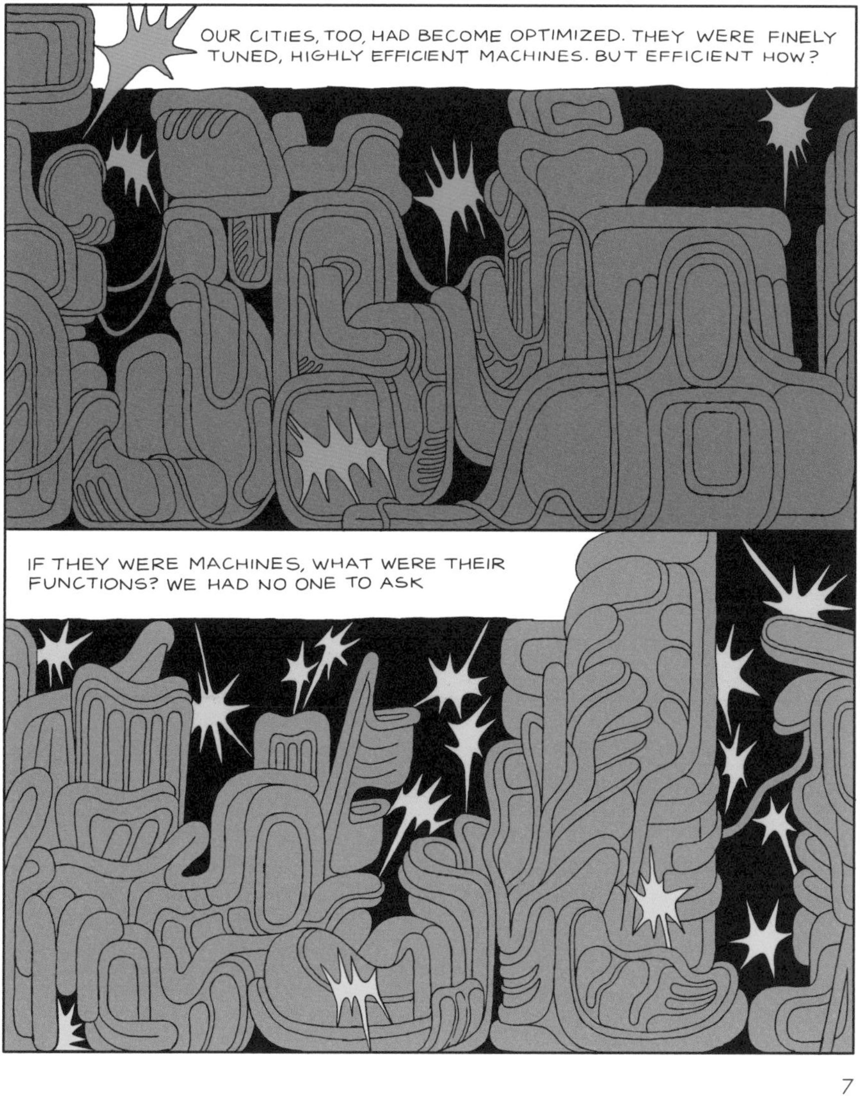
OUR CITIES, TOO, HAD BECOME OPTIMIZED. THEY WERE FINELY TUNED, HIGHLY EFFICIENT MACHINES. BUT EFFICIENT HOW?
IF THEY WERE MACHINES, WHAT WERE THEIR FUNCTIONS? WE HAD NO ONE TO ASK

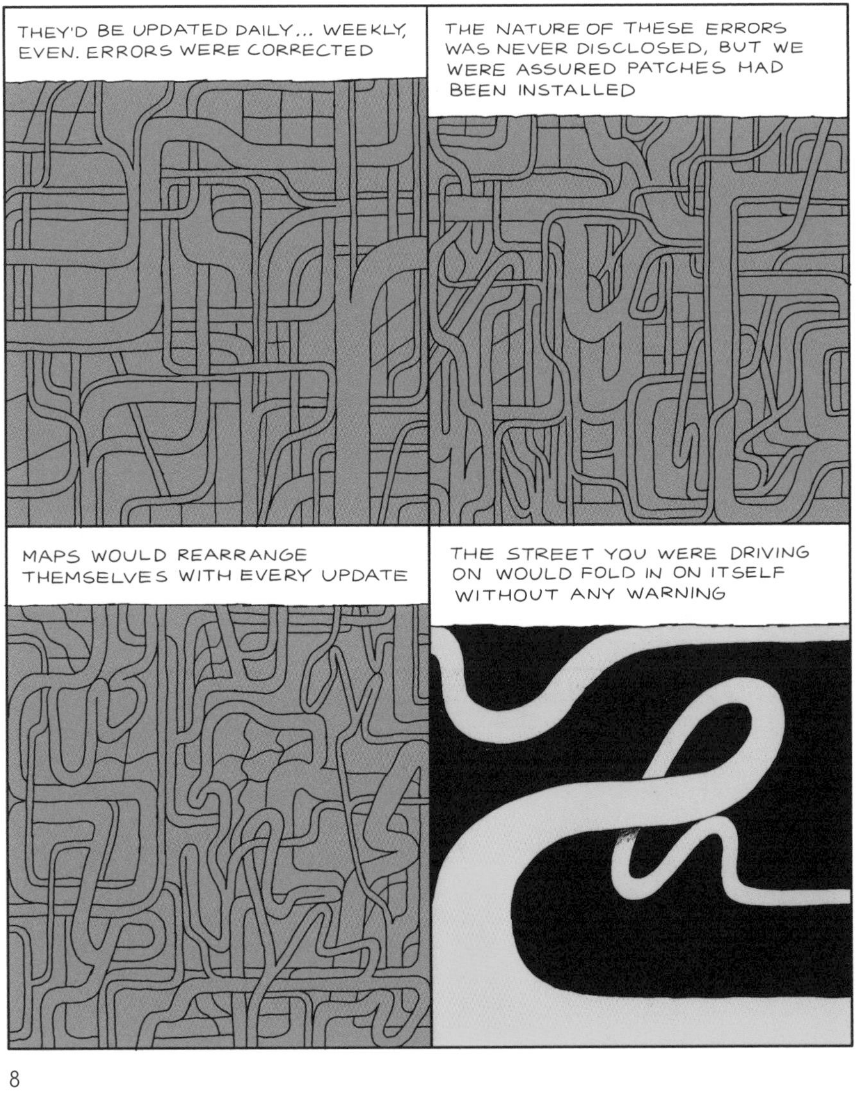
THEY'D BE UPDATED DAILY... WEEKLY, EVEN. ERRORS WERE CORRECTED
THE NATURE OF THESE ERRORS WAS NEVER DISCLOSED, BUT WE WERE ASSURED PATCHES HAD BEEN INSTALLED
MAPS WOULD REARRANGE THEMSELVES WITH EVERY UPDATE
THE STREET YOU WERE DRIVING ON WOULD FOLD IN ON ITSELF WITHOUT ANY WARNING

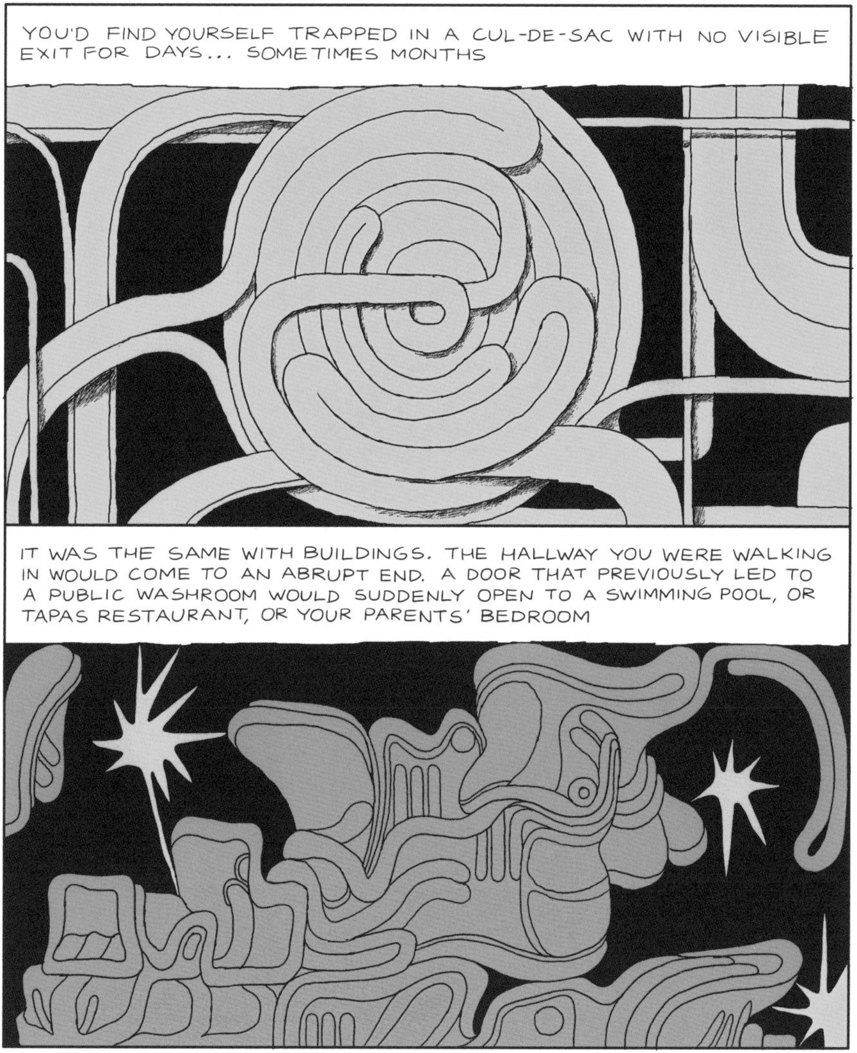
YOU'D FIND YOURSELF TRAPPED IN A CUL-DE-SAC WITH NO VISIBLE EXIT FOR DAYS... SOMETIMES MONTHS
IT WAS THE SAME WITH BUILDINGS. THE HALLWAY YOU WERE WALKING IN WOULD COME TO AN ABRUPT END. A DOOR THAT PREVIOUSLY LED TO A PUBLIC WASHROOM WOULD SUDDENLY OPEN TO A SWIMMING POOL, OR TAPAS RESTAURANT, OR YOUR PARENTS' BEDROOM

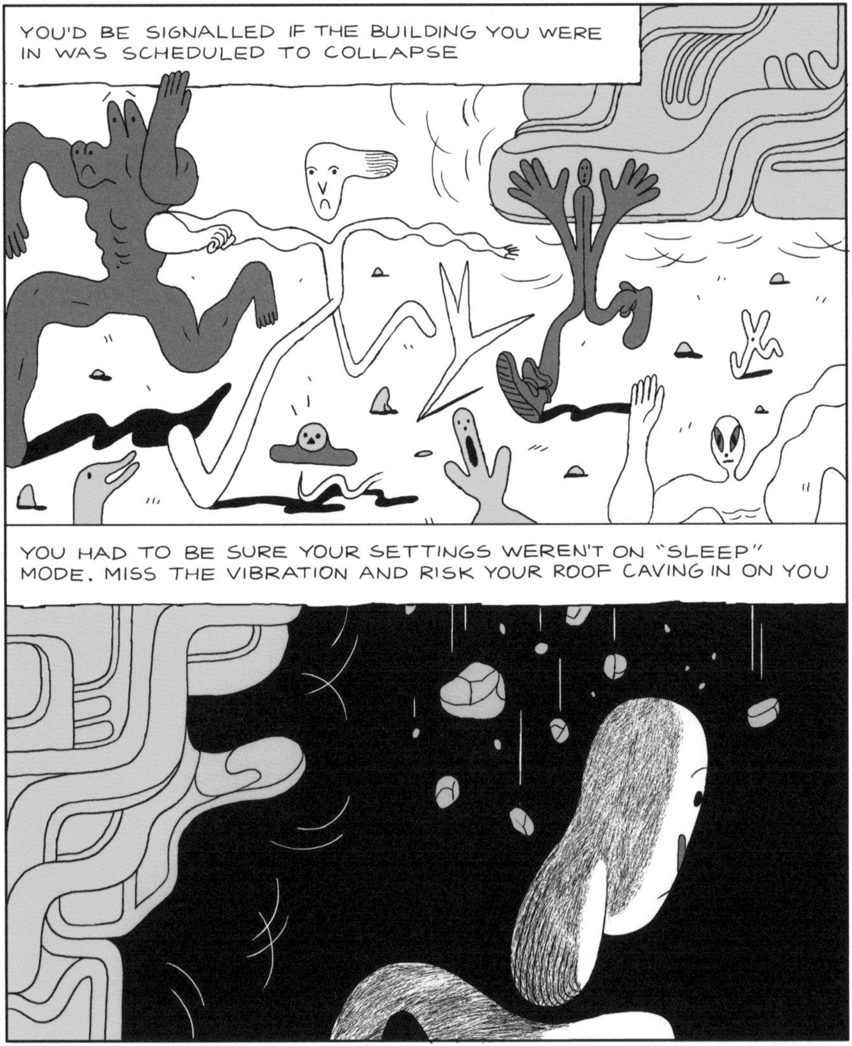
YOU'D BE SIGNALLED IF THE BUILDING YOU WERE IN WAS SCHEDULED TO COLLAPSE
YOU HAD TO BE SURE YOUR SETTINGS WEREN'T ON "SLEEP" MODE. MISS THE VIBRATION AND RISK YOUR ROOF CAVING IN ON YOU

OR BEING SUCKED INTO OBLIVION ALONGSIDE YOUR LIVING ROOM FLOOR

YOU MIGHT BE HOMELESS FOR A TIME, BUT USUALLY – EVENTUALLY – PROVIDED WITH A NEW ABODE

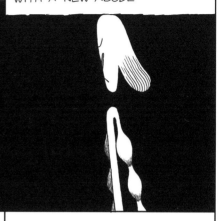

TRANSFORMATIONS TO YOUR BODY WOULD OCCUR AT A SIMILAR FREQUENCY

THE UPDATES OCCURRED WHILE YOU WERE SLEEPING, WITH NO ADVANCE NOTICE

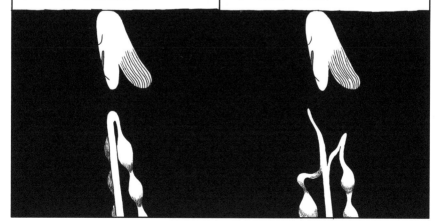

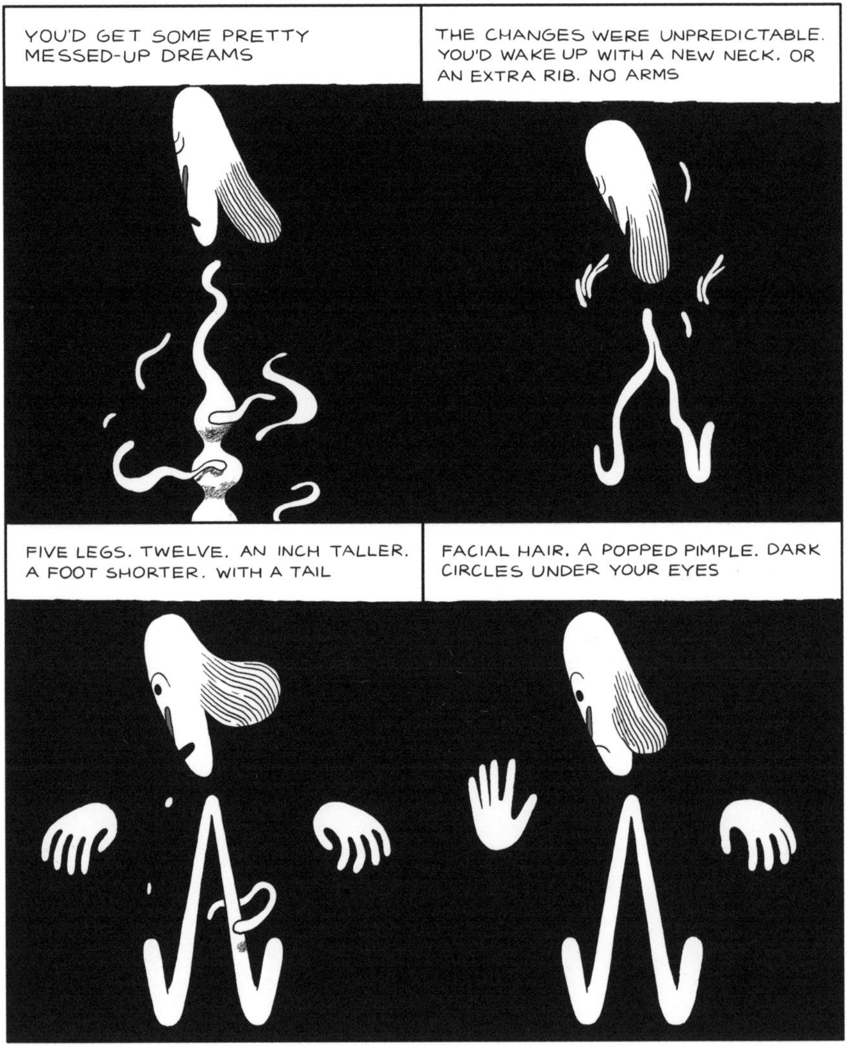
YOU'D GET SOME PRETTY MESSED-UP DREAMS
THE CHANGES WERE UNPREDICTABLE. YOU'D WAKE UP WITH A NEW NECK. OR AN EXTRA RIB. NO ARMS
FIVE LEGS. TWELVE. AN INCH TALLER. A FOOT SHORTER. WITH A TAIL
FACIAL HAIR. A POPPED PIMPLE. DARK CIRCLES UNDER YOUR EYES

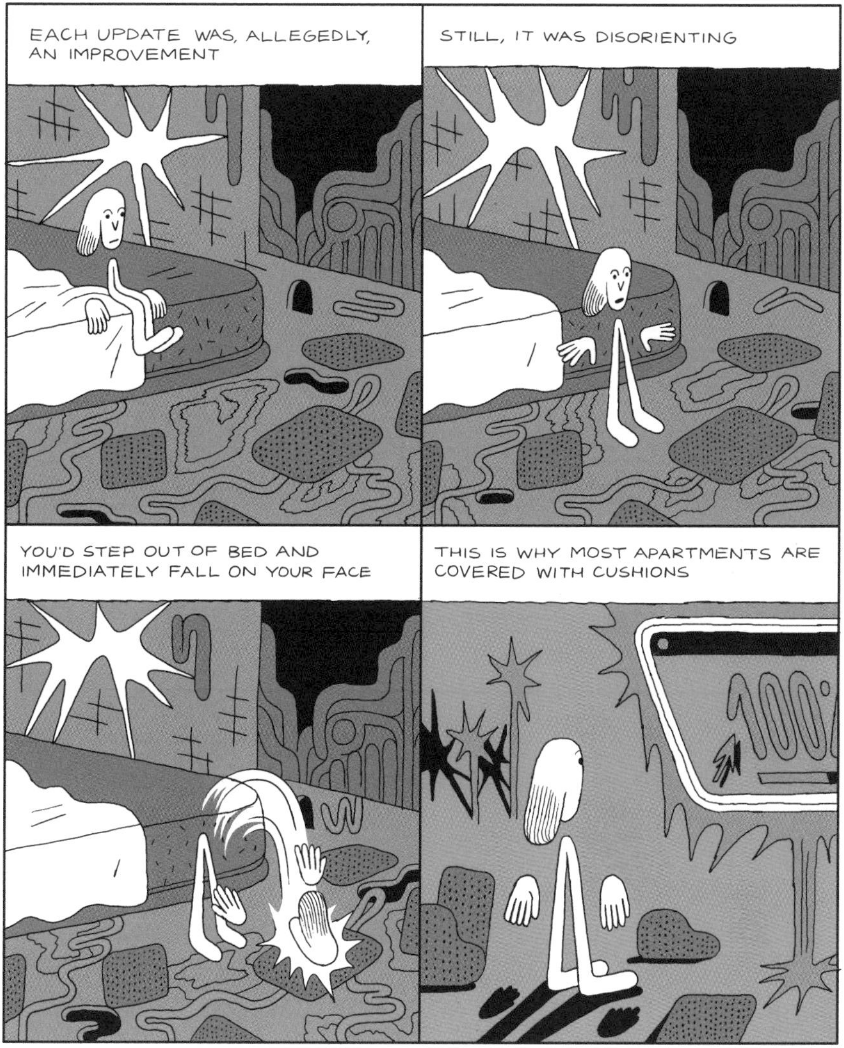
EACH UPDATE WAS, ALLEGEDLY, AN IMPROVEMENT
STILL, IT WAS DISORIENTING
YOU'D STEP OUT OF BED AND IMMEDIATELY FALL ON YOUR FACE
THIS IS WHY MOST APARTMENTS ARE COVERED WITH CUSHIONS

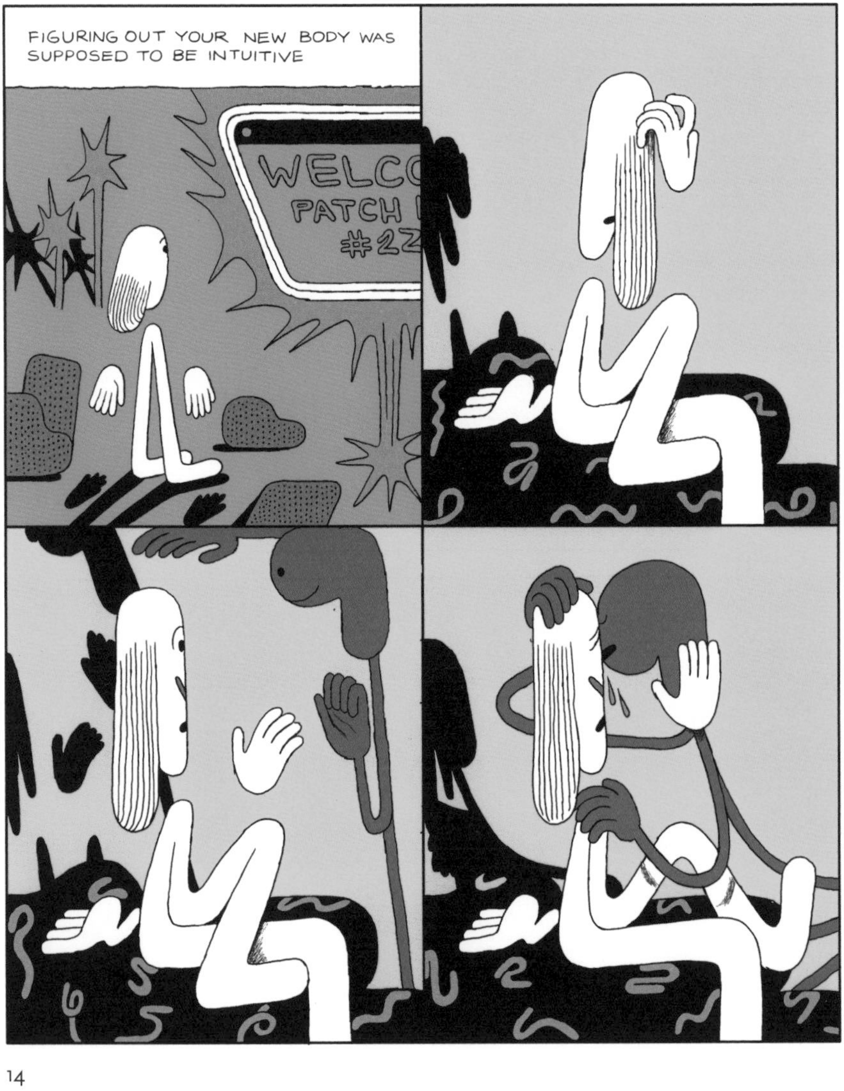
FIGURING OUT YOUR NEW BODY WAS SUPPOSED TO BE INTUITIVE
WELCO
PATCH
#22

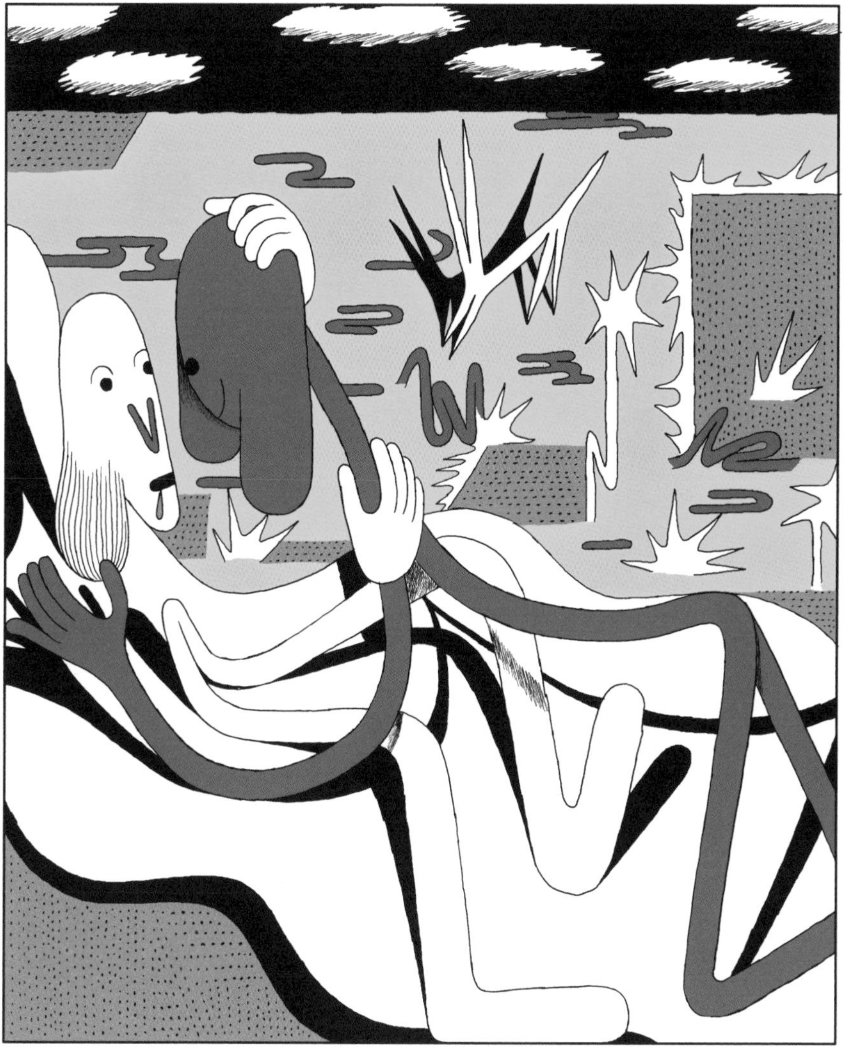

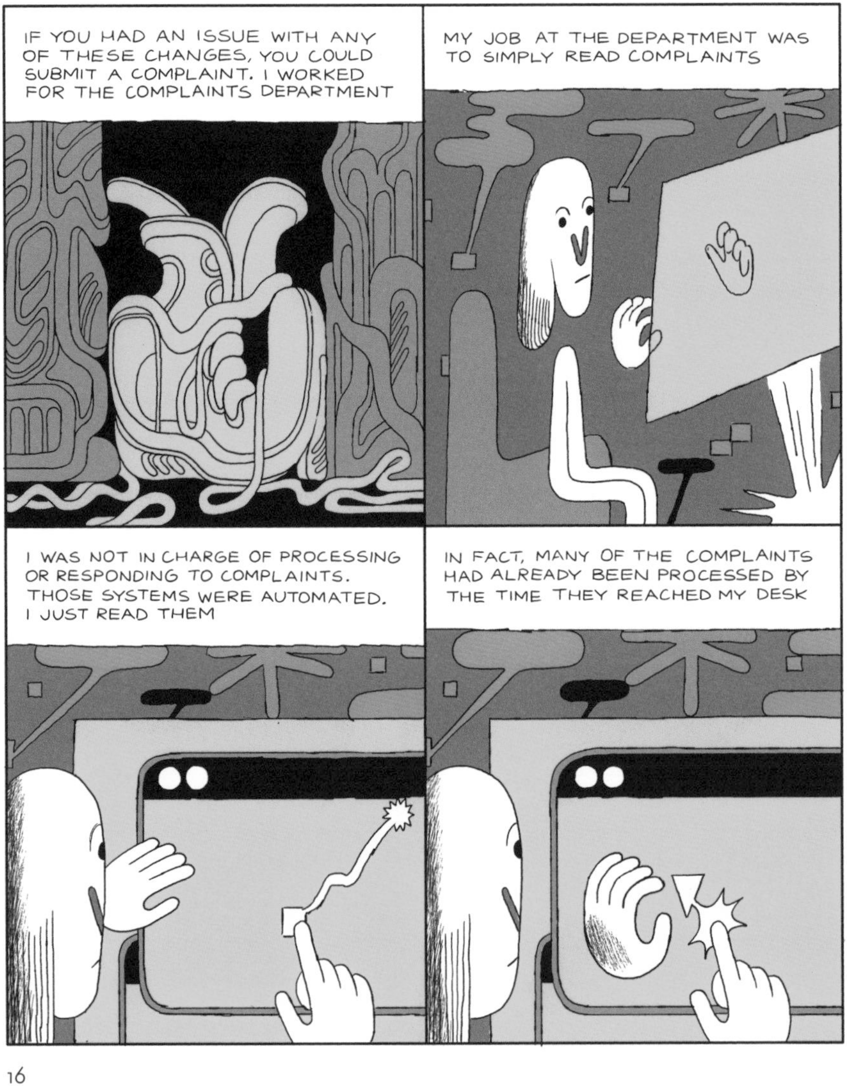
IF YOU HAD AN ISSUE WITH ANY OF THESE CHANGES, YOU COULD SUBMIT A COMPLAINT. I WORKED FOR THE COMPLAINTS DEPARTMENT
MY JOB AT THE DEPARTMENT WAS TO SIMPLY READ COMPLAINTS
I WAS NOT IN CHARGE OF PROCESSING OR RESPONDING TO COMPLAINTS. THOSE SYSTEMS WERE AUTOMATED. I JUST READ THEM
IN FACT, MANY OF THE COMPLAINTS HAD ALREADY BEEN PROCESSED BY THE TIME THEY REACHED MY DESK

THE AUTOMATED SYSTEM CAME UNDER FIRE A FEW YEARS BACK FOR BEING TOO OPAQUE. MY JOB WAS CREATED IN RESPONSE TO THOSE CRITICISMS, AS PART OF AN ACCOUNTABILITY EFFORT

EVEN WHEN THEIR COMPLAINTS WERE LEFT UNADDRESSED, PEOPLE FELT MORE COMFORTABLE KNOWING THERE WAS AT LEAST A PERSON ON THE OTHER END READING WHAT THEY HAD TO SAY

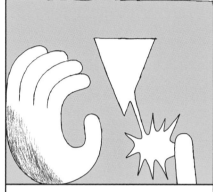

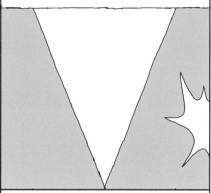

I WAS NEVER TOLD WHEN OR IF A COMPLAINT WAS RESOLVED

THE COMPLAINTS WERE RANDOMIZED AND ANONYMIZED BEFORE THEY WERE GIVEN TO ME

17

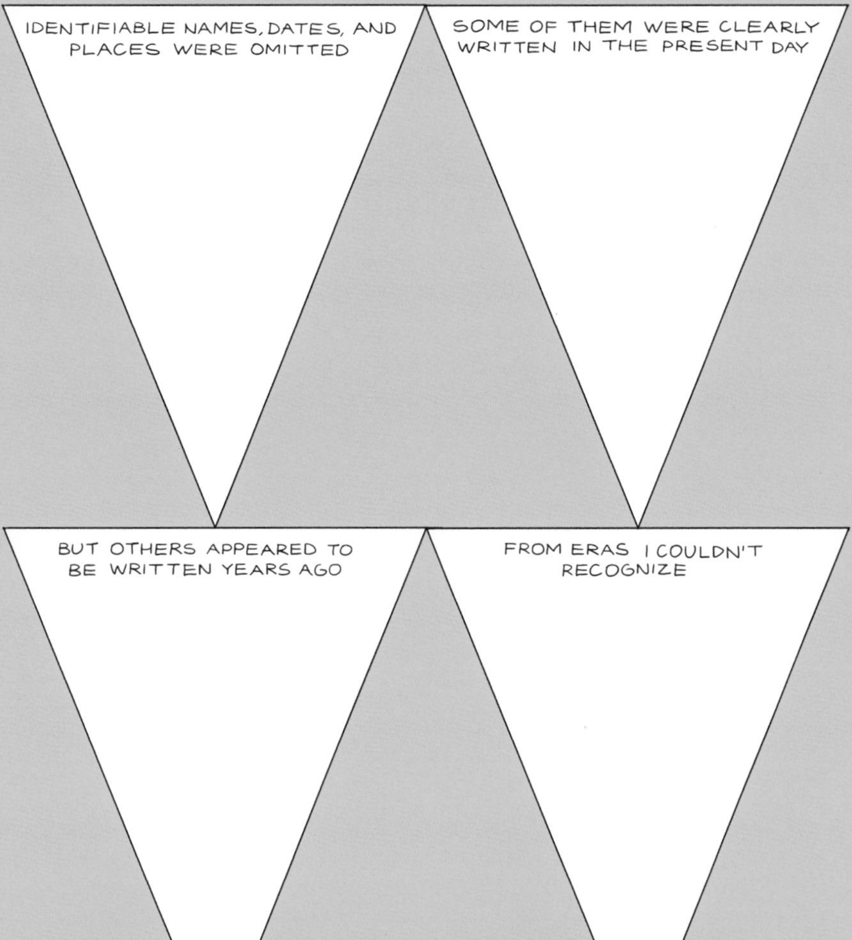
IDENTIFIABLE NAMES, DATES, AND PLACES WERE OMITTED
SOME OF THEM WERE CLEARLY WRITTEN IN THE PRESENT DAY
BUT OTHERS APPEARED TO BE WRITTEN YEARS AGO
FROM ERAS I COULDN'T RECOGNIZE

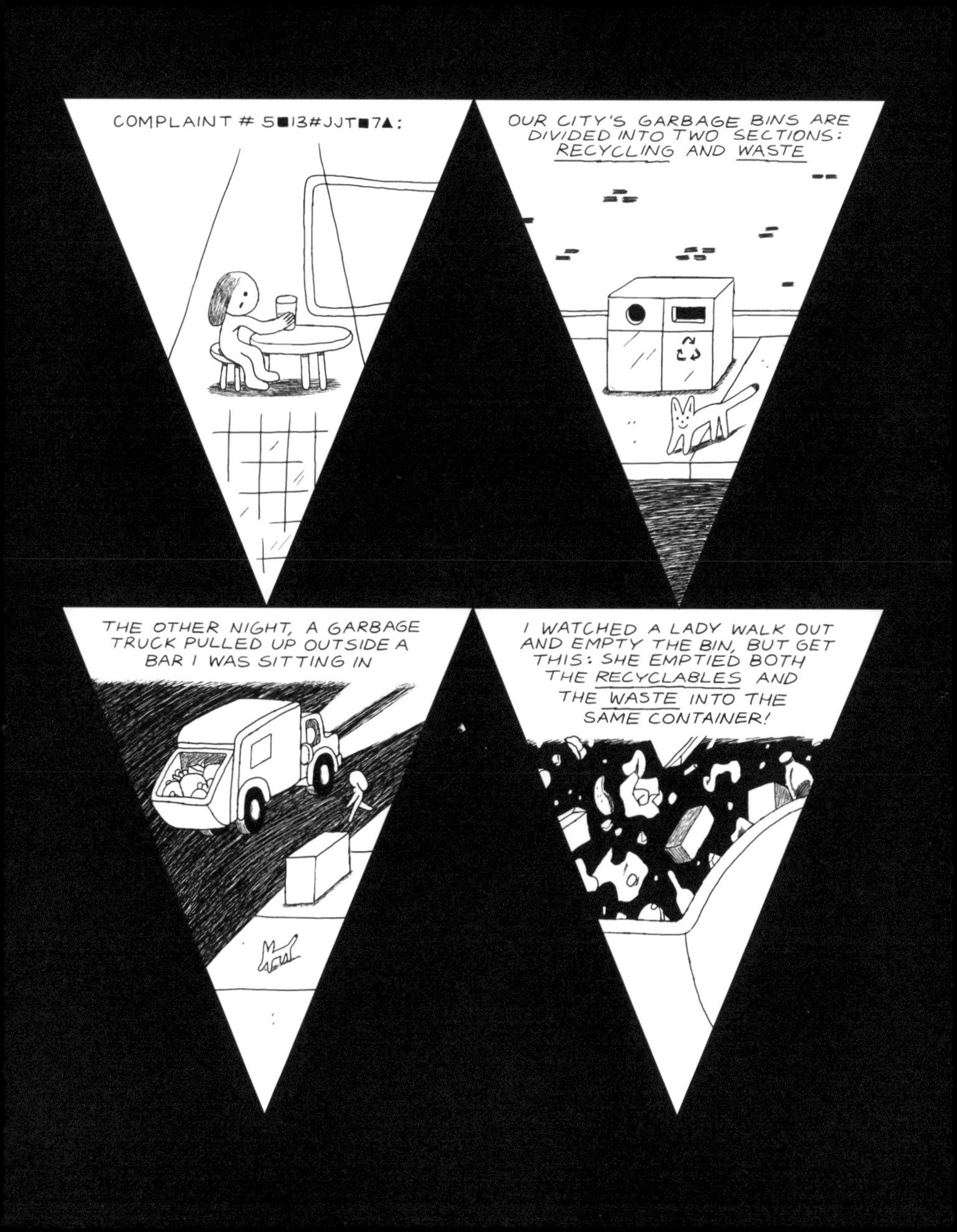
COMPLAINT # 5■13#JJT■7▲:
OUR CITY'S GARBAGE BINS ARE DIVIDED INTO TWO SECTIONS: RECYCLING AND WASTE
THE OTHER NIGHT, A GARBAGE TRUCK PULLED UP OUTSIDE A BAR I WAS SITTING IN
I WATCHED A LADY WALK OUT AND EMPTY THE BIN, BUT GET THIS: SHE EMPTIED BOTH THE RECYCLABLES AND THE WASTE INTO THE SAME CONTAINER!

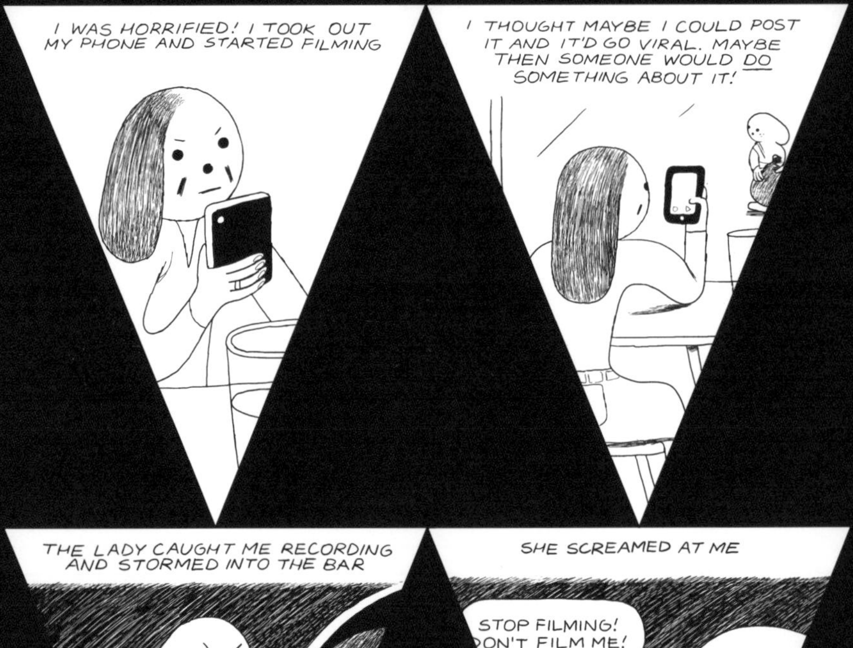
I WAS HORRIFIED! I TOOK OUT MY PHONE AND STARTED FILMING
I THOUGHT MAYBE I COULD POST IT AND IT'D GO VIRAL. MAYBE THEN SOMEONE WOULD DO SOMETHING ABOUT IT!
THE LADY CAUGHT ME RECORDING AND STORMED INTO THE BAR
SHE SCREAMED AT ME
STOP FILMING! DON'T FILM ME!

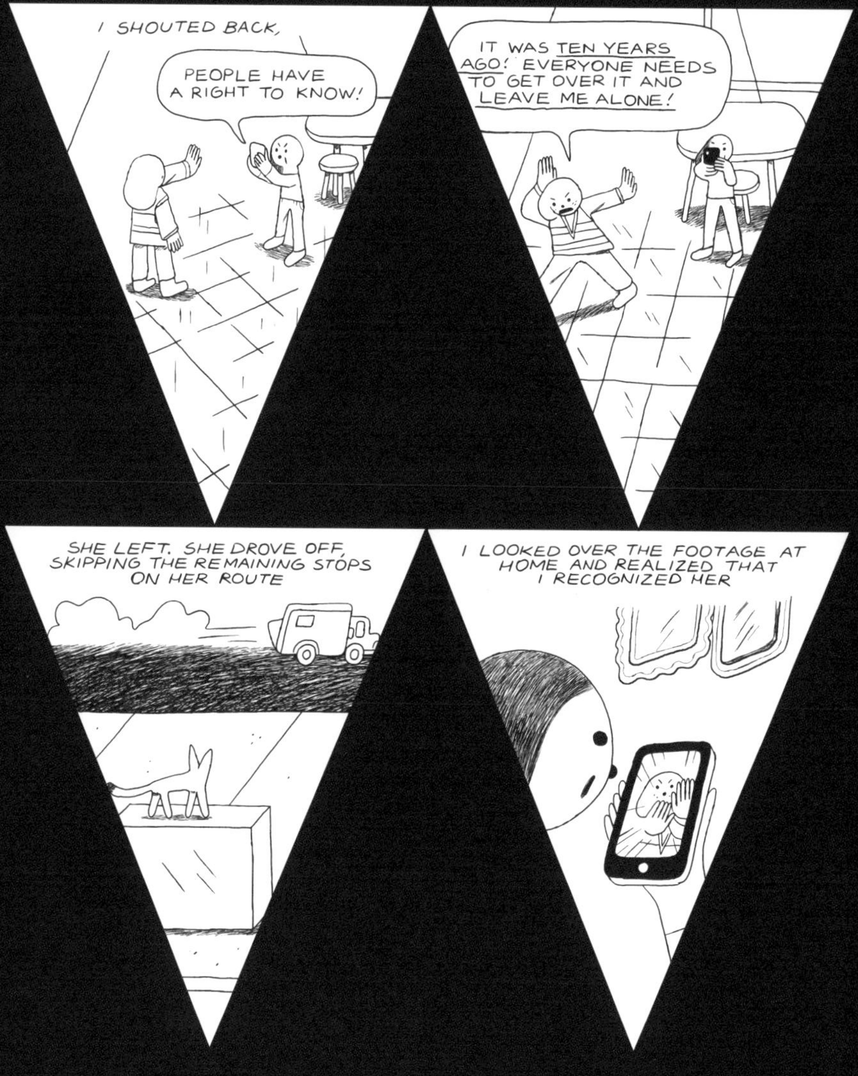
I SHOUTED BACK,
PEOPLE HAVE A RIGHT TO KNOW!
IT WAS TEN YEARS AGO! EVERYONE NEEDS TO GET OVER IT AND LEAVE ME ALONE!
SHE LEFT. SHE DROVE OFF, SKIPPING THE REMAINING STOPS ON HER ROUTE
I LOOKED OVER THE FOOTAGE AT HOME AND REALIZED THAT I RECOGNIZED HER

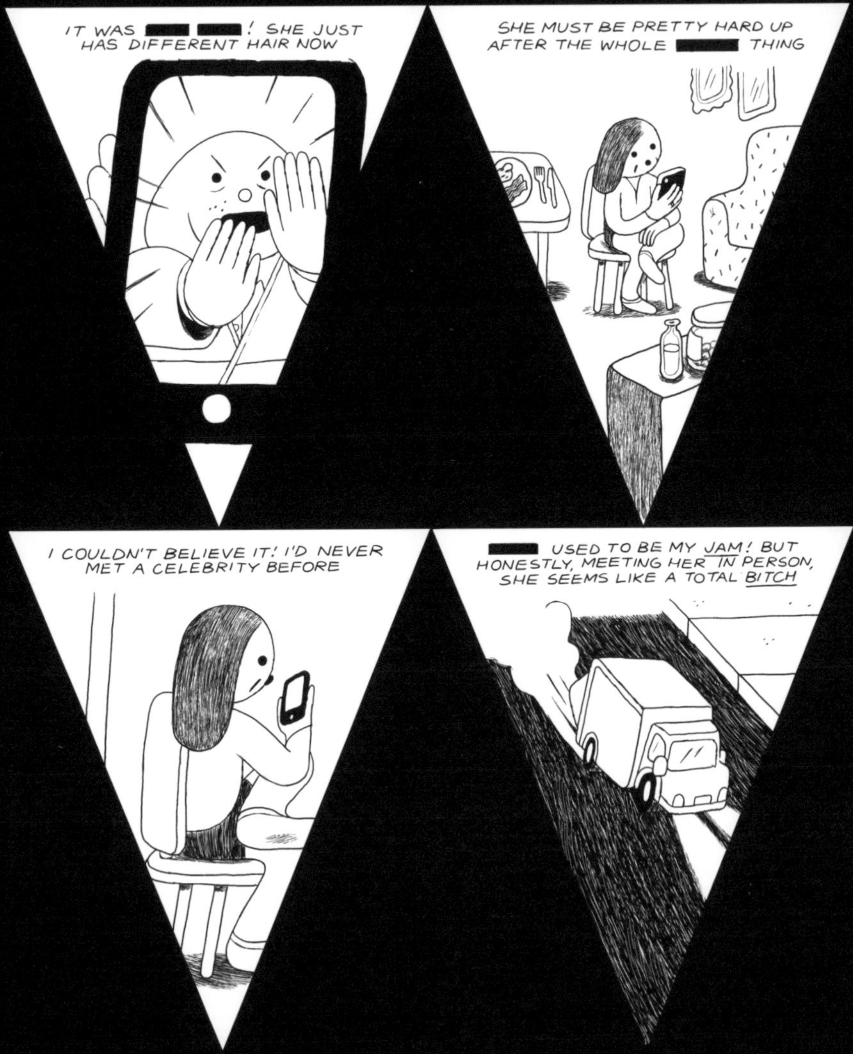
IT WAS [redacted]! SHE JUST HAS DIFFERENT HAIR NOW
SHE MUST BE PRETTY HARD UP AFTER THE WHOLE [redacted] THING
I COULDN'T BELIEVE IT! I'D NEVER MET A CELEBRITY BEFORE
[redacted] USED TO BE MY JAM! BUT HONESTLY, MEETING HER IN PERSON, SHE SEEMS LIKE A TOTAL BITCH

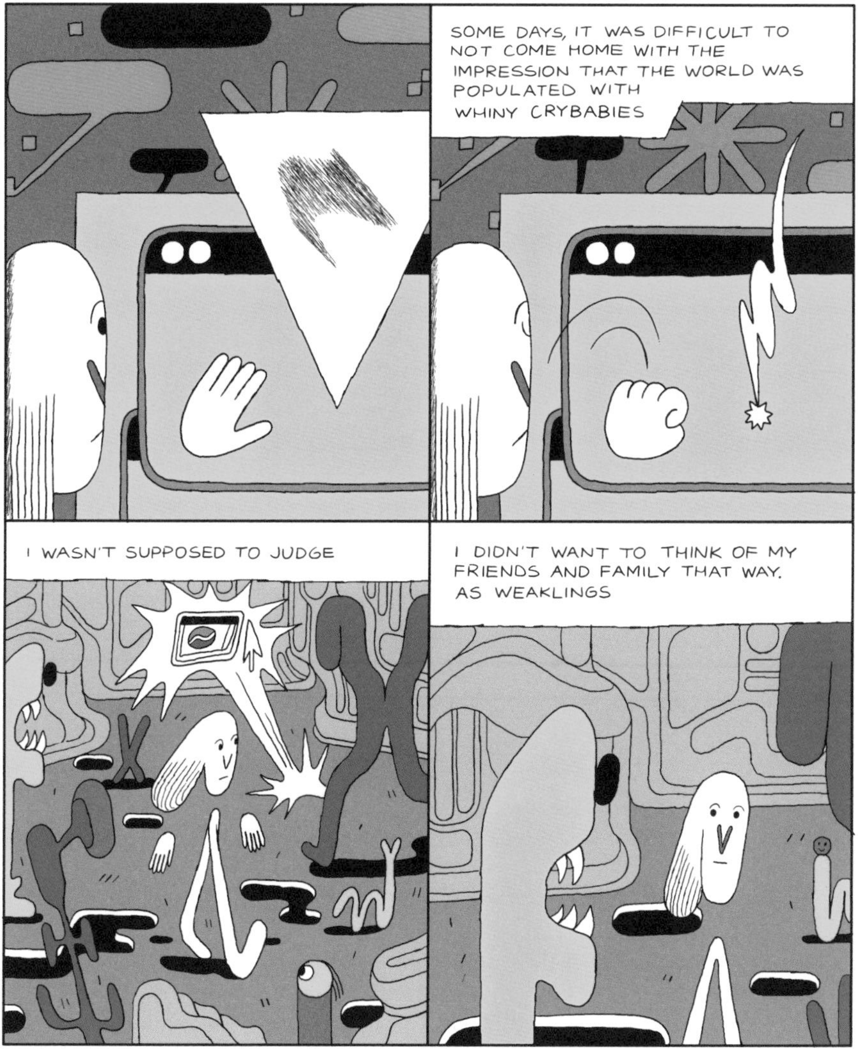
SOME DAYS, IT WAS DIFFICULT TO NOT COME HOME WITH THE IMPRESSION THAT THE WORLD WAS POPULATED WITH WHINY CRYBABIES
I WASN'T SUPPOSED TO JUDGE
I DIDN'T WANT TO THINK OF MY FRIENDS AND FAMILY THAT WAY. AS WEAKLINGS

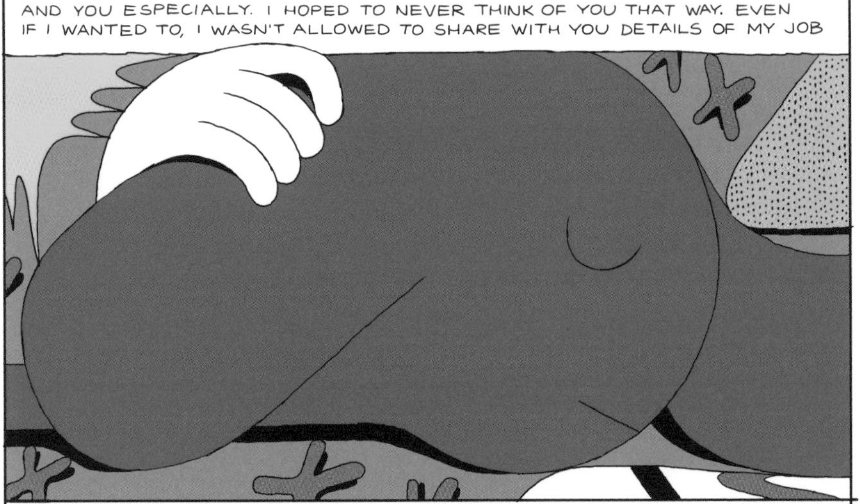
AND YOU ESPECIALLY. I HOPED TO NEVER THINK OF YOU THAT WAY. EVEN IF I WANTED TO, I WASN'T ALLOWED TO SHARE WITH YOU DETAILS OF MY JOB

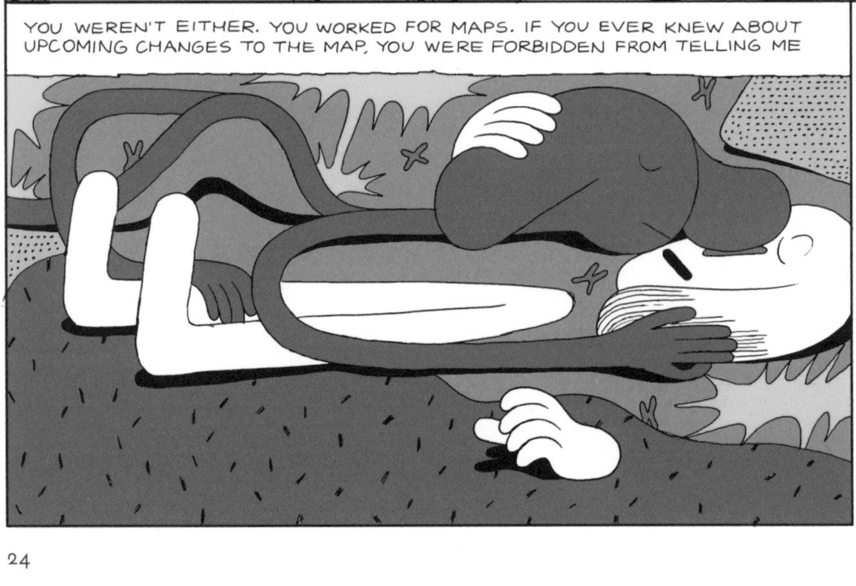
YOU WEREN'T EITHER. YOU WORKED FOR MAPS. IF YOU EVER KNEW ABOUT UPCOMING CHANGES TO THE MAP, YOU WERE FORBIDDEN FROM TELLING ME

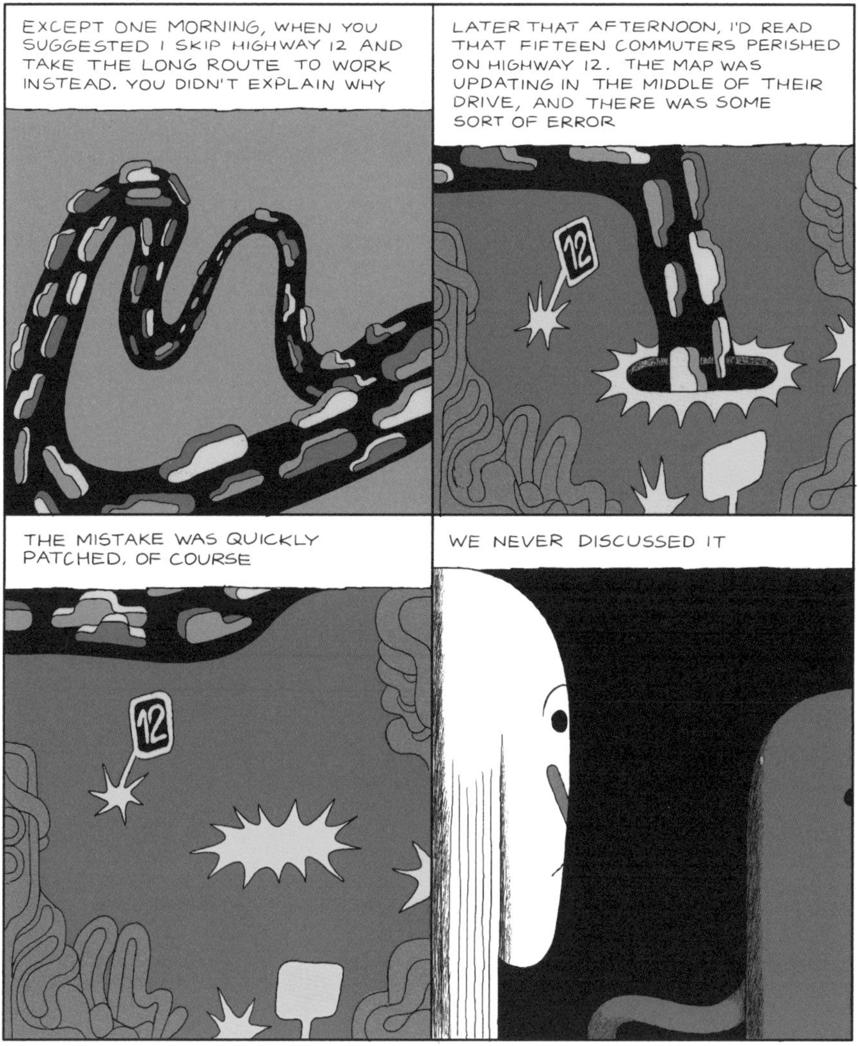

EXCEPT ONE MORNING, WHEN YOU SUGGESTED I SKIP HIGHWAY 12 AND TAKE THE LONG ROUTE TO WORK INSTEAD. YOU DIDN'T EXPLAIN WHY

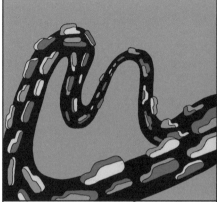

LATER THAT AFTERNOON, I'D READ THAT FIFTEEN COMMUTERS PERISHED ON HIGHWAY 12. THE MAP WAS UPDATING IN THE MIDDLE OF THEIR DRIVE, AND THERE WAS SOME SORT OF ERROR

THE MISTAKE WAS QUICKLY PATCHED, OF COURSE

WE NEVER DISCUSSED IT

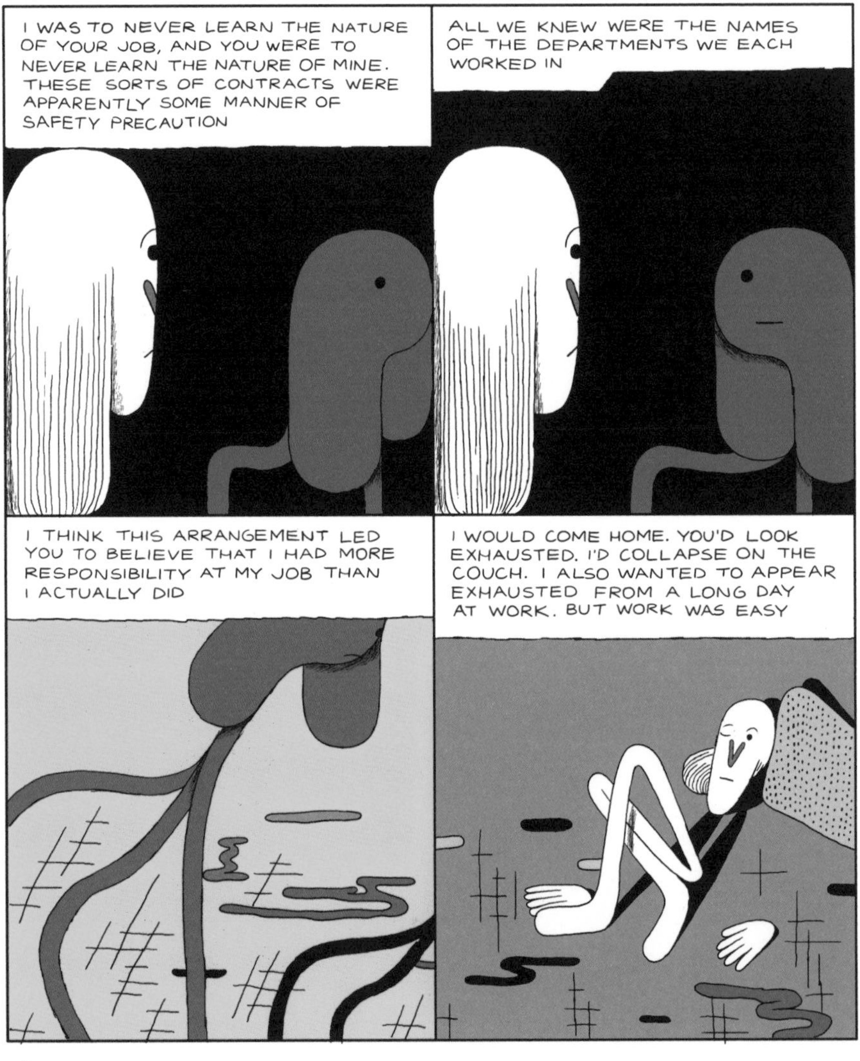
I WAS TO NEVER LEARN THE NATURE OF YOUR JOB, AND YOU WERE TO NEVER LEARN THE NATURE OF MINE. THESE SORTS OF CONTRACTS WERE APPARENTLY SOME MANNER OF SAFETY PRECAUTION
ALL WE KNEW WERE THE NAMES OF THE DEPARTMENTS WE EACH WORKED IN
I THINK THIS ARRANGEMENT LED YOU TO BELIEVE THAT I HAD MORE RESPONSIBILITY AT MY JOB THAN I ACTUALLY DID
I WOULD COME HOME. YOU'D LOOK EXHAUSTED. I'D COLLAPSE ON THE COUCH. I ALSO WANTED TO APPEAR EXHAUSTED FROM A LONG DAY AT WORK. BUT WORK WAS EASY

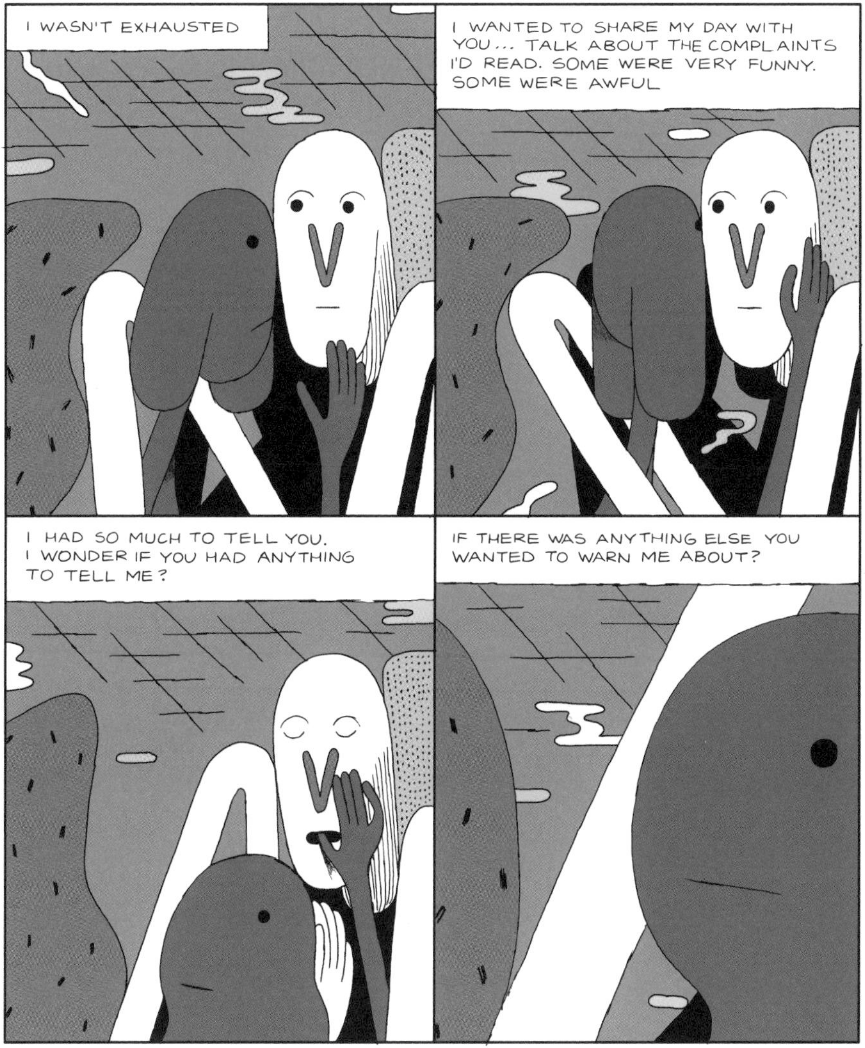
I WASN'T EXHAUSTED
I WANTED TO SHARE MY DAY WITH YOU... TALK ABOUT THE COMPLAINTS I'D READ. SOME WERE VERY FUNNY. SOME WERE AWFUL
I HAD SO MUCH TO TELL YOU. I WONDER IF YOU HAD ANYTHING TO TELL ME?
IF THERE WAS ANYTHING ELSE YOU WANTED TO WARN ME ABOUT?

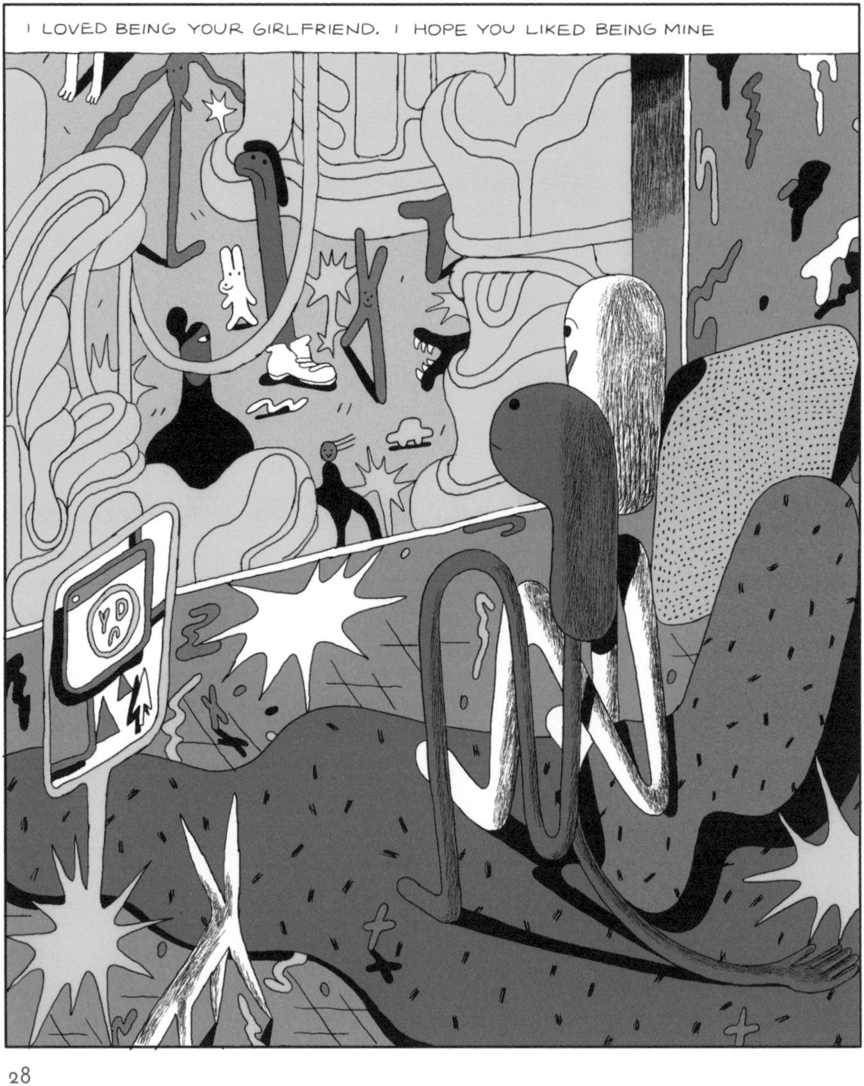
I LOVED BEING YOUR GIRLFRIEND. I HOPE YOU LIKED BEING MINE

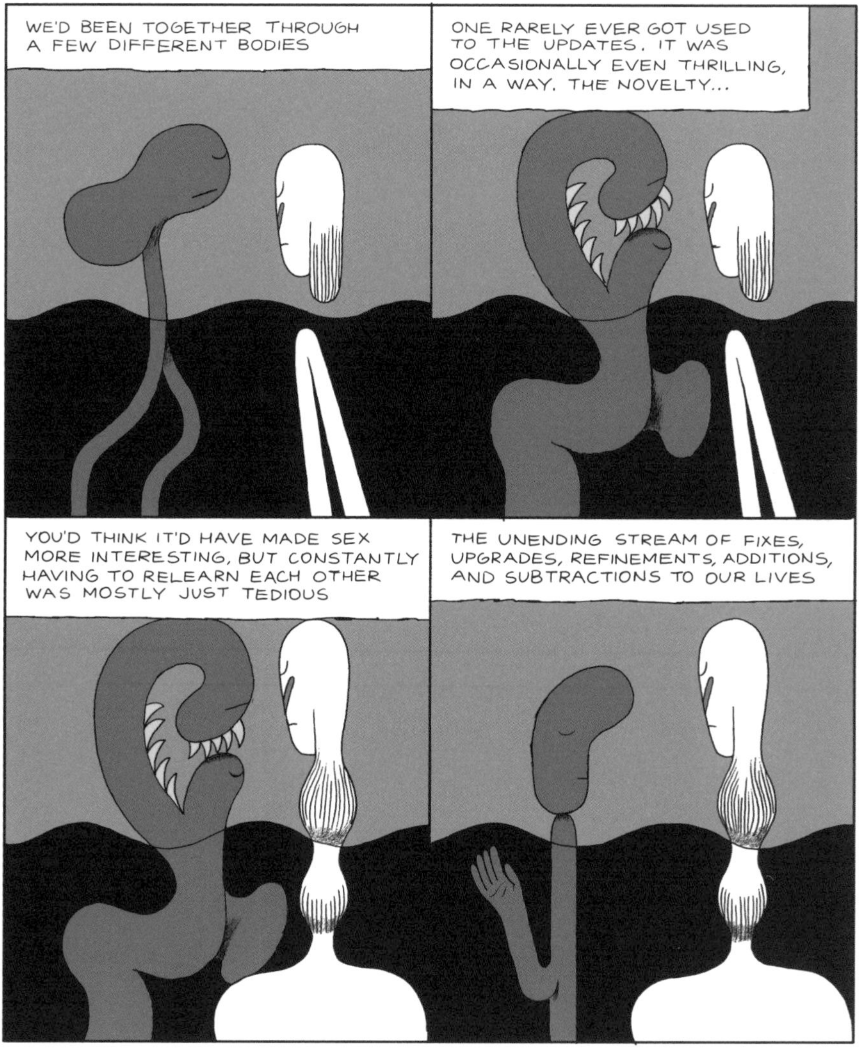
WE'D BEEN TOGETHER THROUGH A FEW DIFFERENT BODIES
ONE RARELY EVER GOT USED TO THE UPDATES. IT WAS OCCASIONALLY EVEN THRILLING, IN A WAY. THE NOVELTY...
YOU'D THINK IT'D HAVE MADE SEX MORE INTERESTING, BUT CONSTANTLY HAVING TO RELEARN EACH OTHER WAS MOSTLY JUST TEDIOUS
THE UNENDING STREAM OF FIXES, UPGRADES, REFINEMENTS, ADDITIONS, AND SUBTRACTIONS TO OUR LIVES

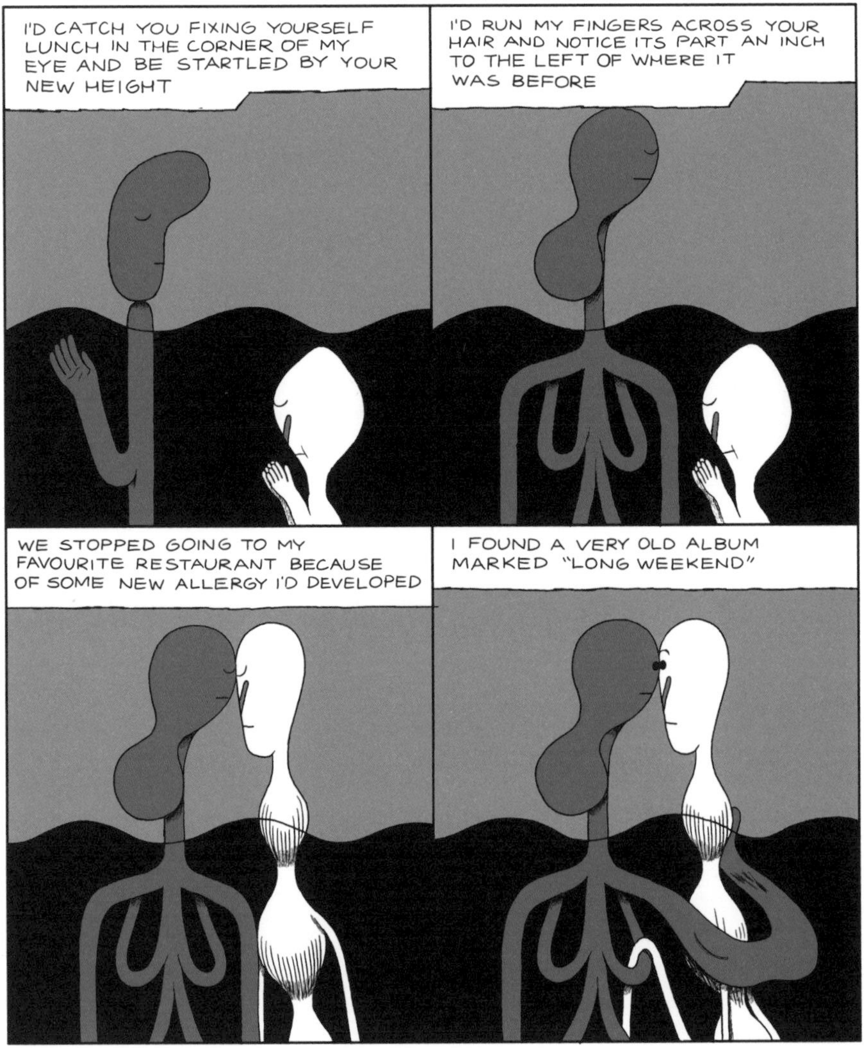
I'D CATCH YOU FIXING YOURSELF LUNCH IN THE CORNER OF MY EYE AND BE STARTLED BY YOUR NEW HEIGHT
I'D RUN MY FINGERS ACROSS YOUR HAIR AND NOTICE ITS PART AN INCH TO THE LEFT OF WHERE IT WAS BEFORE
WE STOPPED GOING TO MY FAVOURITE RESTAURANT BECAUSE OF SOME NEW ALLERGY I'D DEVELOPED
I FOUND A VERY OLD ALBUM MARKED "LONG WEEKEND"

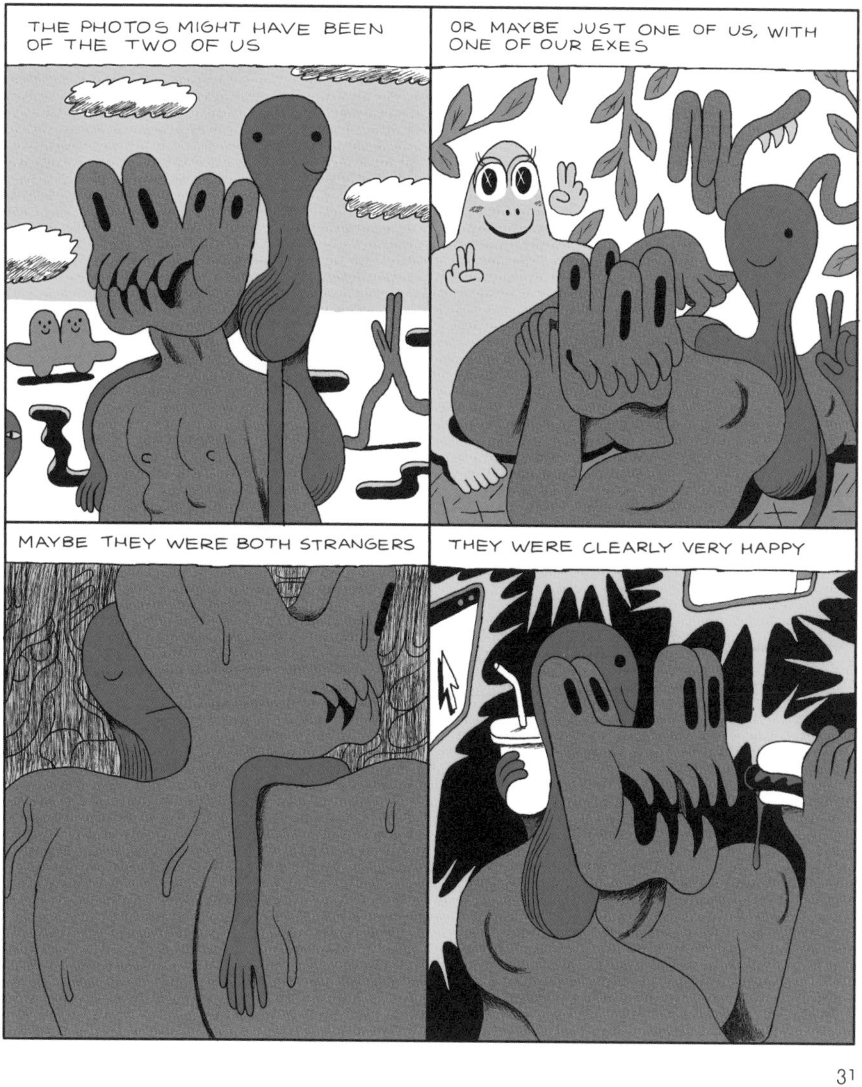
THE PHOTOS MIGHT HAVE BEEN OF THE TWO OF US
OR MAYBE JUST ONE OF US, WITH ONE OF OUR EXES
MAYBE THEY WERE BOTH STRANGERS
THEY WERE CLEARLY VERY HAPPY

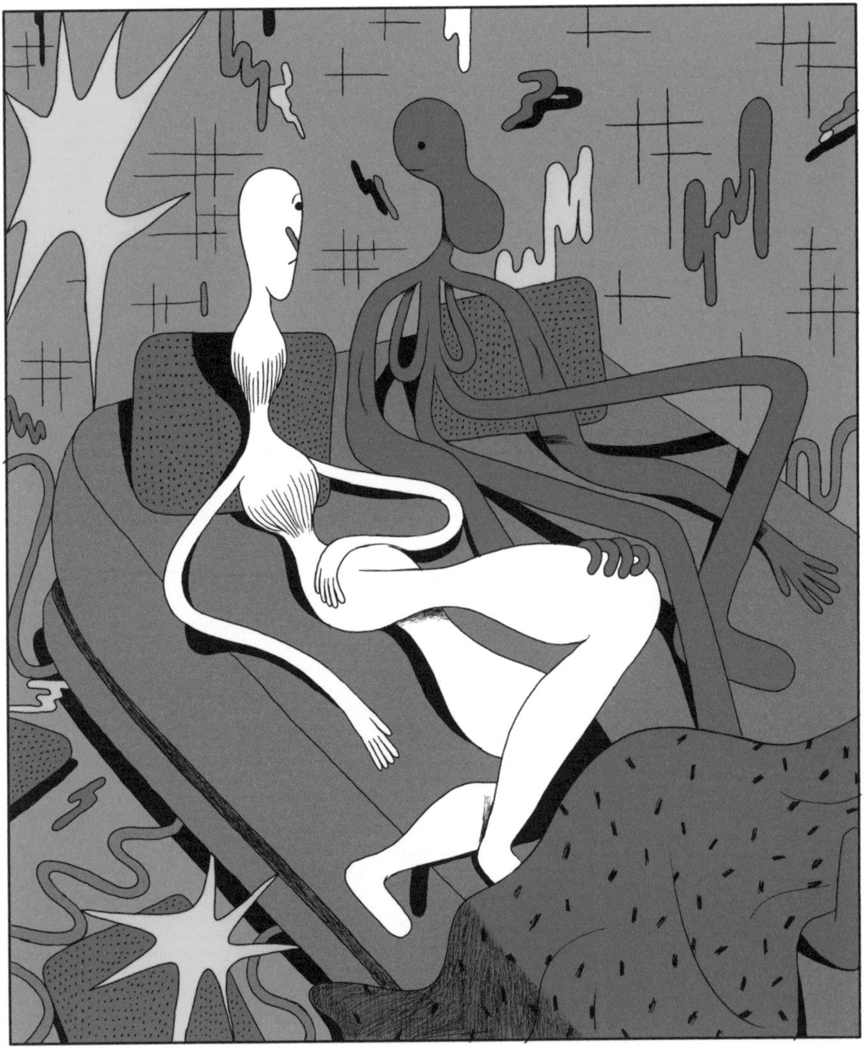

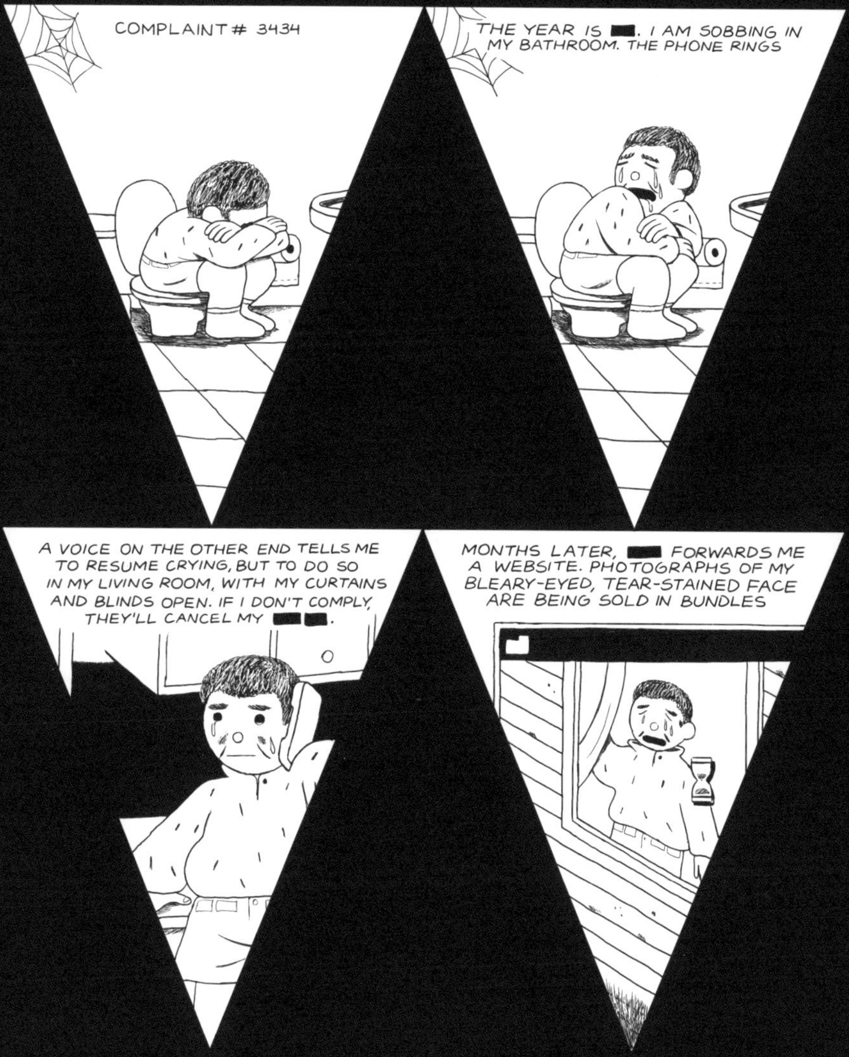
COMPLAINT # 3434
THE YEAR IS [redacted]. I AM SOBBING IN MY BATHROOM. THE PHONE RINGS
A VOICE ON THE OTHER END TELLS ME TO RESUME CRYING, BUT TO DO SO IN MY LIVING ROOM, WITH MY CURTAINS AND BLINDS OPEN. IF I DON'T COMPLY, THEY'LL CANCEL MY [redacted].
MONTHS LATER, [redacted] FORWARDS ME A WEBSITE. PHOTOGRAPHS OF MY BLEARY-EYED, TEAR-STAINED FACE ARE BEING SOLD IN BUNDLES

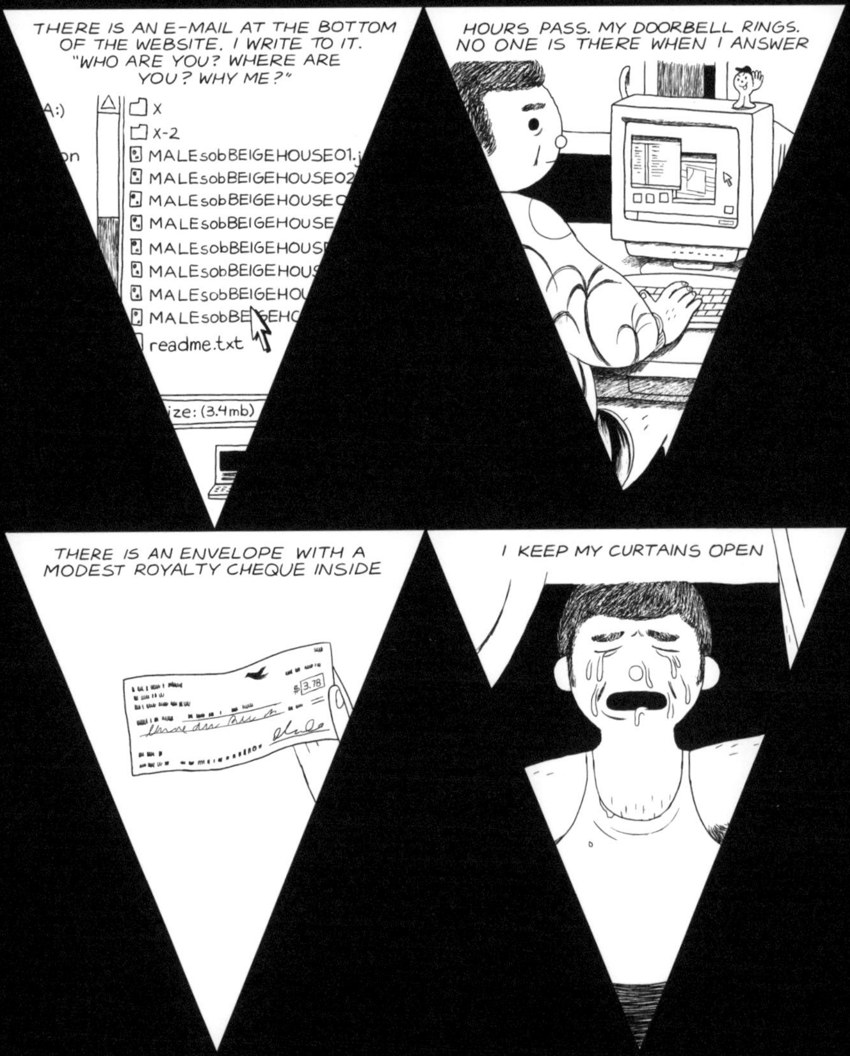
THERE IS AN E-MAIL AT THE BOTTOM OF THE WEBSITE. I WRITE TO IT. "WHO ARE YOU? WHERE ARE YOU? WHY ME?"
X
X-2
MALEsobBEIGEHOUSE01.j
readme.txt
HOURS PASS. MY DOORBELL RINGS. NO ONE IS THERE WHEN I ANSWER
THERE IS AN ENVELOPE WITH A MODEST ROYALTY CHEQUE INSIDE
$3.78
I KEEP MY CURTAINS OPEN

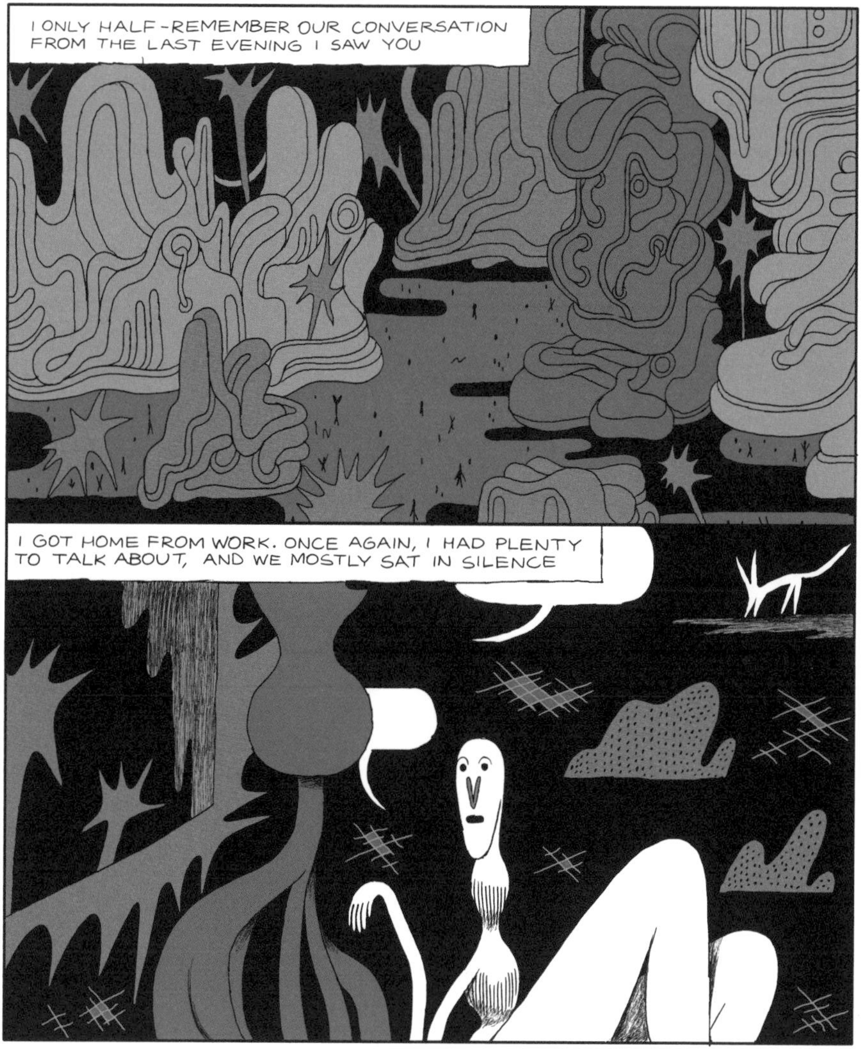
I ONLY HALF-REMEMBER OUR CONVERSATION FROM THE LAST EVENING I SAW YOU
I GOT HOME FROM WORK. ONCE AGAIN, I HAD PLENTY TO TALK ABOUT, AND WE MOSTLY SAT IN SILENCE

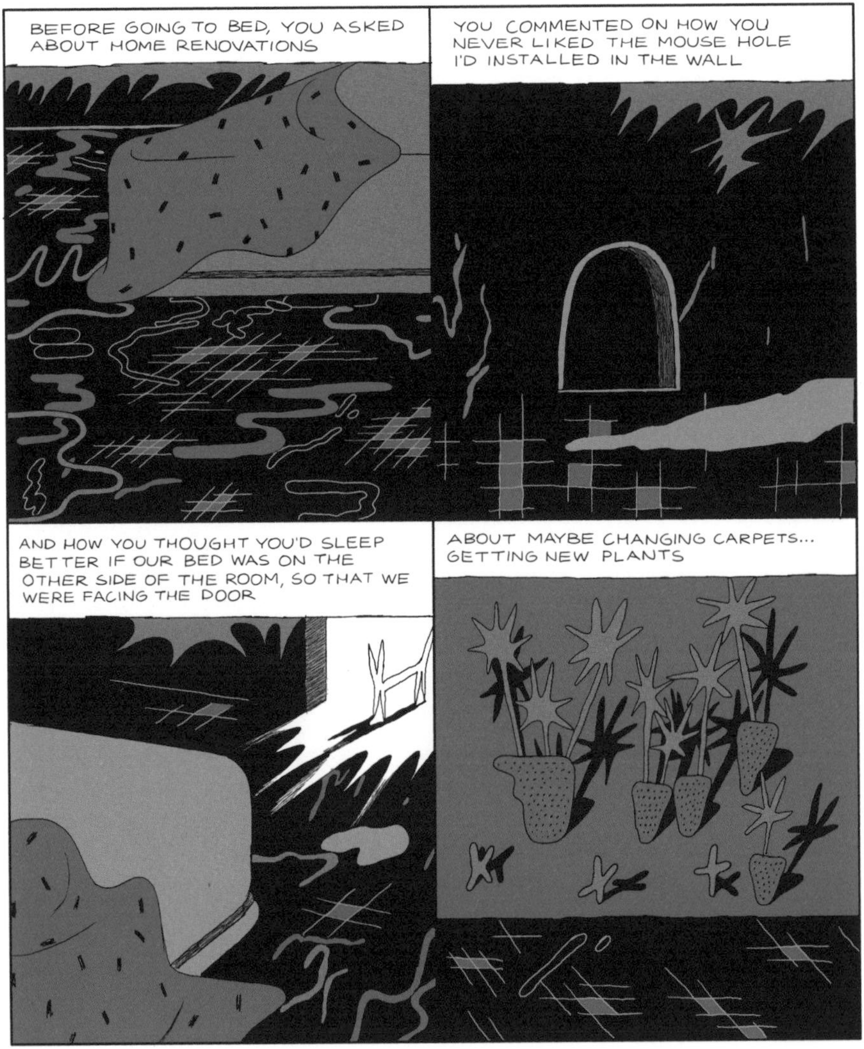
BEFORE GOING TO BED, YOU ASKED ABOUT HOME RENOVATIONS
YOU COMMENTED ON HOW YOU NEVER LIKED THE MOUSE HOLE I'D INSTALLED IN THE WALL
AND HOW YOU THOUGHT YOU'D SLEEP BETTER IF OUR BED WAS ON THE OTHER SIDE OF THE ROOM, SO THAT WE WERE FACING THE DOOR
ABOUT MAYBE CHANGING CARPETS... GETTING NEW PLANTS

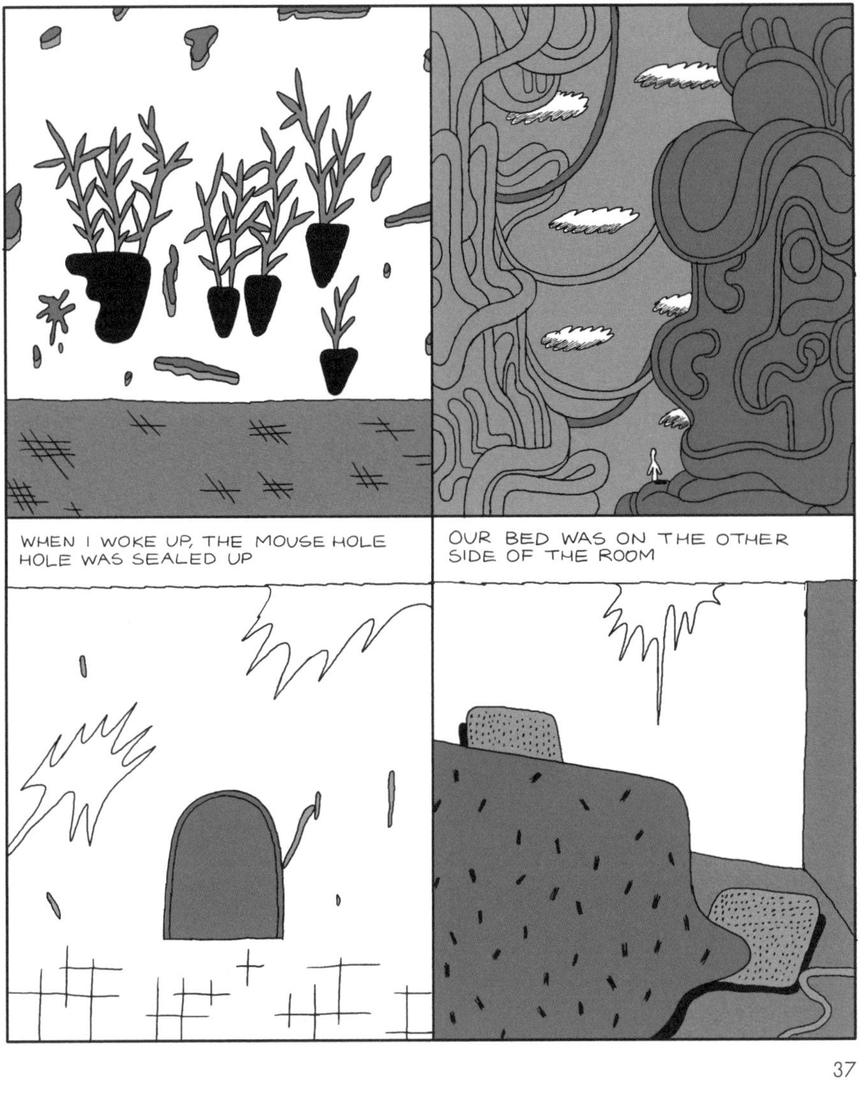
WHEN I WOKE UP, THE MOUSE HOLE HOLE WAS SEALED UP
OUR BED WAS ON THE OTHER SIDE OF THE ROOM

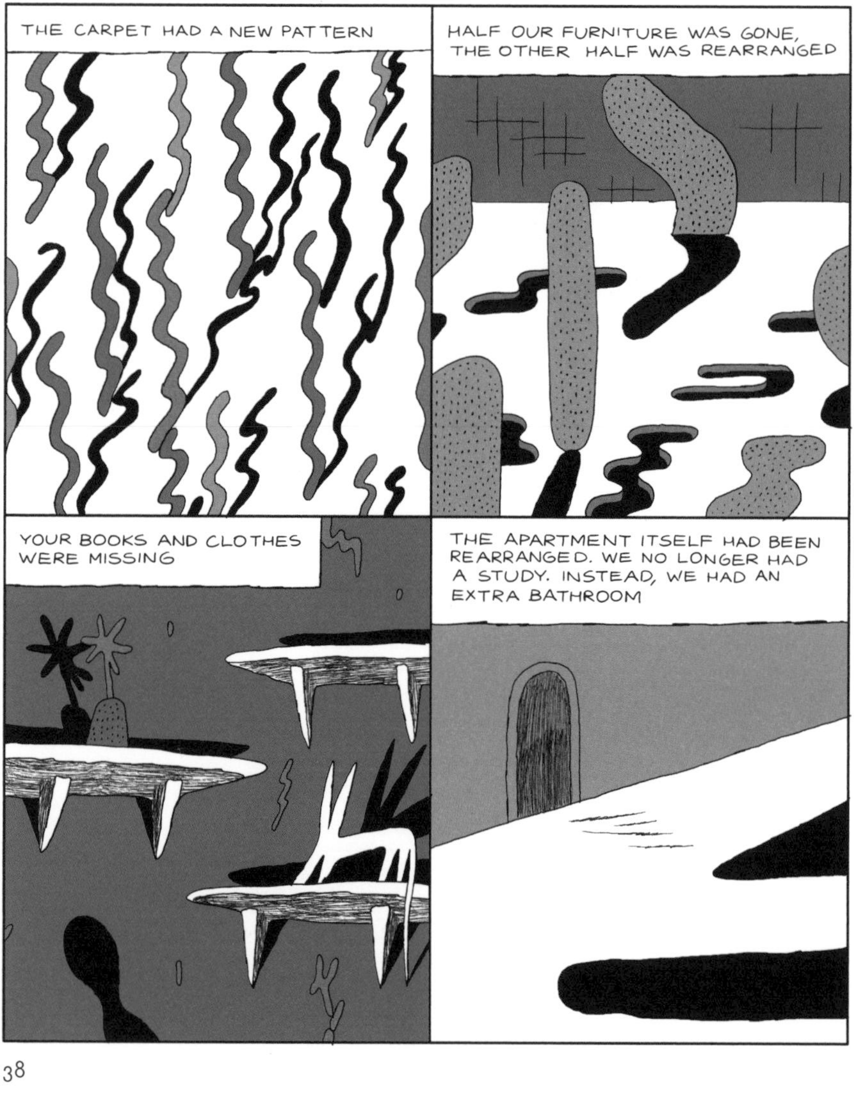
THE CARPET HAD A NEW PATTERN
HALF OUR FURNITURE WAS GONE, THE OTHER HALF WAS REARRANGED
YOUR BOOKS AND CLOTHES WERE MISSING
THE APARTMENT ITSELF HAD BEEN REARRANGED. WE NO LONGER HAD A STUDY. INSTEAD, WE HAD AN EXTRA BATHROOM

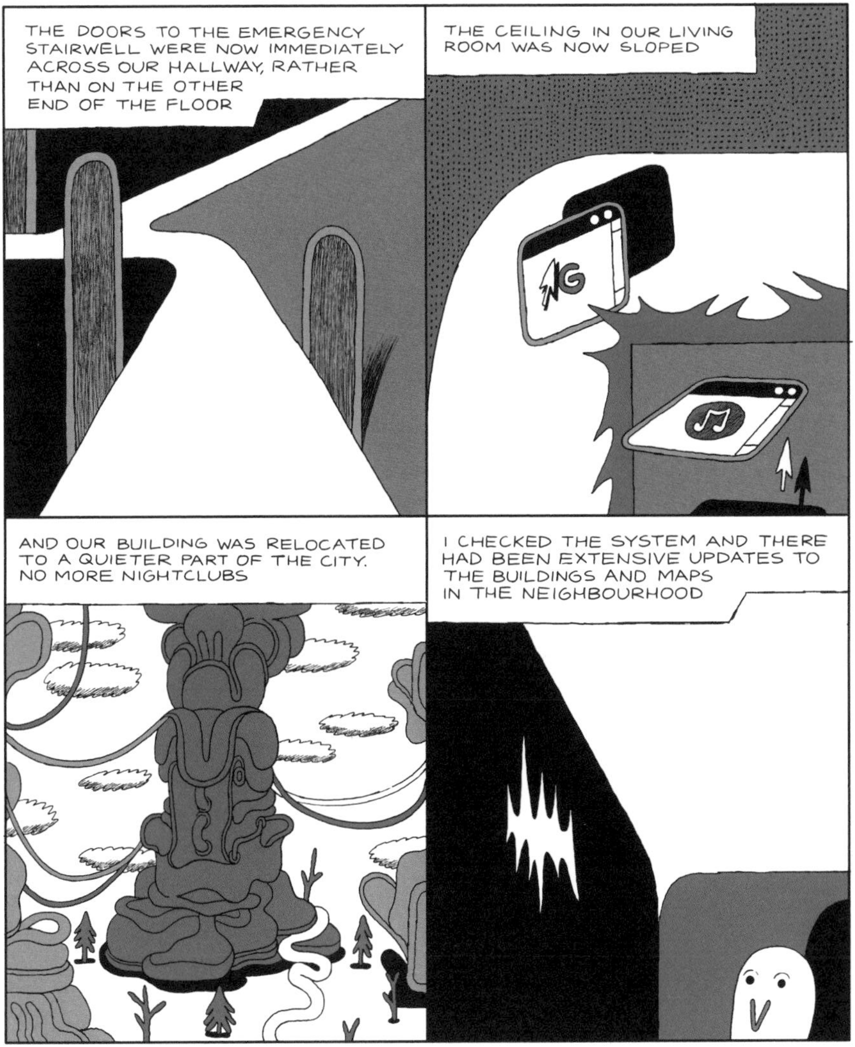
THE DOORS TO THE EMERGENCY STAIRWELL WERE NOW IMMEDIATELY ACROSS OUR HALLWAY, RATHER THAN ON THE OTHER END OF THE FLOOR
THE CEILING IN OUR LIVING ROOM WAS NOW SLOPED
G
AND OUR BUILDING WAS RELOCATED TO A QUIETER PART OF THE CITY. NO MORE NIGHTCLUBS
I CHECKED THE SYSTEM AND THERE HAD BEEN EXTENSIVE UPDATES TO THE BUILDINGS AND MAPS IN THE NEIGHBOURHOOD

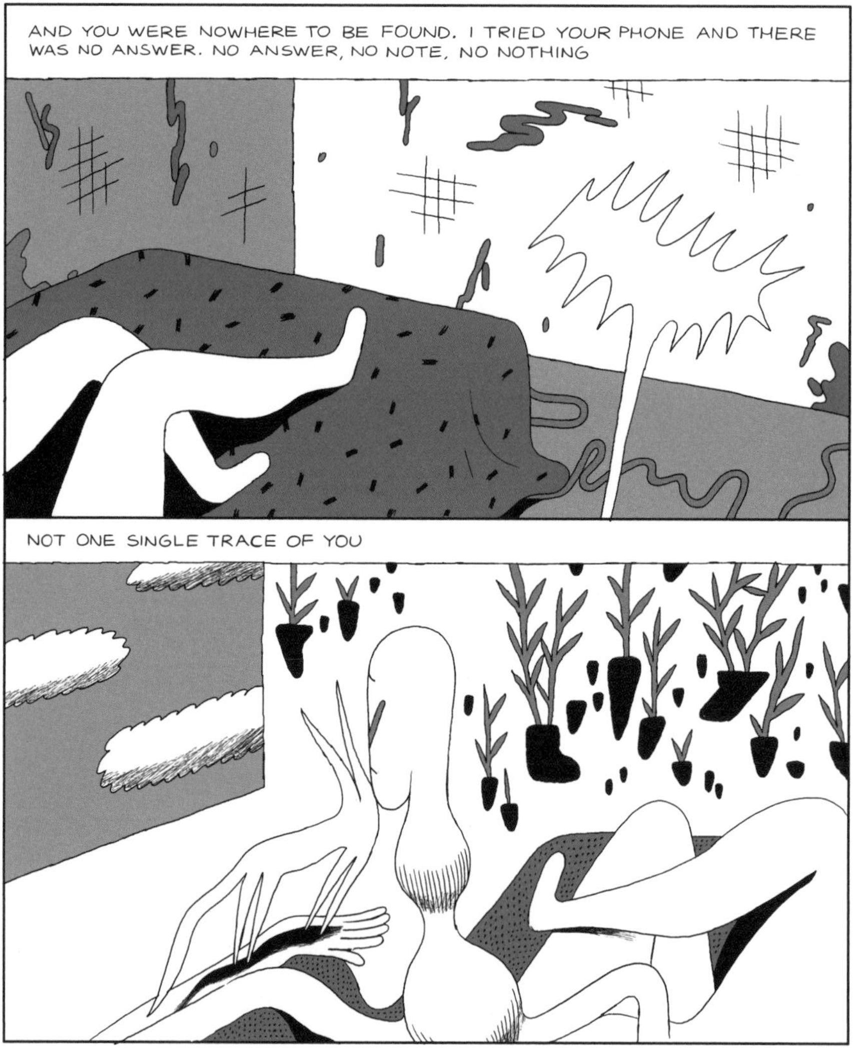
AND YOU WERE NOWHERE TO BE FOUND. I TRIED YOUR PHONE AND THERE WAS NO ANSWER. NO ANSWER, NO NOTE, NO NOTHING
NOT ONE SINGLE TRACE OF YOU

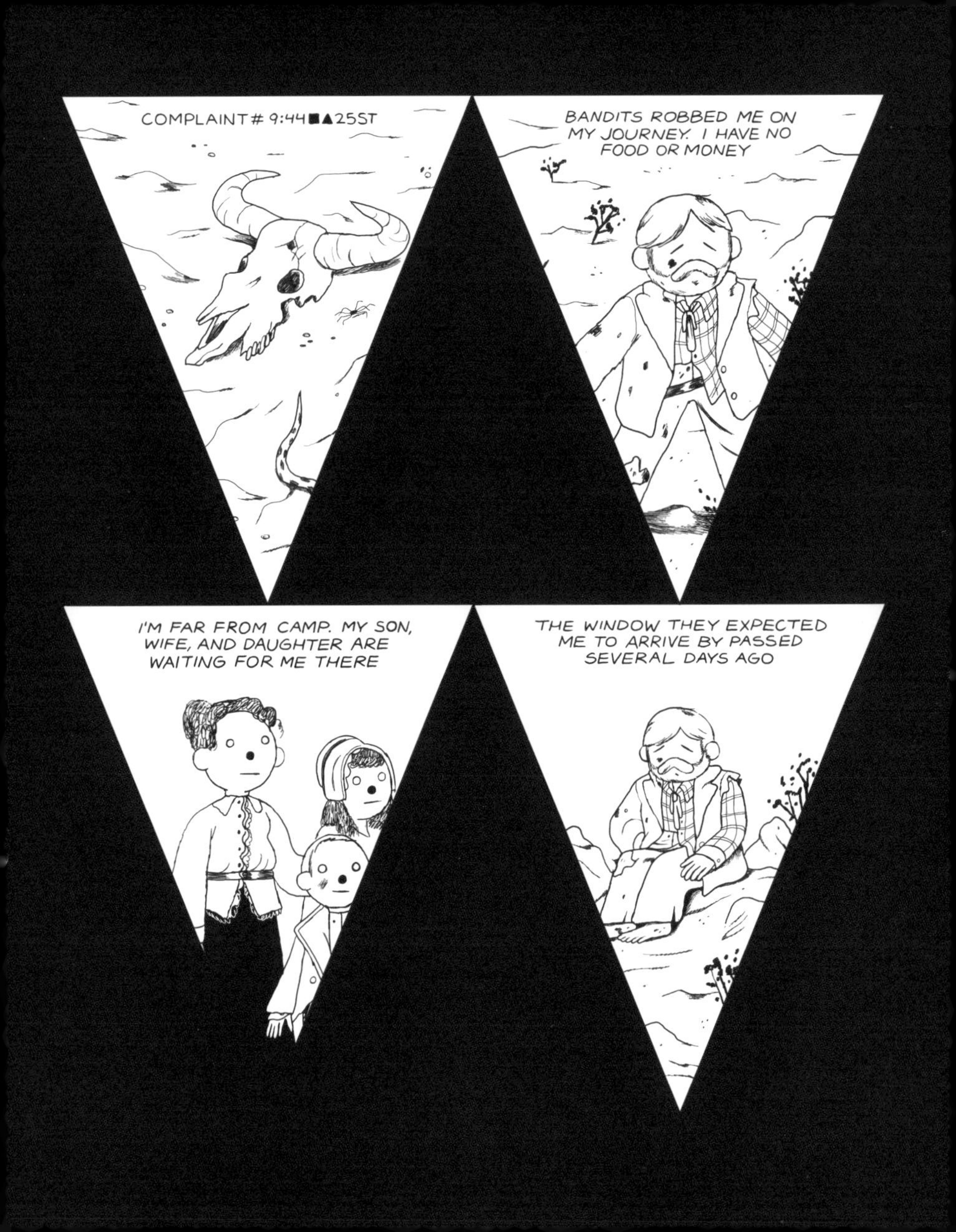
COMPLAINT # 9:44■▲25ST
BANDITS ROBBED ME ON MY JOURNEY. I HAVE NO FOOD OR MONEY
I'M FAR FROM CAMP. MY SON, WIFE, AND DAUGHTER ARE WAITING FOR ME THERE
THE WINDOW THEY EXPECTED ME TO ARRIVE BY PASSED SEVERAL DAYS AGO

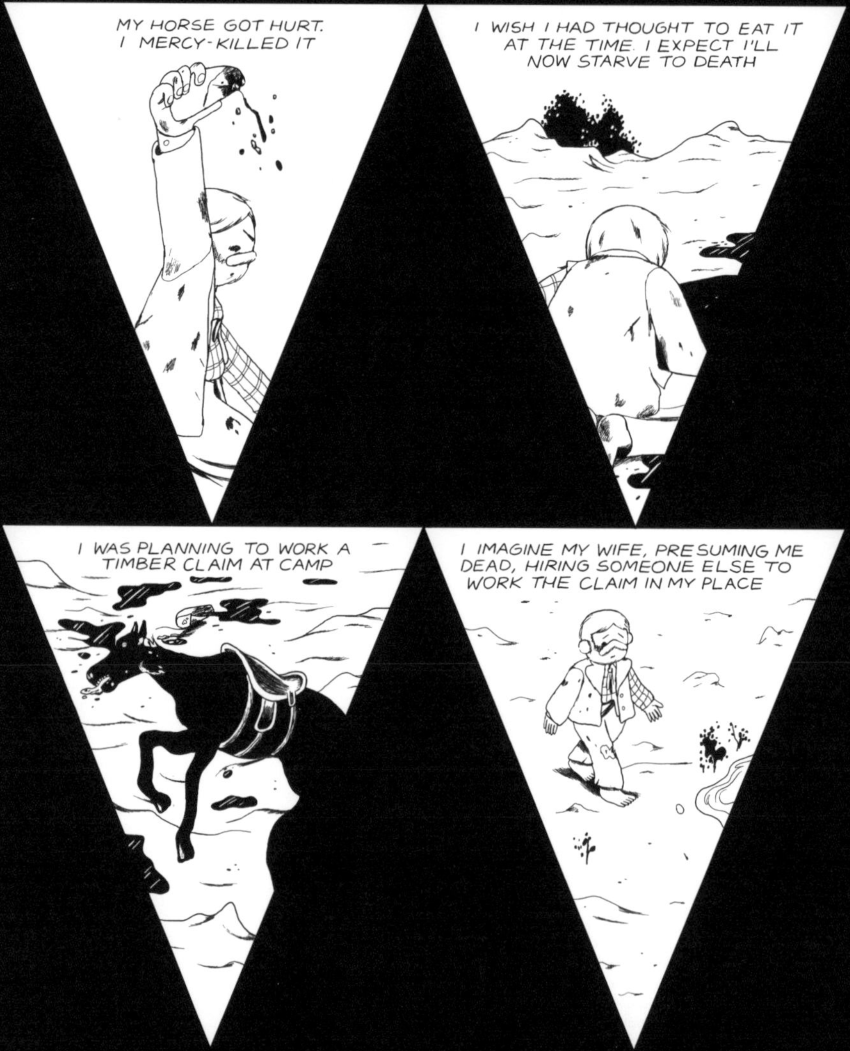
MY HORSE GOT HURT. I MERCY-KILLED IT
I WISH I HAD THOUGHT TO EAT IT AT THE TIME. I EXPECT I'LL NOW STARVE TO DEATH
I WAS PLANNING TO WORK A TIMBER CLAIM AT CAMP
I IMAGINE MY WIFE, PRESUMING ME DEAD, HIRING SOMEONE ELSE TO WORK THE CLAIM IN MY PLACE

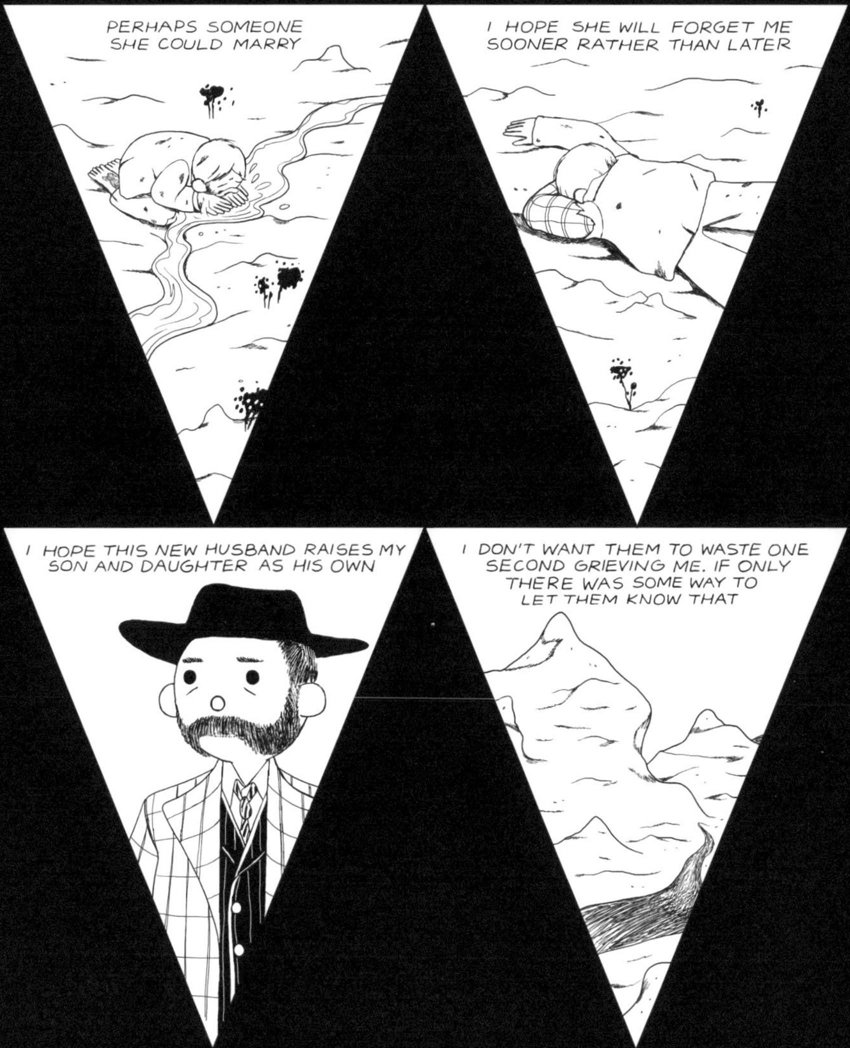
PERHAPS SOMEONE SHE COULD MARRY
I HOPE SHE WILL FORGET ME SOONER RATHER THAN LATER
I HOPE THIS NEW HUSBAND RAISES MY SON AND DAUGHTER AS HIS OWN
I DON'T WANT THEM TO WASTE ONE SECOND GRIEVING ME. IF ONLY THERE WAS SOME WAY TO LET THEM KNOW THAT

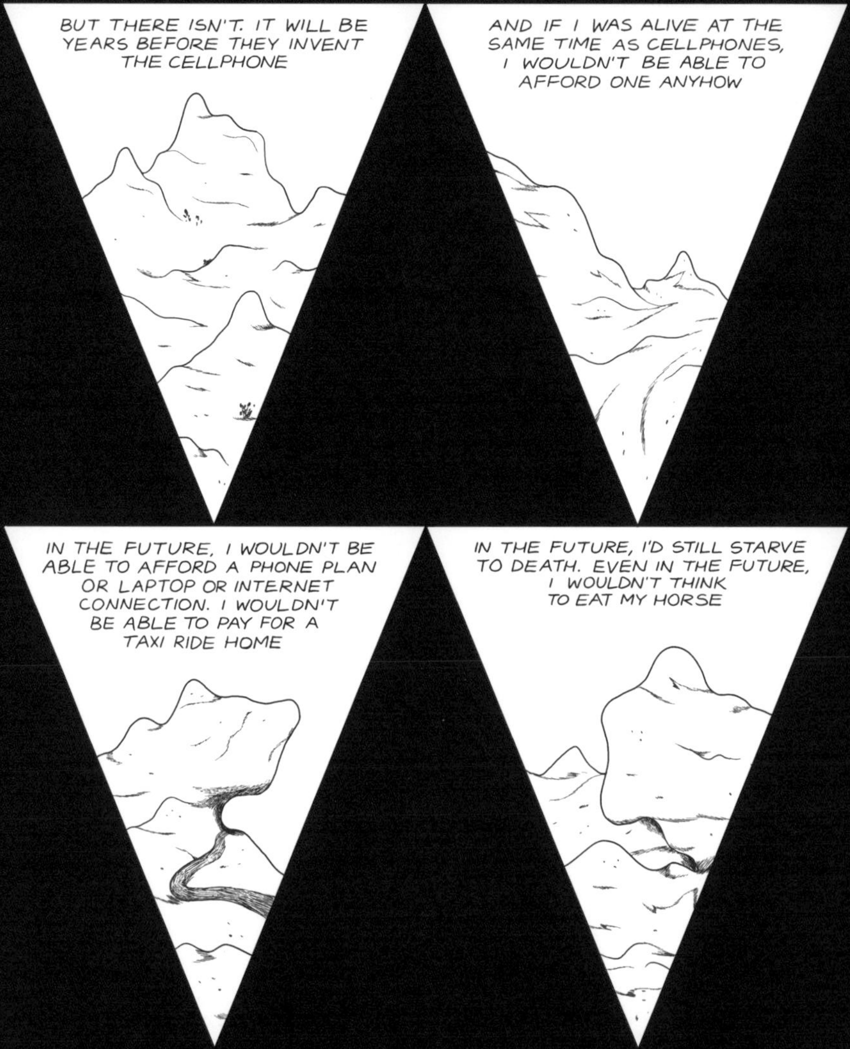
BUT THERE ISN'T. IT WILL BE YEARS BEFORE THEY INVENT THE CELLPHONE
AND IF I WAS ALIVE AT THE SAME TIME AS CELLPHONES, I WOULDN'T BE ABLE TO AFFORD ONE ANYHOW
IN THE FUTURE, I WOULDN'T BE ABLE TO AFFORD A PHONE PLAN OR LAPTOP OR INTERNET CONNECTION. I WOULDN'T BE ABLE TO PAY FOR A TAXI RIDE HOME
IN THE FUTURE, I'D STILL STARVE TO DEATH. EVEN IN THE FUTURE, I WOULDN'T THINK TO EAT MY HORSE

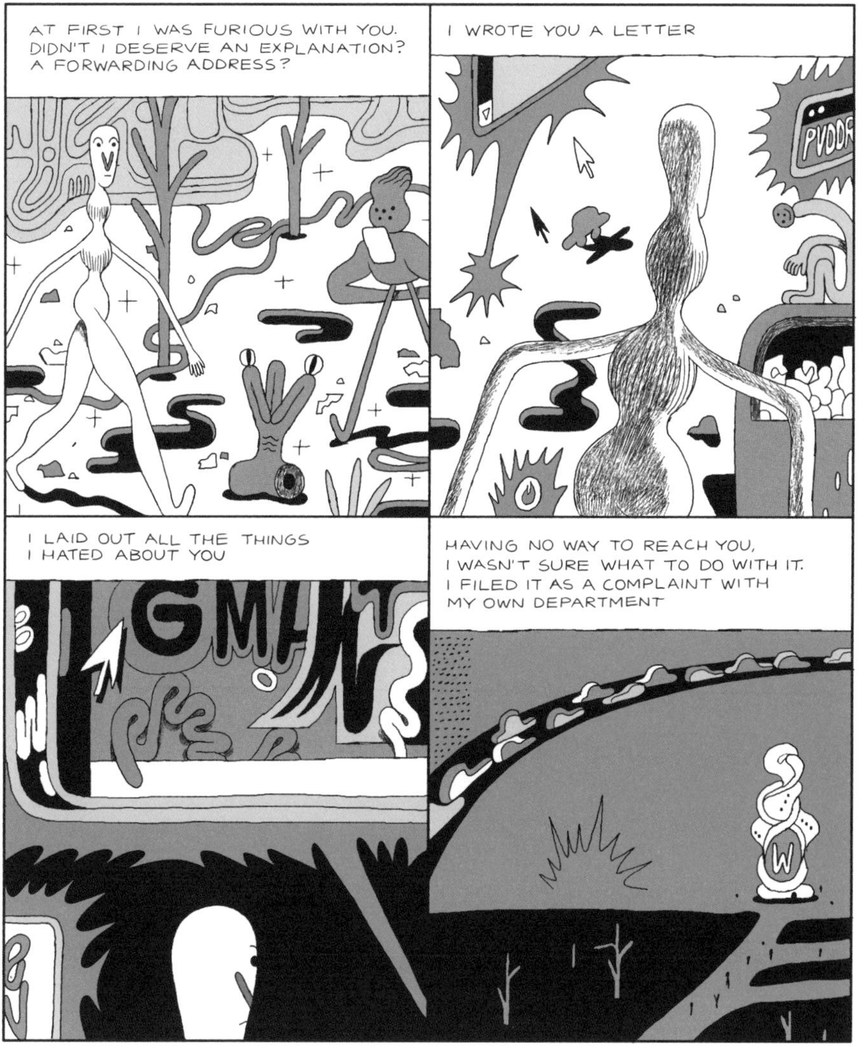
AT FIRST I WAS FURIOUS WITH YOU. DIDN'T I DESERVE AN EXPLANATION? A FORWARDING ADDRESS?
I WROTE YOU A LETTER
PVDDR
I LAID OUT ALL THE THINGS I HATED ABOUT YOU
GM
HAVING NO WAY TO REACH YOU, I WASN'T SURE WHAT TO DO WITH IT. I FILED IT AS A COMPLAINT WITH MY OWN DEPARTMENT
W

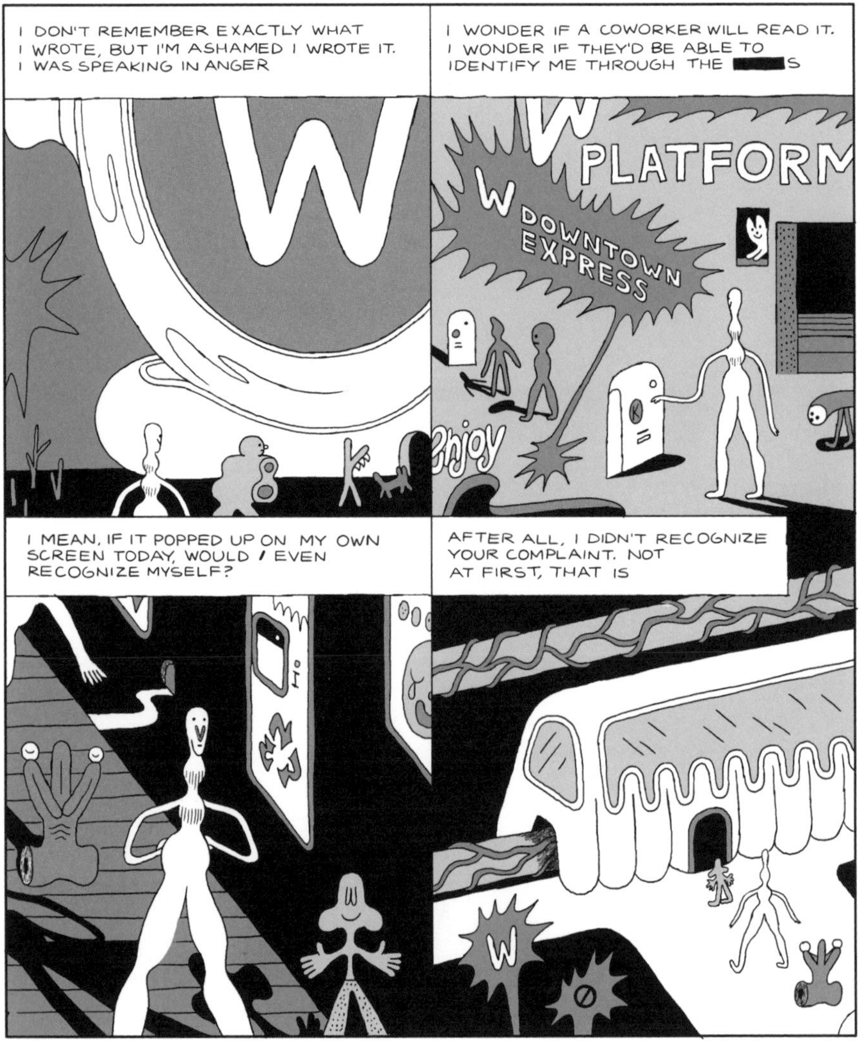
I DON'T REMEMBER EXACTLY WHAT I WROTE, BUT I'M ASHAMED I WROTE IT. I WAS SPEAKING IN ANGER
W
I WONDER IF A COWORKER WILL READ IT. I WONDER IF THEY'D BE ABLE TO IDENTIFY ME THROUGH THE [redacted]S
W
PLATFORM
W
DOWNTOWN EXPRESS
enjoy
I MEAN, IF IT POPPED UP ON MY OWN SCREEN TODAY, WOULD I EVEN RECOGNIZE MYSELF?
AFTER ALL, I DIDN'T RECOGNIZE YOUR COMPLAINT. NOT AT FIRST, THAT IS
W

BUT I WAS ALL OVER THE PLACE THAT DAY. OUR CAR HAD VANISHED ALONG WITH YOU. MAYBE IT HAD RELOCATED TO SOME NEW PARKING SPACE?

ANYWAY, I WAS TAKING THE TRAIN. MY COMMUTE TO WORK TOOK AN EXTRA HOUR AND A HALF WITH THE LAST MAP UPDATE

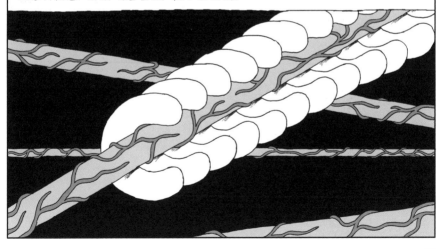

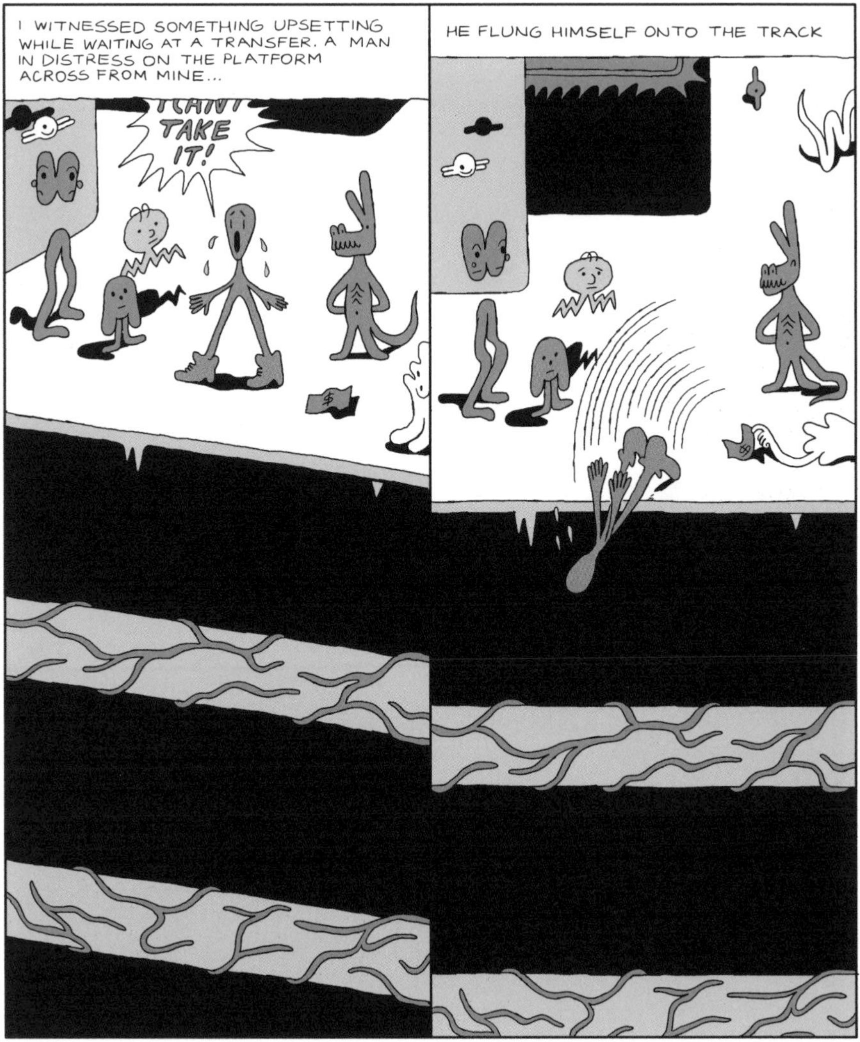
I WITNESSED SOMETHING UPSETTING WHILE WAITING AT A TRANSFER. A MAN IN DISTRESS ON THE PLATFORM ACROSS FROM MINE...
TAKE IT!
HE FLUNG HIMSELF ONTO THE TRACK

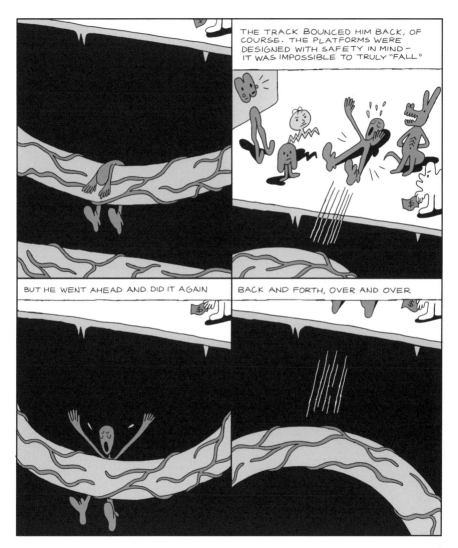

THE TRACK BOUNCED HIM BACK, OF COURSE. THE PLATFORMS WERE DESIGNED WITH SAFETY IN MIND — IT WAS IMPOSSIBLE TO TRULY "FALL"

BUT HE WENT AHEAD AND DID IT AGAIN

BACK AND FORTH, OVER AND OVER

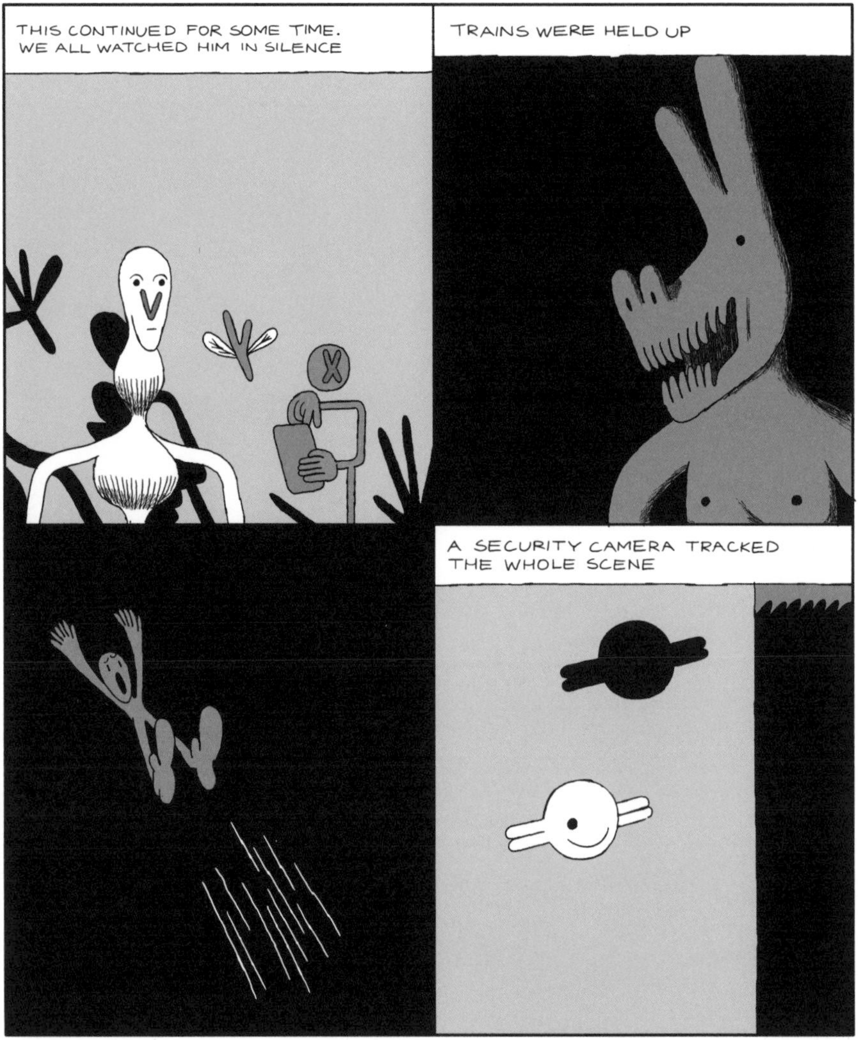
THIS CONTINUED FOR SOME TIME. WE ALL WATCHED HIM IN SILENCE
TRAINS WERE HELD UP
A SECURITY CAMERA TRACKED THE WHOLE SCENE

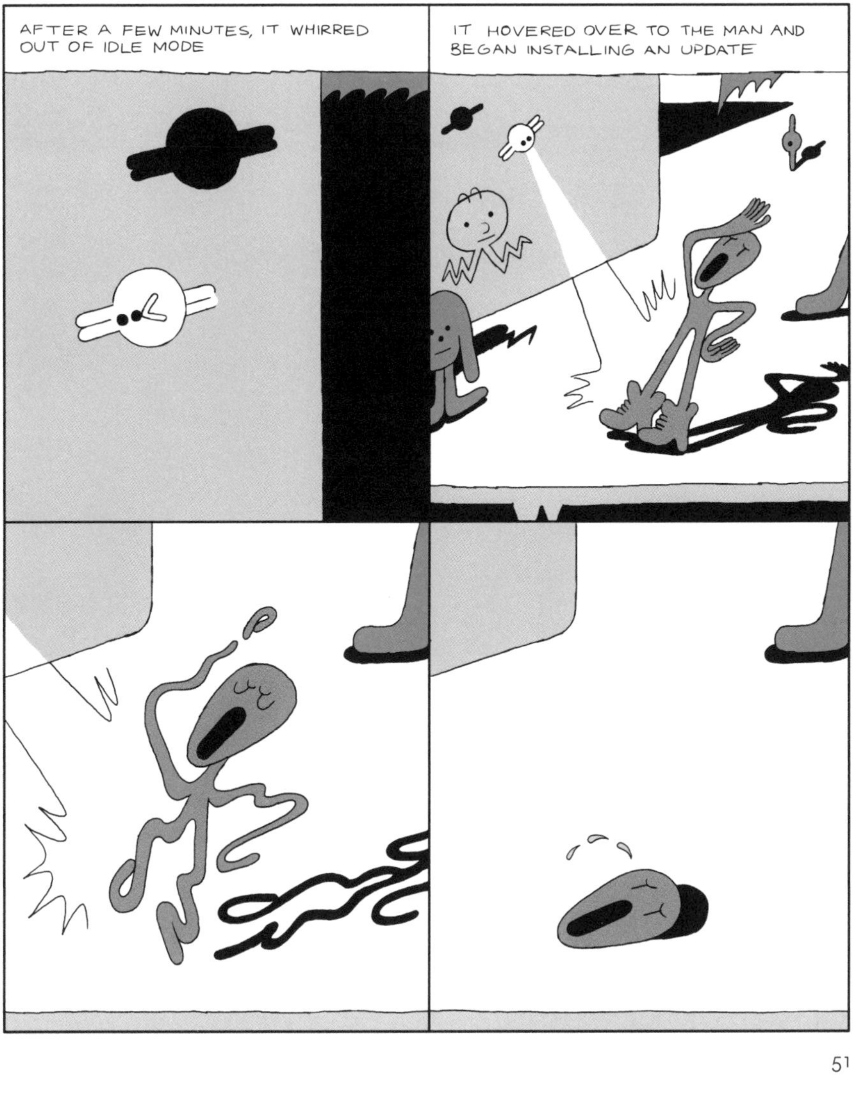
AFTER A FEW MINUTES, IT WHIRRED OUT OF IDLE MODE
IT HOVERED OVER TO THE MAN AND BEGAN INSTALLING AN UPDATE

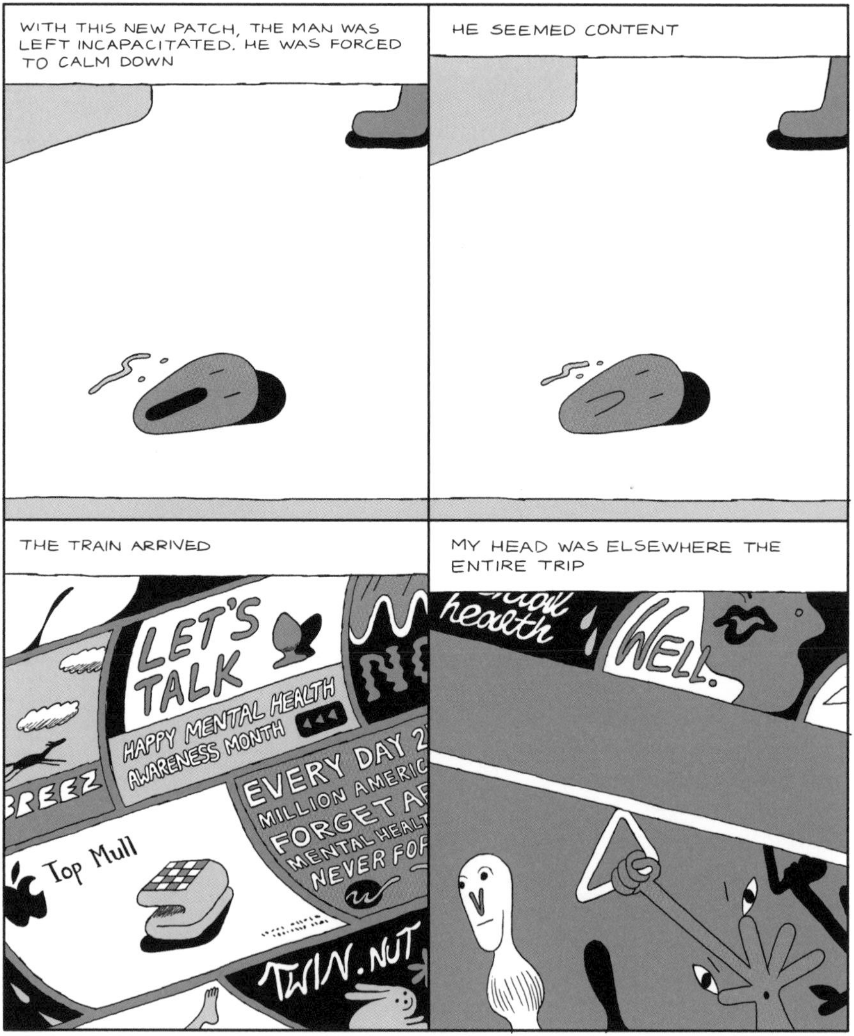
WITH THIS NEW PATCH, THE MAN WAS LEFT INCAPACITATED. HE WAS FORCED TO CALM DOWN
HE SEEMED CONTENT
THE TRAIN ARRIVED
LET'S TALK
HAPPY MENTAL HEALTH AWARENESS MONTH
Top Mull
TWIN.NUT
MY HEAD WAS ELSEWHERE THE ENTIRE TRIP
health
WELL.

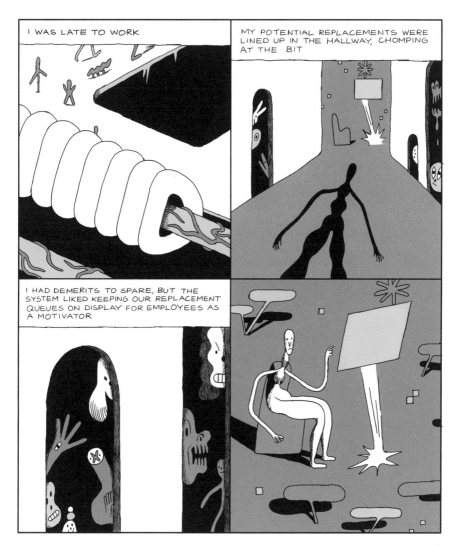

I WAS LATE TO WORK

MY POTENTIAL REPLACEMENTS WERE LINED UP IN THE HALLWAY, CHOMPING AT THE BIT

I HAD DEMERITS TO SPARE, BUT THE SYSTEM LIKED KEEPING OUR REPLACEMENT QUEUES ON DISPLAY FOR EMPLOYEES AS A MOTIVATOR

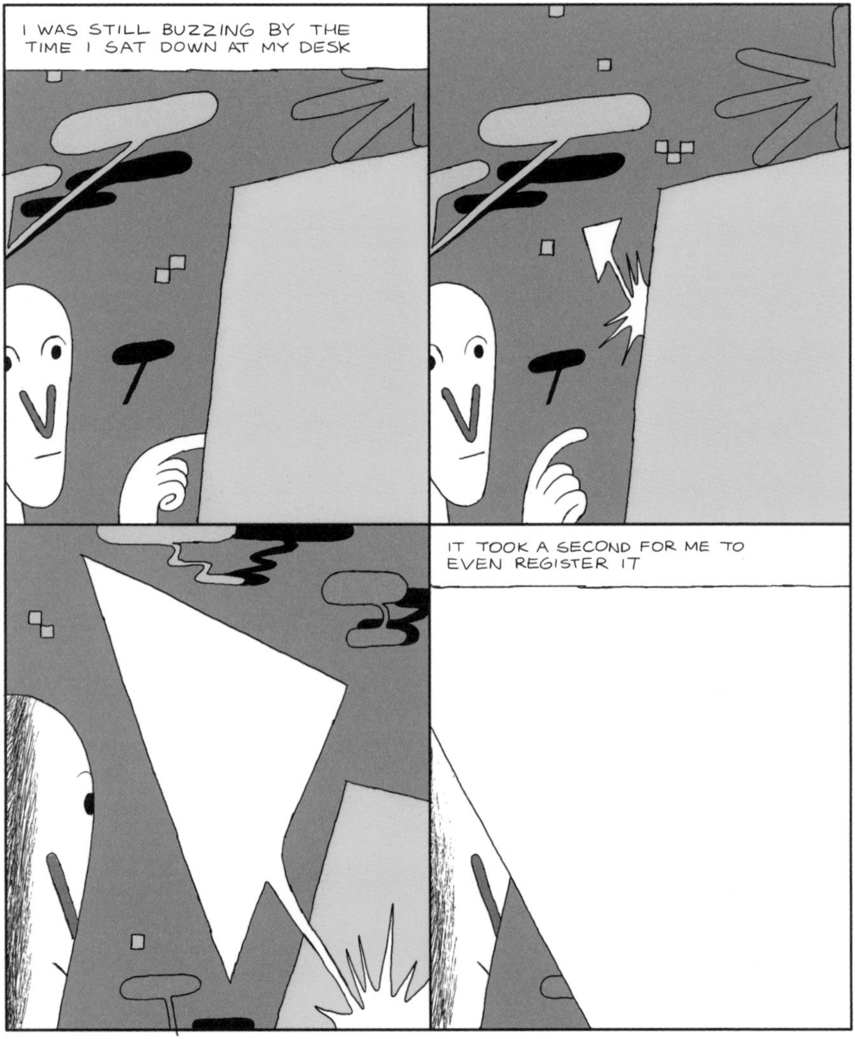
I WAS STILL BUZZING BY THE TIME I SAT DOWN AT MY DESK
IT TOOK A SECOND FOR ME TO EVEN REGISTER IT

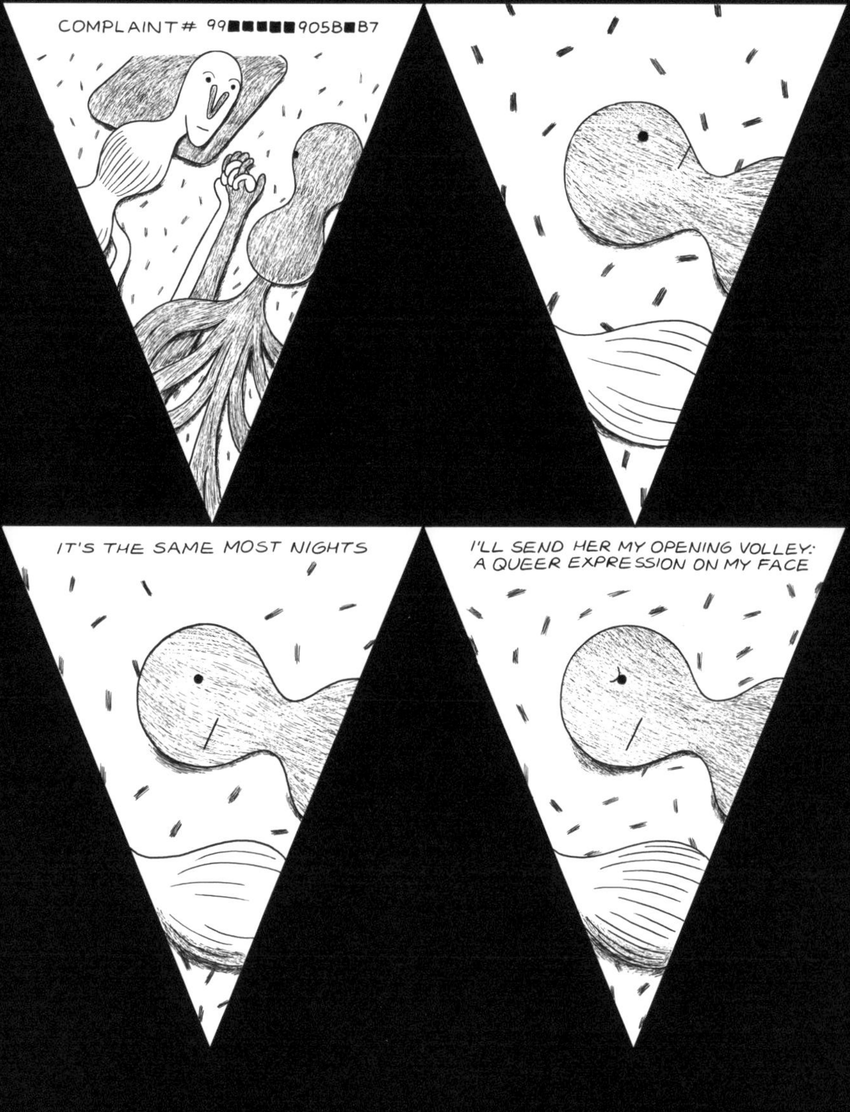
COMPLAINT # 99[redacted]905B[redacted]B7
IT'S THE SAME MOST NIGHTS
I'LL SEND HER MY OPENING VOLLEY:
A QUEER EXPRESSION ON MY FACE

SHE LOBS BACK: NOTHING. SHE NEVER SAYS A THING. THIS STALEMATE GOES ON ALL NIGHT
I USED TO CONFUSE IT WITH GRACE. OR STOICISM?
NOW I IMAGINE HER AS AN ENORMOUS THROAT, WITH AN ENORMOUS LUMP SITTING INSIDE OF IT
I FANTASIZE ABOUT CRACKING AN EGG IN OUR BED

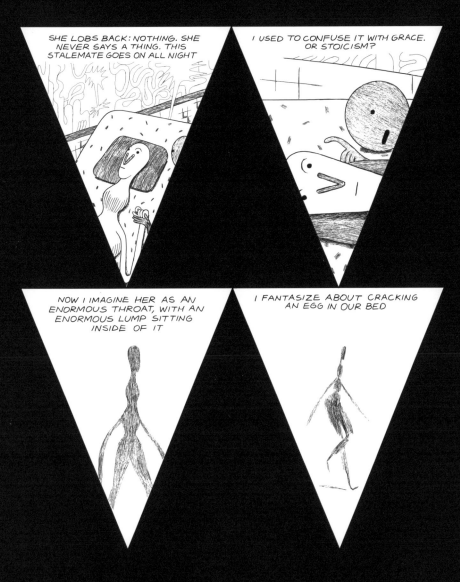

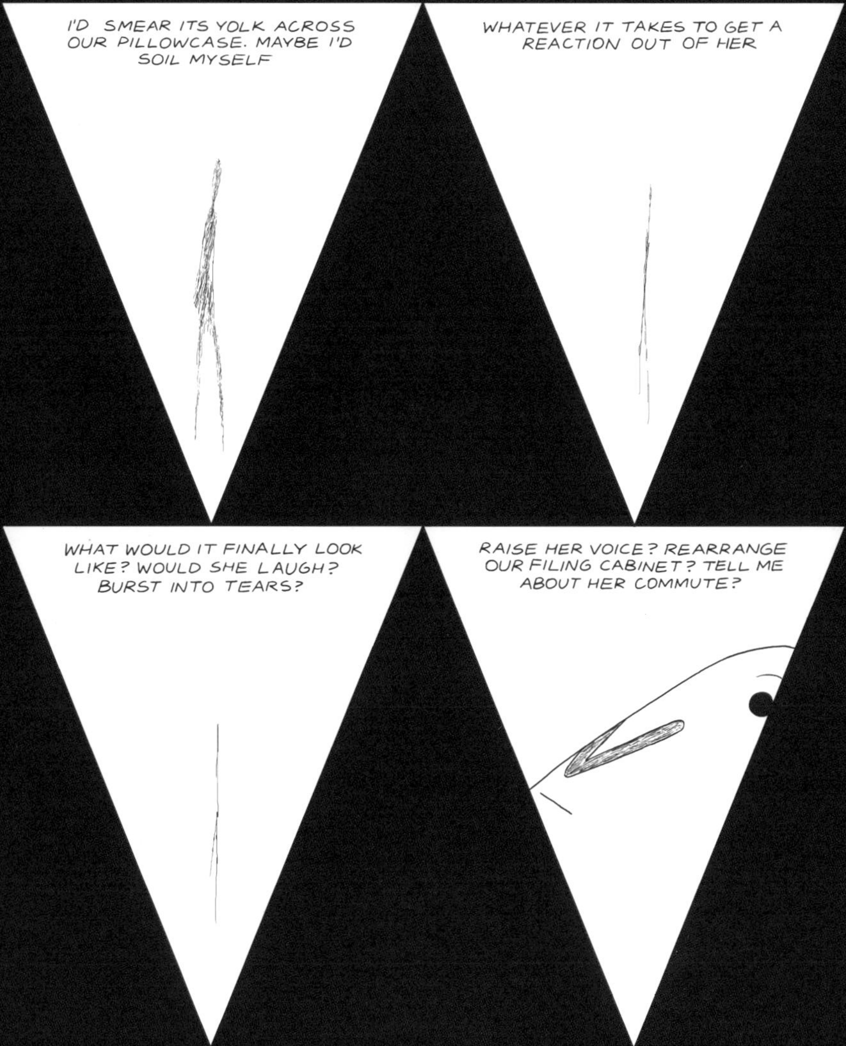
I'D SMEAR ITS YOLK ACROSS OUR PILLOWCASE. MAYBE I'D SOIL MYSELF
WHATEVER IT TAKES TO GET A REACTION OUT OF HER
WHAT WOULD IT FINALLY LOOK LIKE? WOULD SHE LAUGH? BURST INTO TEARS?
RAISE HER VOICE? REARRANGE OUR FILING CABINET? TELL ME ABOUT HER COMMUTE?

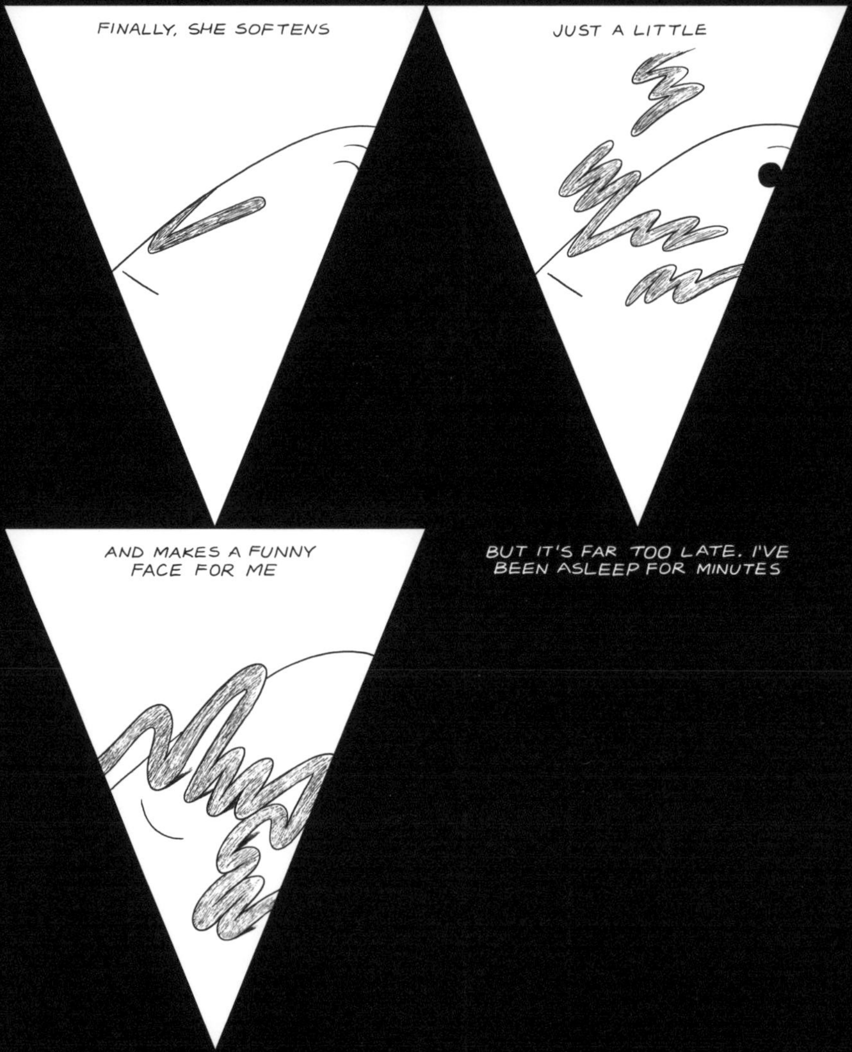
FINALLY, SHE SOFTENS
JUST A LITTLE
AND MAKES A FUNNY FACE FOR ME
BUT IT'S FAR TOO LATE. I'VE BEEN ASLEEP FOR MINUTES

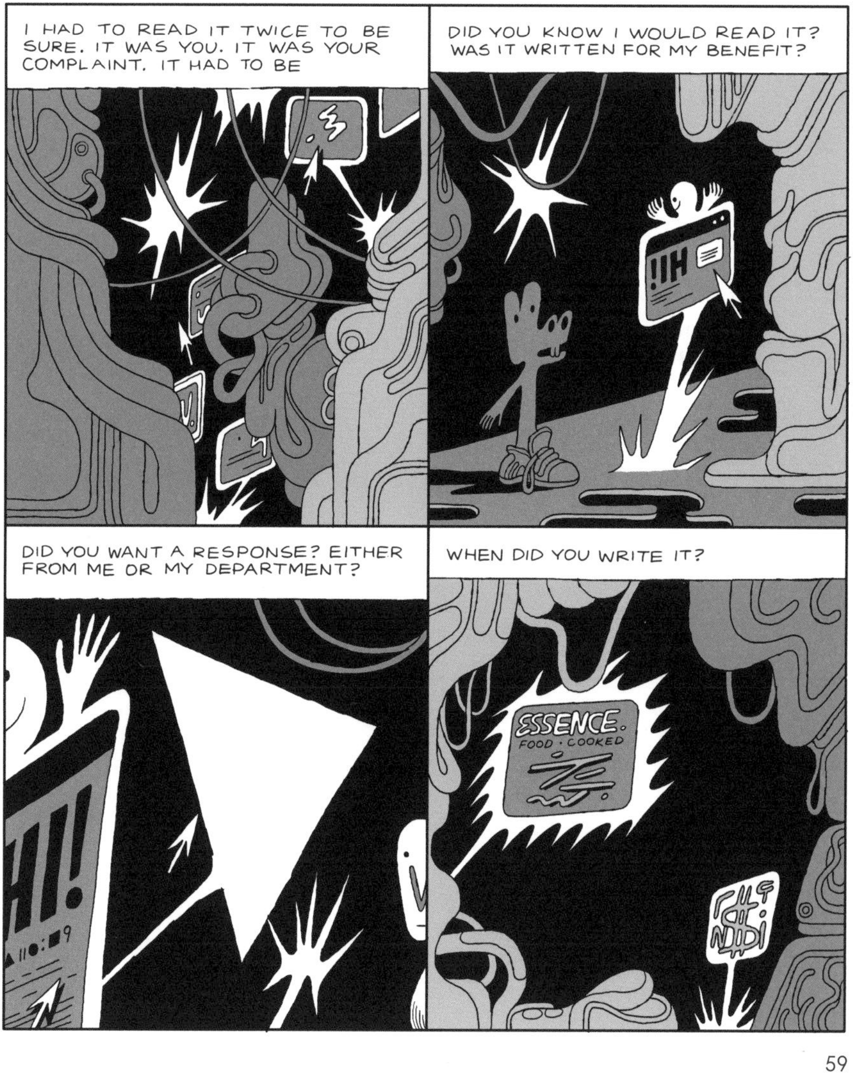
I HAD TO READ IT TWICE TO BE SURE. IT WAS YOU. IT WAS YOUR COMPLAINT. IT HAD TO BE
DID YOU KNOW I WOULD READ IT? WAS IT WRITTEN FOR MY BENEFIT?
!!H
DID YOU WANT A RESPONSE? EITHER FROM ME OR MY DEPARTMENT?
HI!
WHEN DID YOU WRITE IT?
ESSENCE.
FOOD · COOKED

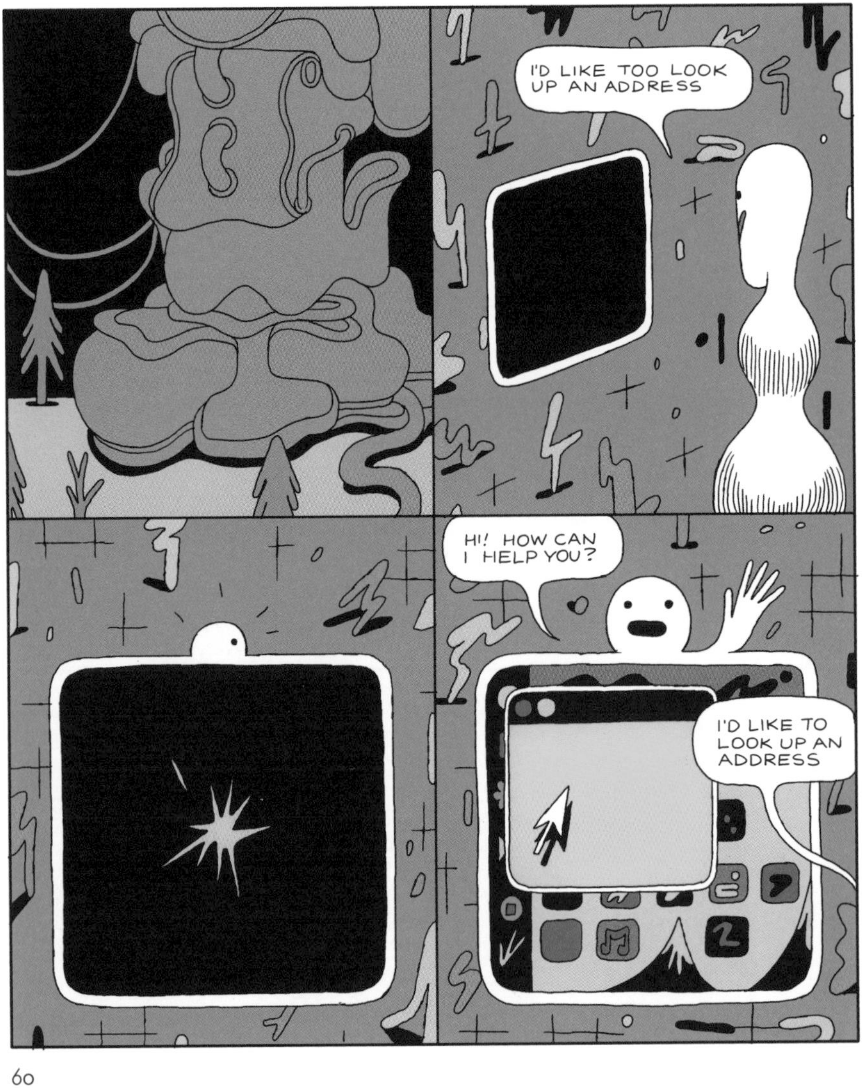
I'D LIKE TOO LOOK UP AN ADDRESS
HI! HOW CAN I HELP YOU?
I'D LIKE TO LOOK UP AN ADDRESS

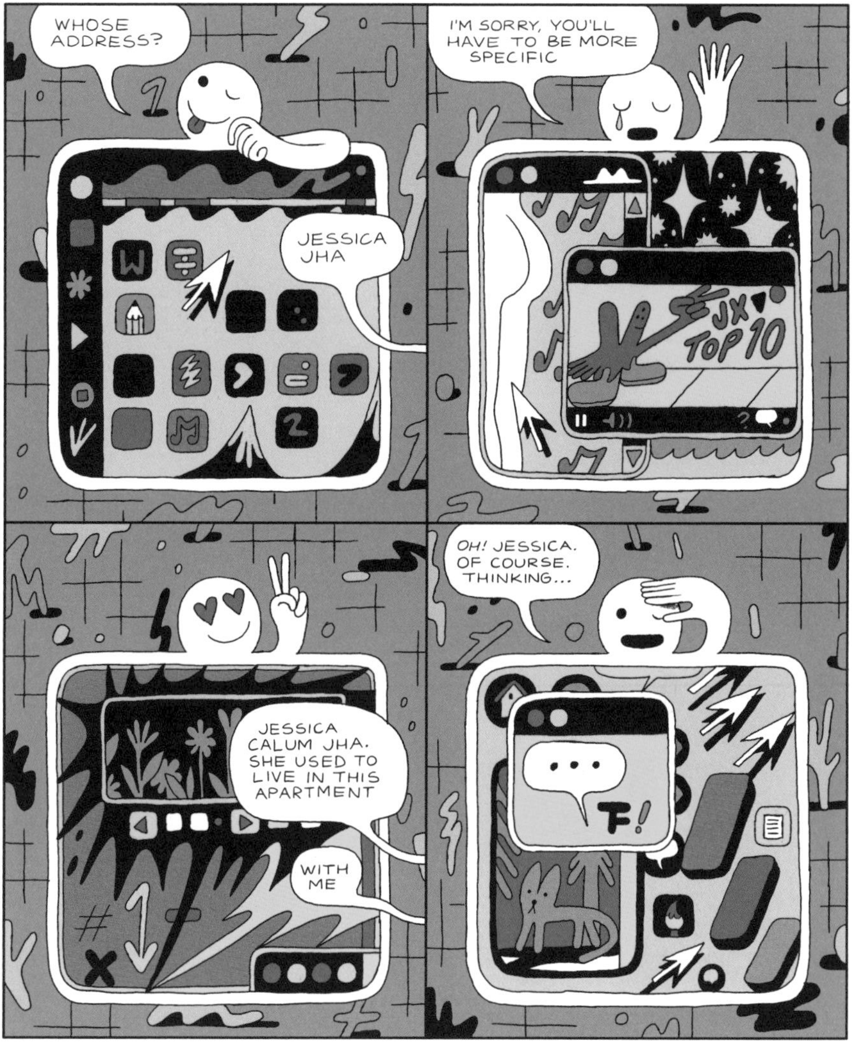
WHOSE ADDRESS?
JESSICA JHA
I'M SORRY, YOU'LL HAVE TO BE MORE SPECIFIC
JX TOP 10
JESSICA CALUM JHA. SHE USED TO LIVE IN THIS APARTMENT
WITH ME
OH! JESSICA. OF COURSE. THINKING...

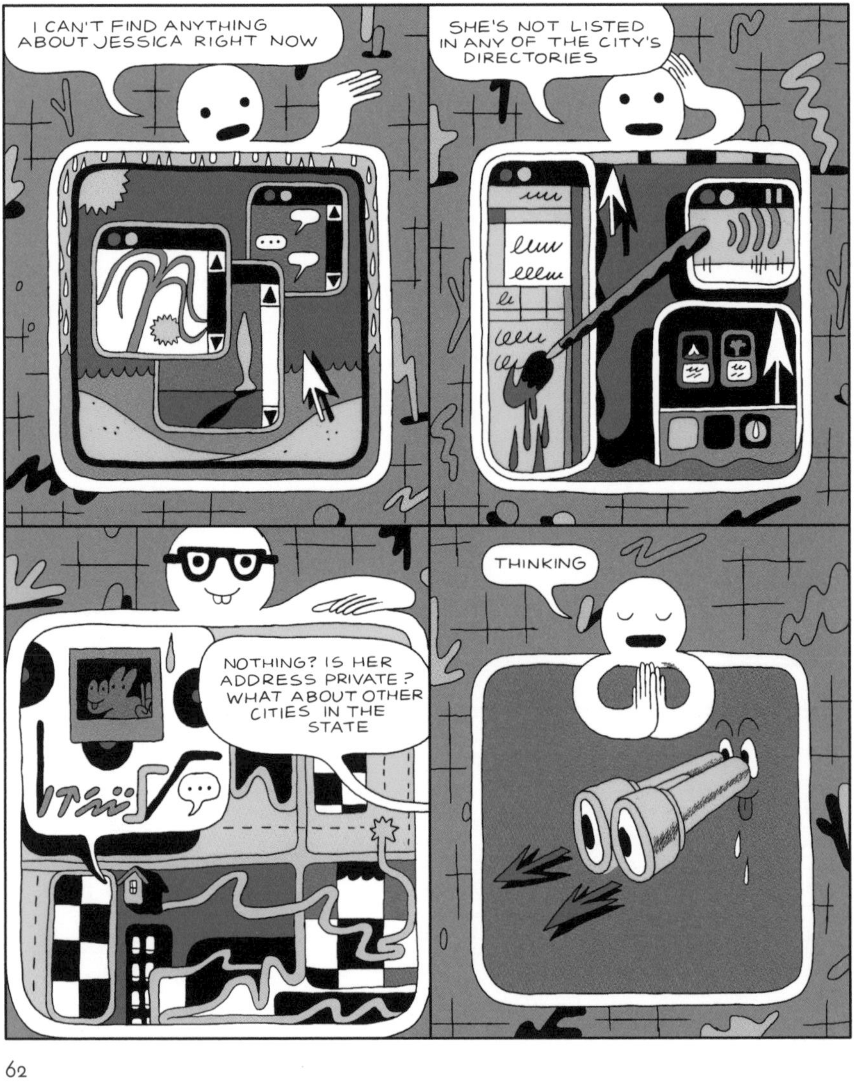
I CAN'T FIND ANYTHING ABOUT JESSICA RIGHT NOW
SHE'S NOT LISTED IN ANY OF THE CITY'S DIRECTORIES
NOTHING? IS HER ADDRESS PRIVATE? WHAT ABOUT OTHER CITIES IN THE STATE
THINKING

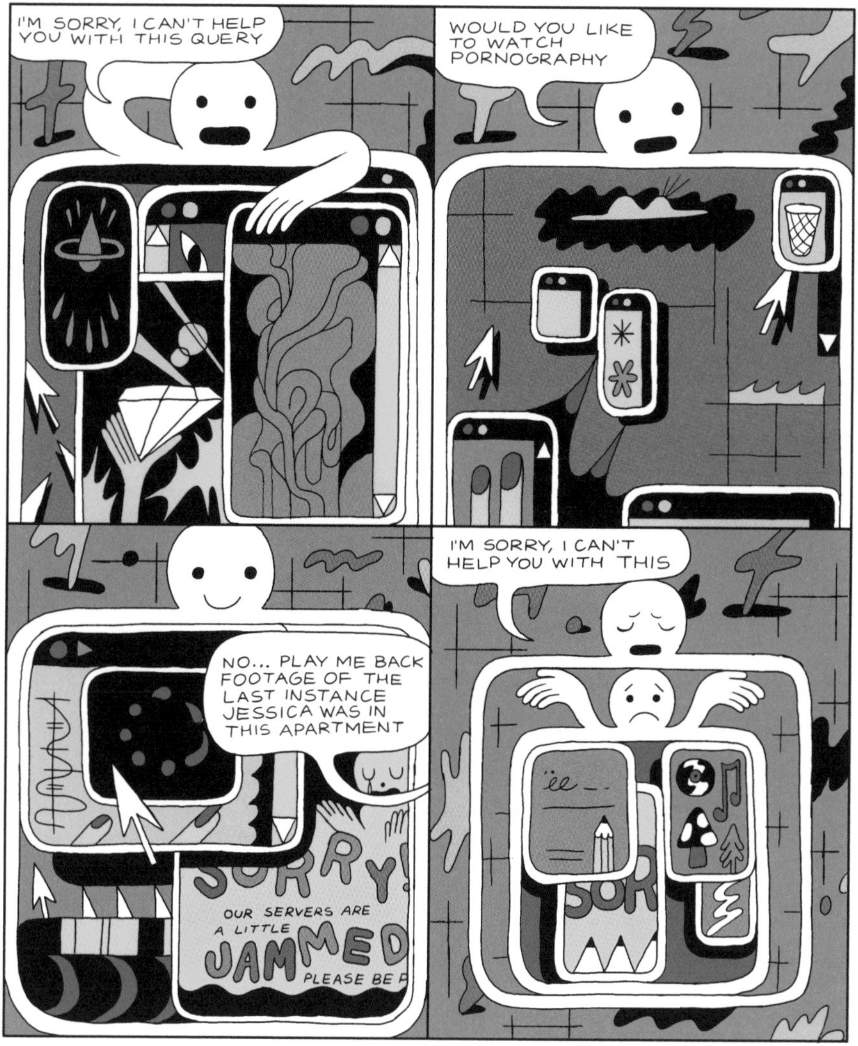

I'M SORRY, I CAN'T HELP YOU WITH THIS QUERY
WOULD YOU LIKE TO WATCH PORNOGRAPHY
NO... PLAY ME BACK FOOTAGE OF THE LAST INSTANCE JESSICA WAS IN THIS APARTMENT
SORRY!
OUR SERVERS ARE A LITTLE JAMMED
PLEASE BE P
I'M SORRY, I CAN'T HELP YOU WITH THIS

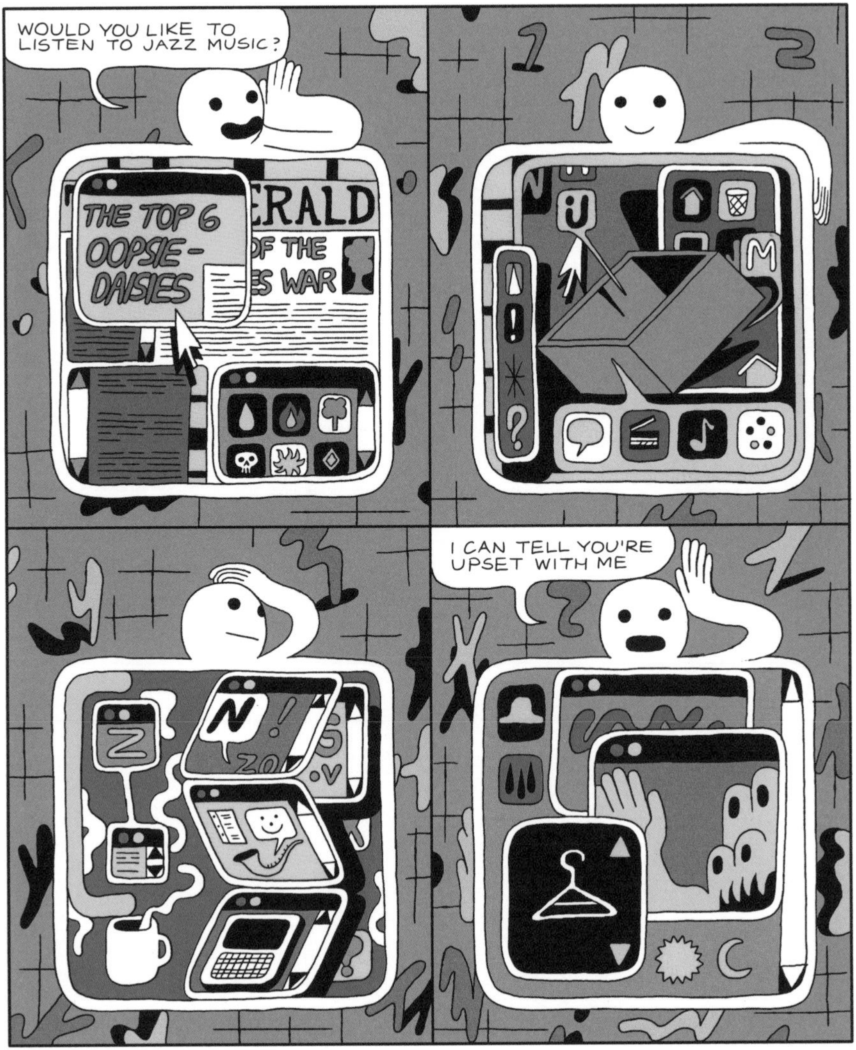
WOULD YOU LIKE TO LISTEN TO JAZZ MUSIC?
ERALD
THE TOP 6 OOPSIE-DAISIES
OF THE
ES WAR
I CAN TELL YOU'RE UPSET WITH ME

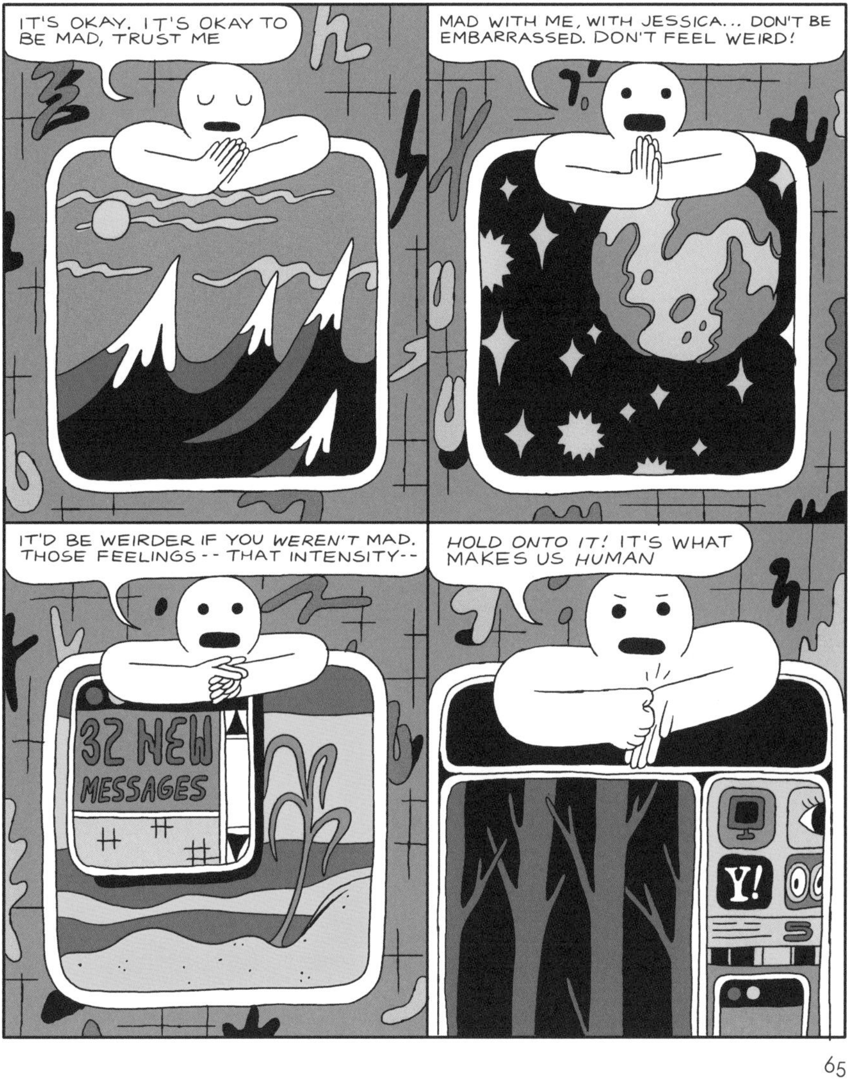
IT'S OKAY. IT'S OKAY TO BE MAD, TRUST ME
MAD WITH ME, WITH JESSICA... DON'T BE EMBARRASSED. DON'T FEEL WEIRD!
IT'D BE WEIRDER IF YOU *WEREN'T* MAD. THOSE FEELINGS -- THAT INTENSITY --
HOLD ONTO IT! IT'S WHAT MAKES US *HUMAN*
32 NEW MESSAGES
Y!

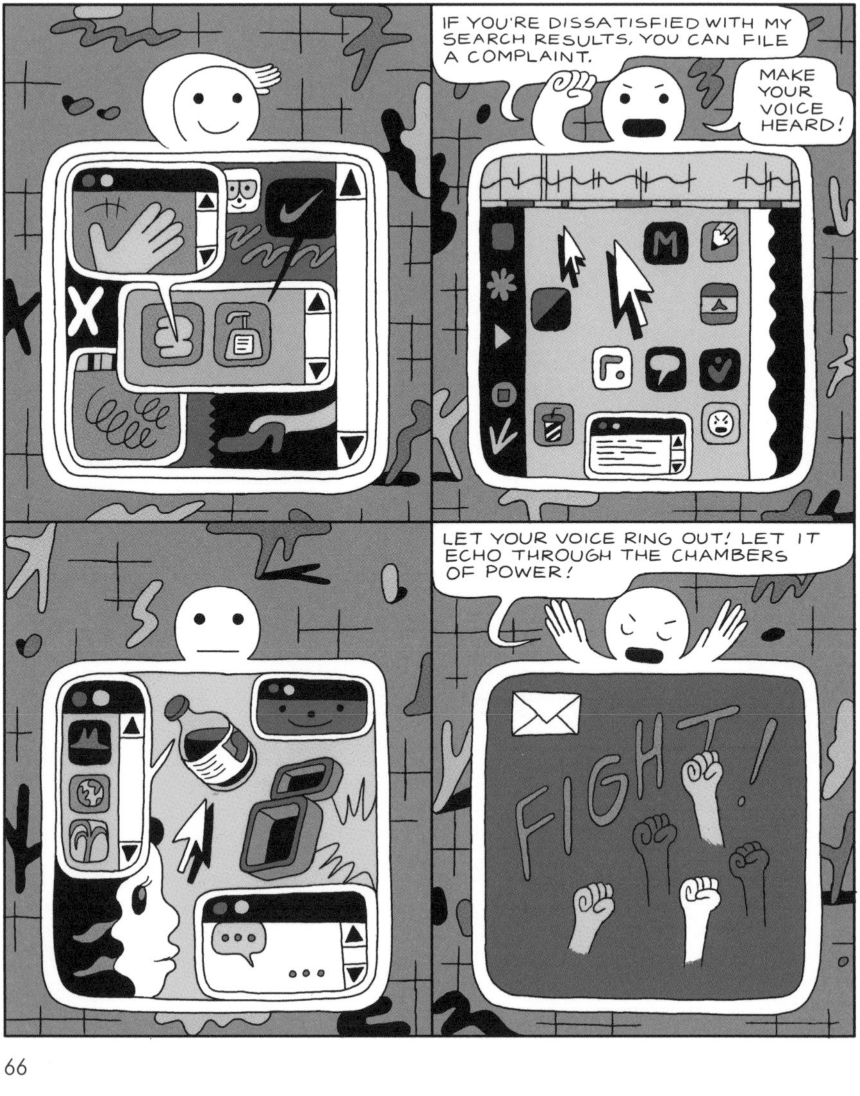
IF YOU'RE DISSATISFIED WITH MY SEARCH RESULTS, YOU CAN FILE A COMPLAINT.
MAKE YOUR VOICE HEARD!
LET YOUR VOICE RING OUT! LET IT ECHO THROUGH THE CHAMBERS OF POWER!
FIGHT!

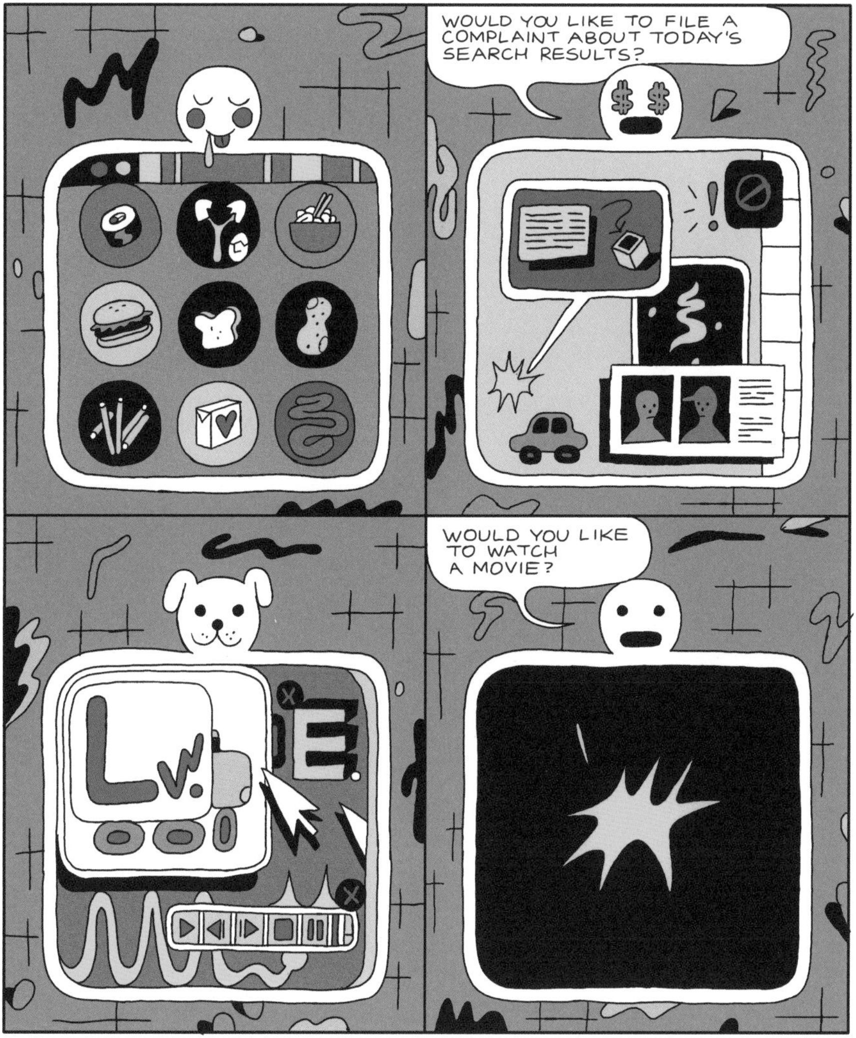
WOULD YOU LIKE TO FILE A COMPLAINT ABOUT TODAY'S SEARCH RESULTS?
WOULD YOU LIKE TO WATCH A MOVIE?

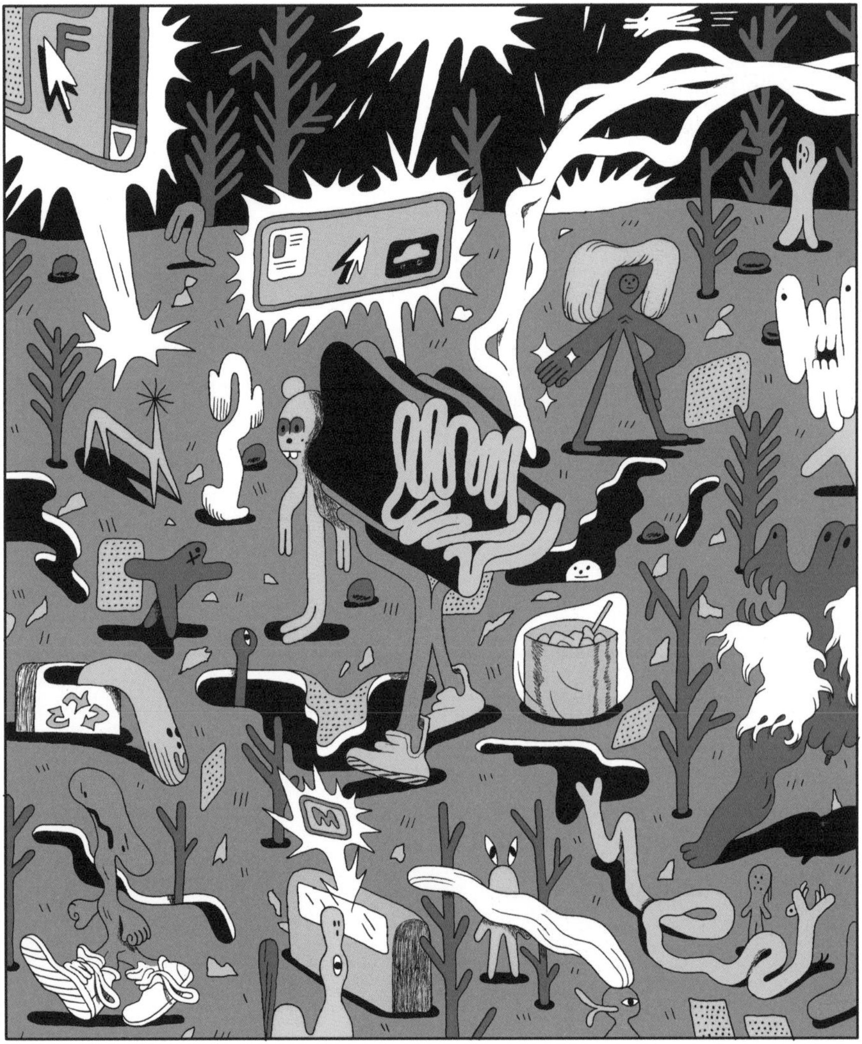

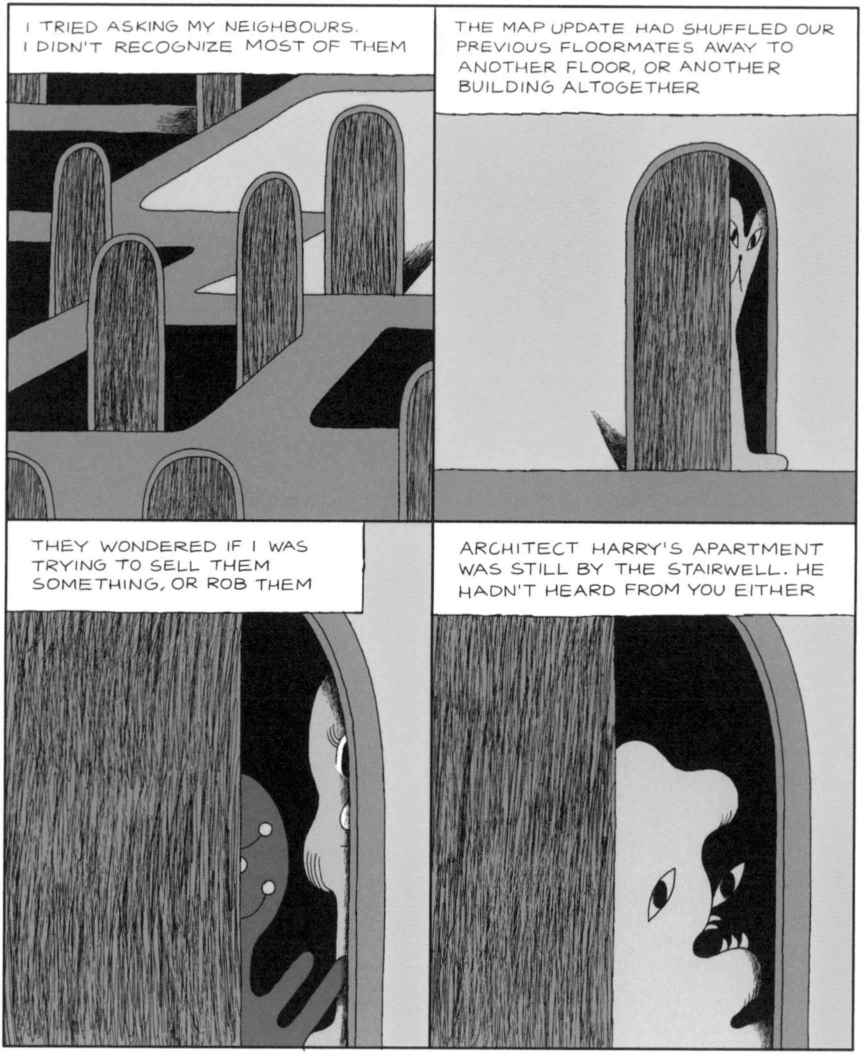
I TRIED ASKING MY NEIGHBOURS.
I DIDN'T RECOGNIZE MOST OF THEM
THE MAP UPDATE HAD SHUFFLED OUR PREVIOUS FLOORMATES AWAY TO ANOTHER FLOOR, OR ANOTHER BUILDING ALTOGETHER
THEY WONDERED IF I WAS TRYING TO SELL THEM SOMETHING, OR ROB THEM
ARCHITECT HARRY'S APARTMENT WAS STILL BY THE STAIRWELL. HE HADN'T HEARD FROM YOU EITHER

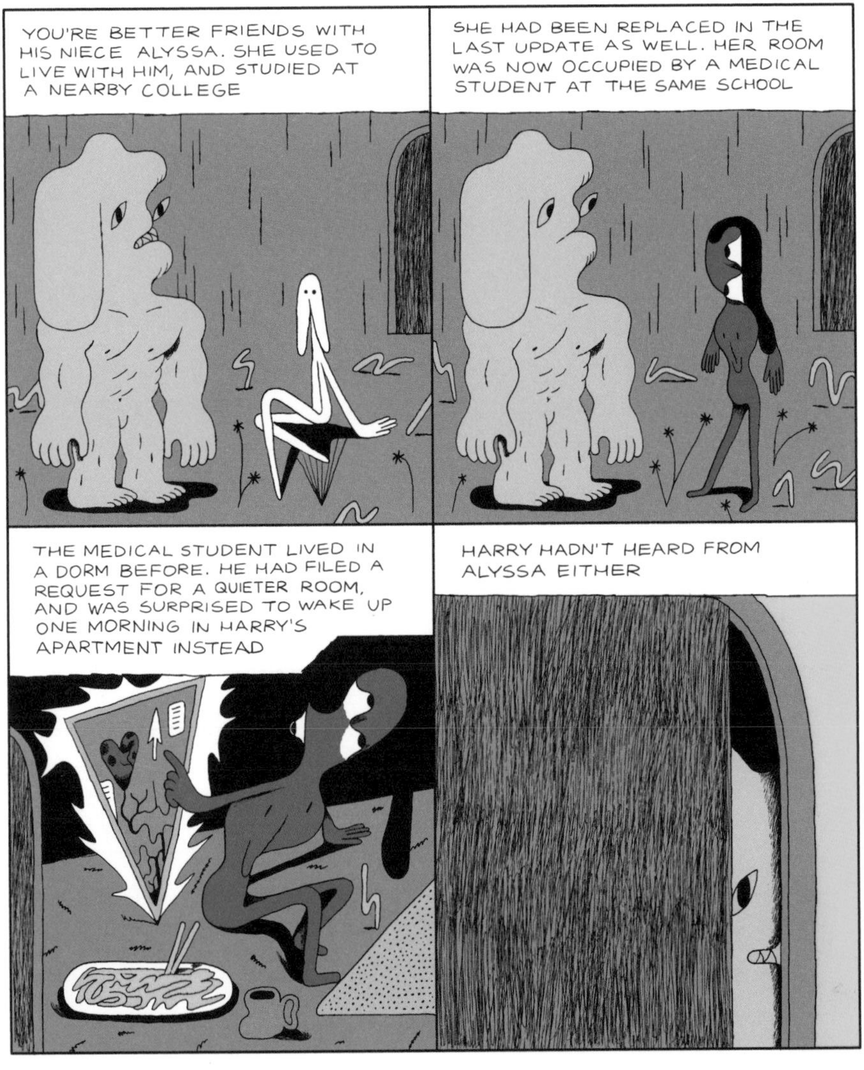
YOU'RE BETTER FRIENDS WITH HIS NIECE ALYSSA. SHE USED TO LIVE WITH HIM, AND STUDIED AT A NEARBY COLLEGE
SHE HAD BEEN REPLACED IN THE LAST UPDATE AS WELL. HER ROOM WAS NOW OCCUPIED BY A MEDICAL STUDENT AT THE SAME SCHOOL
THE MEDICAL STUDENT LIVED IN A DORM BEFORE. HE HAD FILED A REQUEST FOR A QUIETER ROOM, AND WAS SURPRISED TO WAKE UP ONE MORNING IN HARRY'S APARTMENT INSTEAD
HARRY HADN'T HEARD FROM ALYSSA EITHER

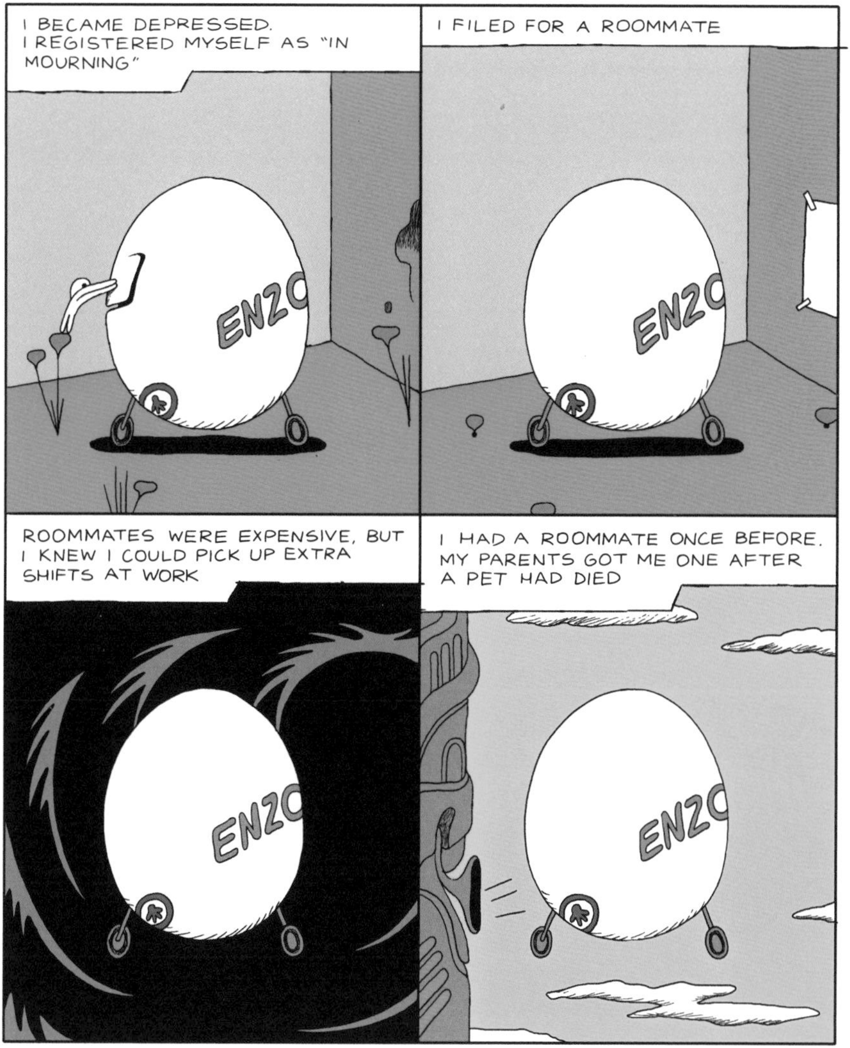
I BECAME DEPRESSED.
I REGISTERED MYSELF AS "IN MOURNING"
ENZO
I FILED FOR A ROOMMATE
ENZO
ROOMMATES WERE EXPENSIVE, BUT I KNEW I COULD PICK UP EXTRA SHIFTS AT WORK
ENZO
I HAD A ROOMMATE ONCE BEFORE. MY PARENTS GOT ME ONE AFTER A PET HAD DIED
ENZO

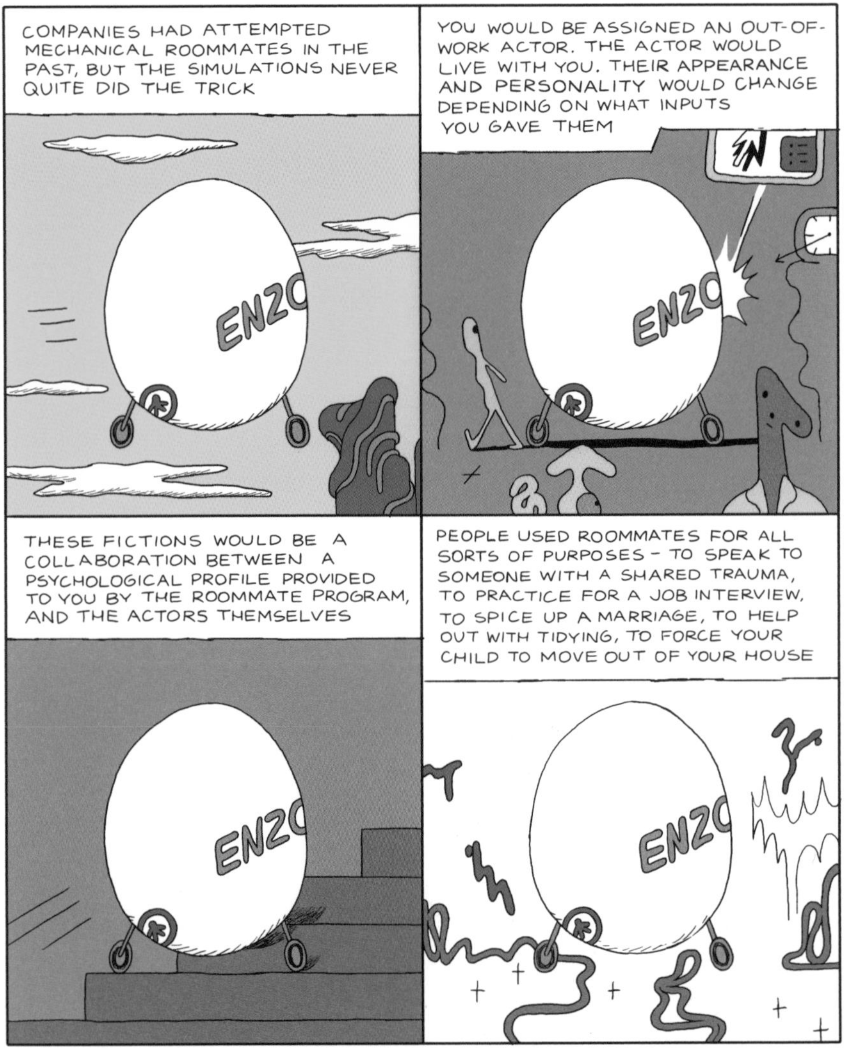
COMPANIES HAD ATTEMPTED MECHANICAL ROOMMATES IN THE PAST, BUT THE SIMULATIONS NEVER QUITE DID THE TRICK
ENZO
YOU WOULD BE ASSIGNED AN OUT-OF-WORK ACTOR. THE ACTOR WOULD LIVE WITH YOU. THEIR APPEARANCE AND PERSONALITY WOULD CHANGE DEPENDING ON WHAT INPUTS YOU GAVE THEM
ENZO
THESE FICTIONS WOULD BE A COLLABORATION BETWEEN A PSYCHOLOGICAL PROFILE PROVIDED TO YOU BY THE ROOMMATE PROGRAM, AND THE ACTORS THEMSELVES
ENZO
PEOPLE USED ROOMMATES FOR ALL SORTS OF PURPOSES - TO SPEAK TO SOMEONE WITH A SHARED TRAUMA, TO PRACTICE FOR A JOB INTERVIEW, TO SPICE UP A MARRIAGE, TO HELP OUT WITH TIDYING, TO FORCE YOUR CHILD TO MOVE OUT OF YOUR HOUSE
ENZO

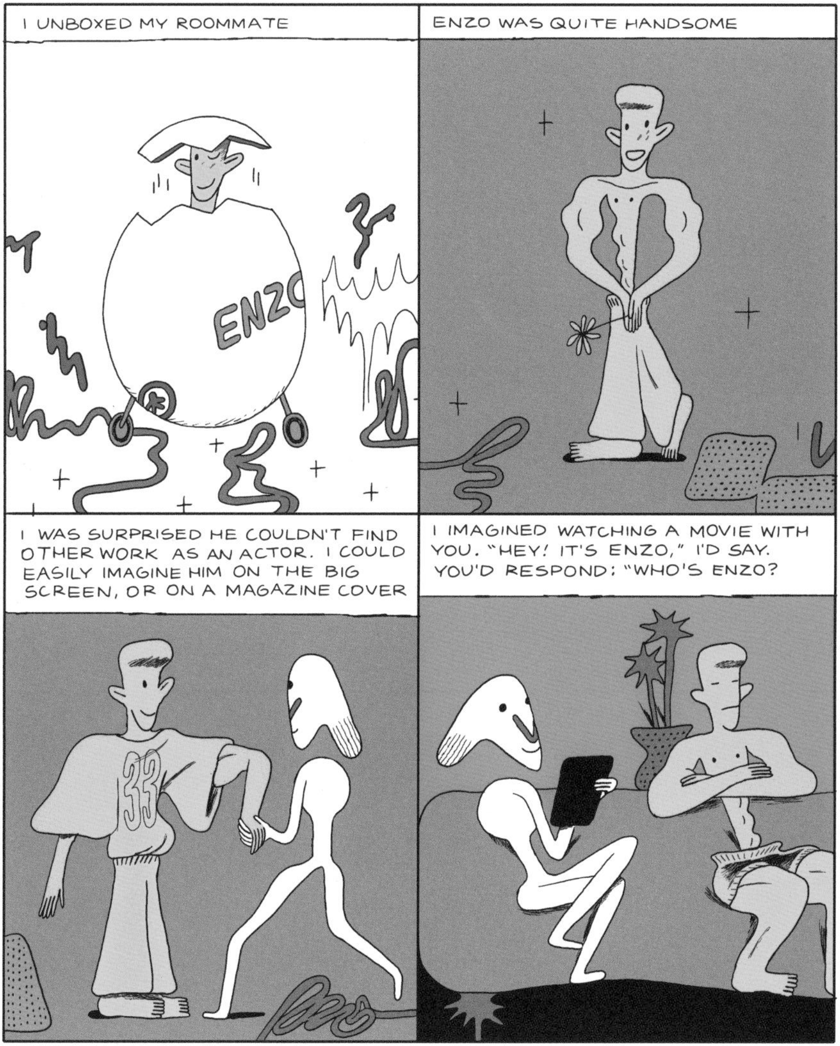
I UNBOXED MY ROOMMATE
ENZO
ENZO WAS QUITE HANDSOME
I WAS SURPRISED HE COULDN'T FIND OTHER WORK AS AN ACTOR. I COULD EASILY IMAGINE HIM ON THE BIG SCREEN, OR ON A MAGAZINE COVER
33
I IMAGINED WATCHING A MOVIE WITH YOU. "HEY! IT'S ENZO," I'D SAY. YOU'D RESPOND: "WHO'S ENZO?

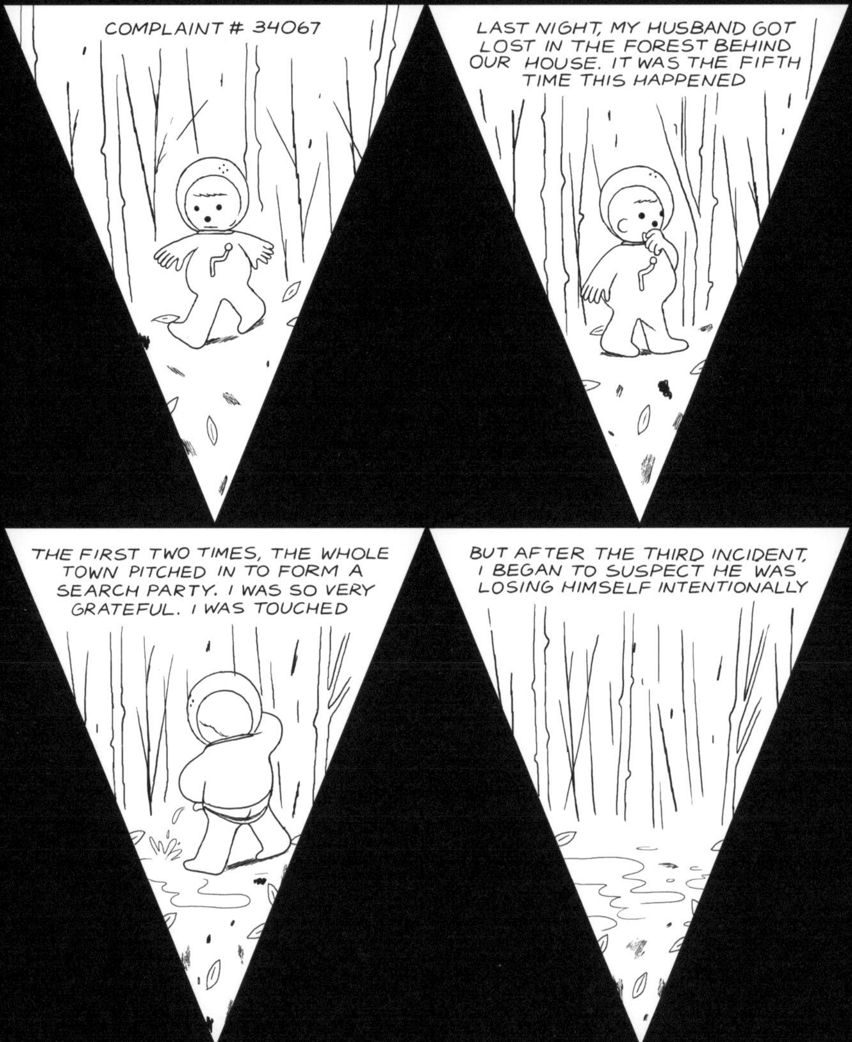
COMPLAINT # 34067
LAST NIGHT, MY HUSBAND GOT LOST IN THE FOREST BEHIND OUR HOUSE. IT WAS THE FIFTH TIME THIS HAPPENED
THE FIRST TWO TIMES, THE WHOLE TOWN PITCHED IN TO FORM A SEARCH PARTY. I WAS SO VERY GRATEFUL. I WAS TOUCHED
BUT AFTER THE THIRD INCIDENT, I BEGAN TO SUSPECT HE WAS LOSING HIMSELF INTENTIONALLY

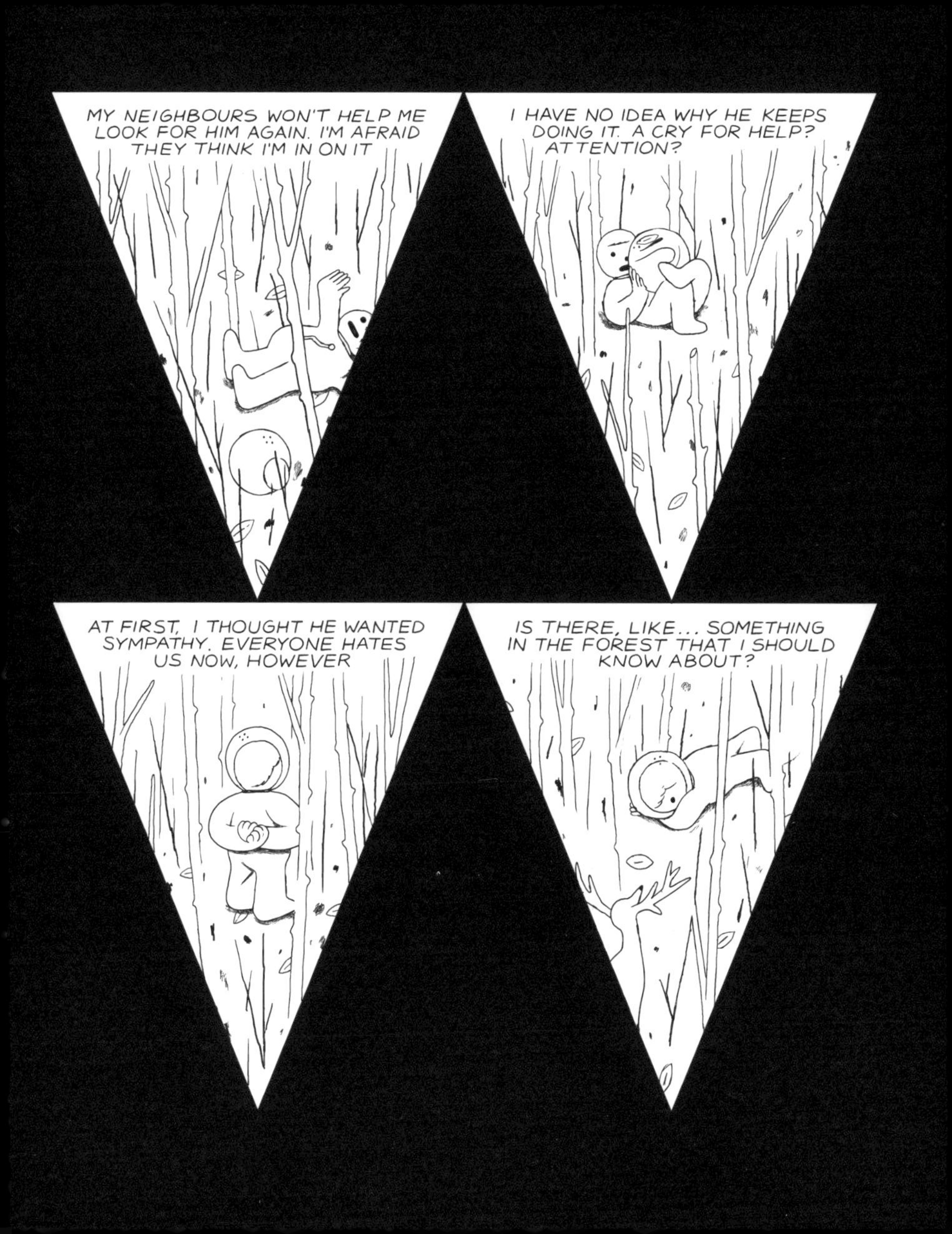
MY NEIGHBOURS WON'T HELP ME LOOK FOR HIM AGAIN. I'M AFRAID THEY THINK I'M IN ON IT
I HAVE NO IDEA WHY HE KEEPS DOING IT. A CRY FOR HELP? ATTENTION?
AT FIRST, I THOUGHT HE WANTED SYMPATHY. EVERYONE HATES US NOW, HOWEVER
IS THERE, LIKE... SOMETHING IN THE FOREST THAT I SHOULD KNOW ABOUT?

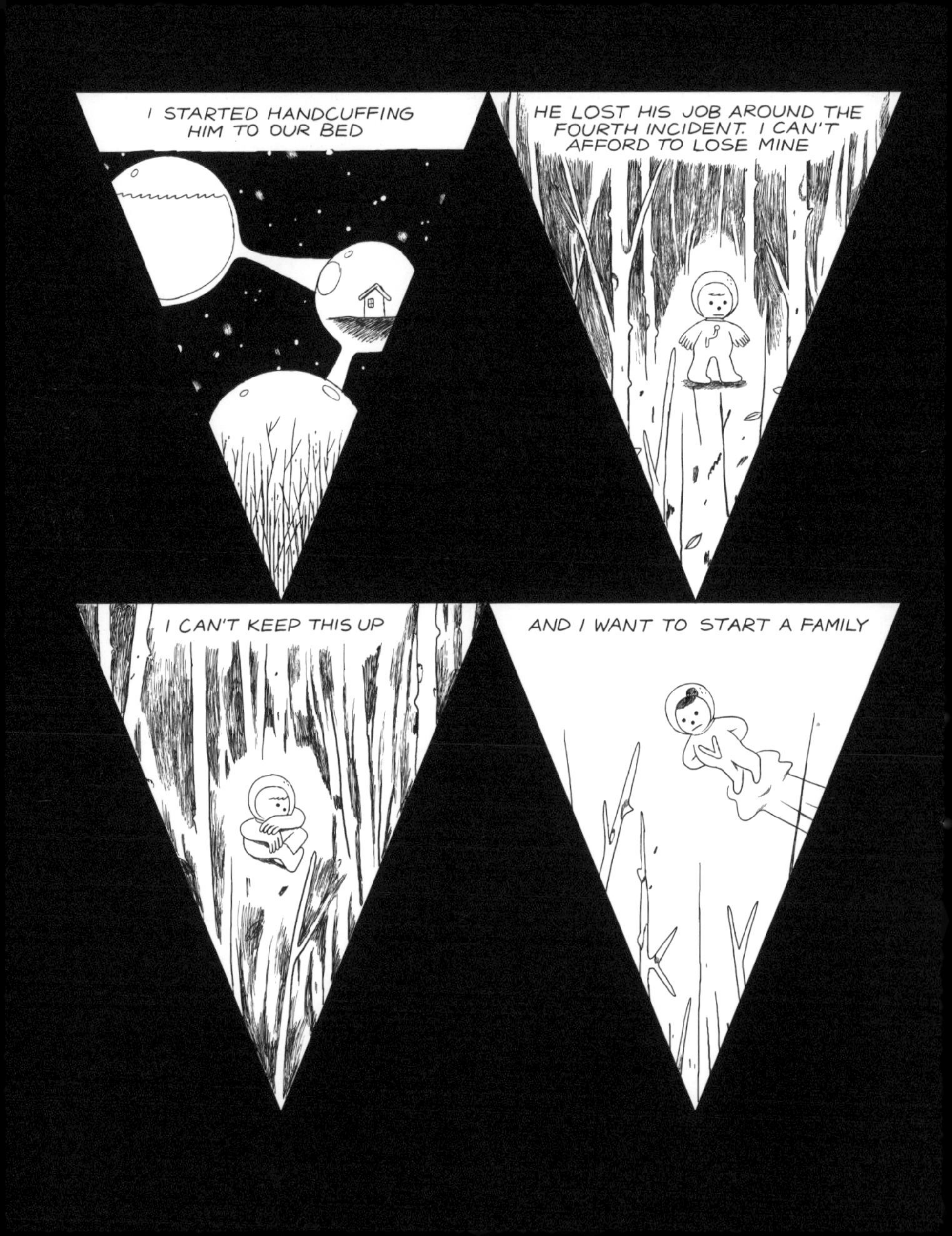
I STARTED HANDCUFFING HIM TO OUR BED
HE LOST HIS JOB AROUND THE FOURTH INCIDENT. I CAN'T AFFORD TO LOSE MINE
I CAN'T KEEP THIS UP
AND I WANT TO START A FAMILY

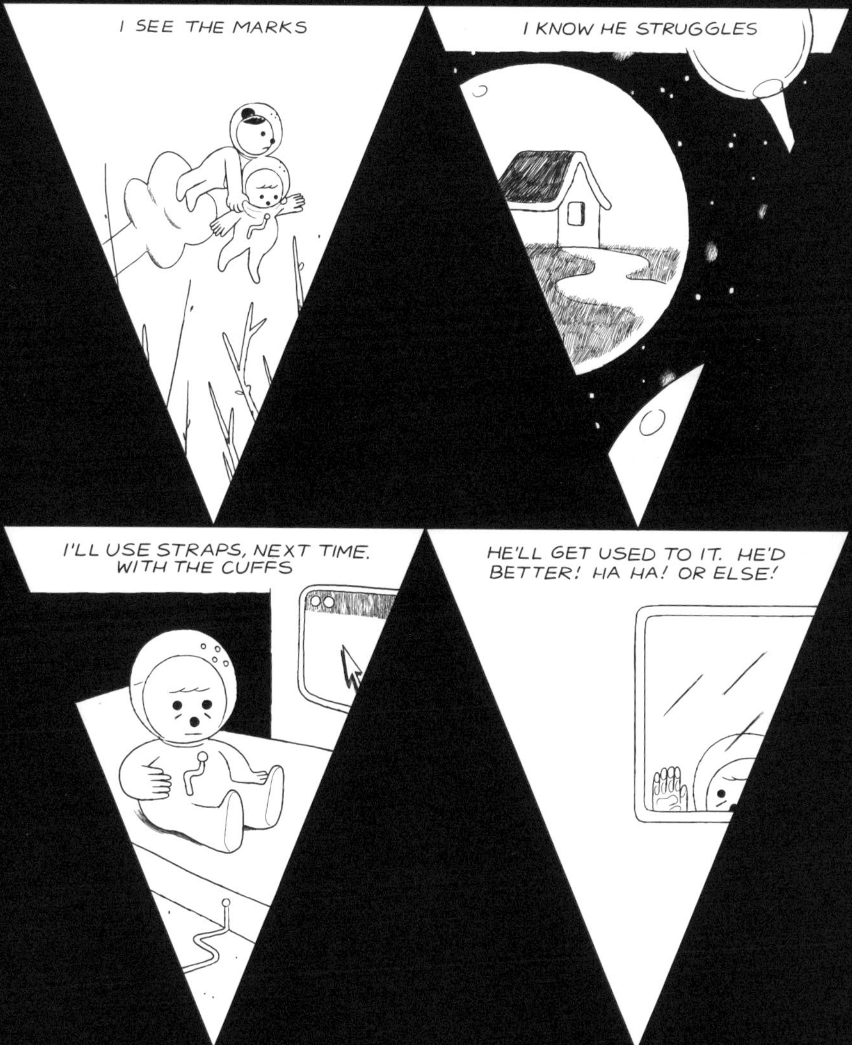
I SEE THE MARKS
I KNOW HE STRUGGLES
I'LL USE STRAPS, NEXT TIME. WITH THE CUFFS
HE'LL GET USED TO IT. HE'D BETTER! HA HA! OR ELSE!

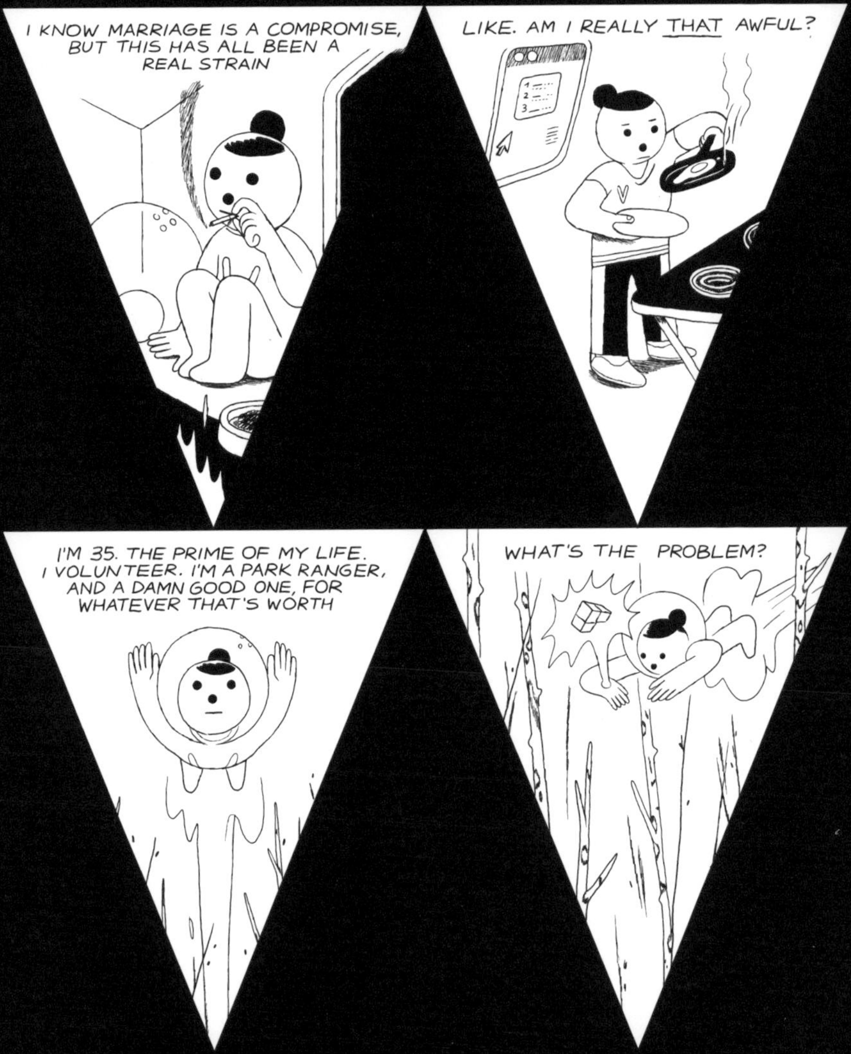
I KNOW MARRIAGE IS A COMPROMISE, BUT THIS HAS ALL BEEN A REAL STRAIN
LIKE. AM I REALLY THAT AWFUL?
I'M 35. THE PRIME OF MY LIFE. I VOLUNTEER. I'M A PARK RANGER, AND A DAMN GOOD ONE, FOR WHATEVER THAT'S WORTH
WHAT'S THE PROBLEM?

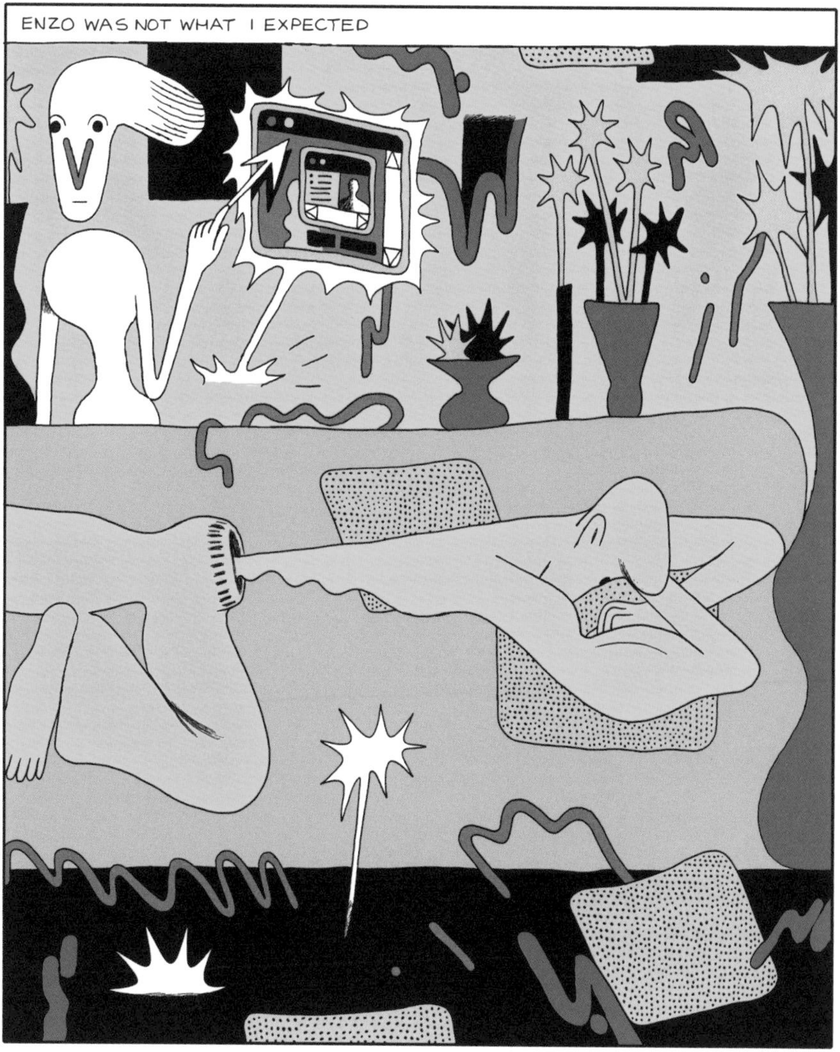
ENZO WAS NOT WHAT I EXPECTED

I UNDERSTOOD THAT HIS PRESENCE WAS SUPPOSED TO BE THERAPEUTIC, BUT WAS UNCLEAR IN WHAT WAY IT WAS THERAPEUTIC

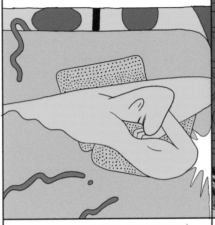

I'D TRY TO TALK TO HIM ABOUT YOU, BUT HE'D CHANGE THE SUBJECT TO HIS OWN LIFE

THE (USUALLY QUITE CONVINCING) BIOGRAPHICAL DETAILS GENERATED BY THE SERVICE WAS NORMALLY MEANT TO COMPLIMENT YOUR OWN PREDICAMENT IN SOME WAY

FOR INSTANCE, SOMEONE COPING WITH THE DEATH OF THEIR MOTHER MIGHT BE PROVIDED WITH AN OLDER, NURTURING FEMALE FIGURE AS A ROOMMATE

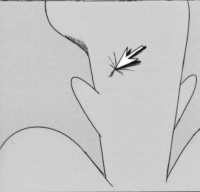

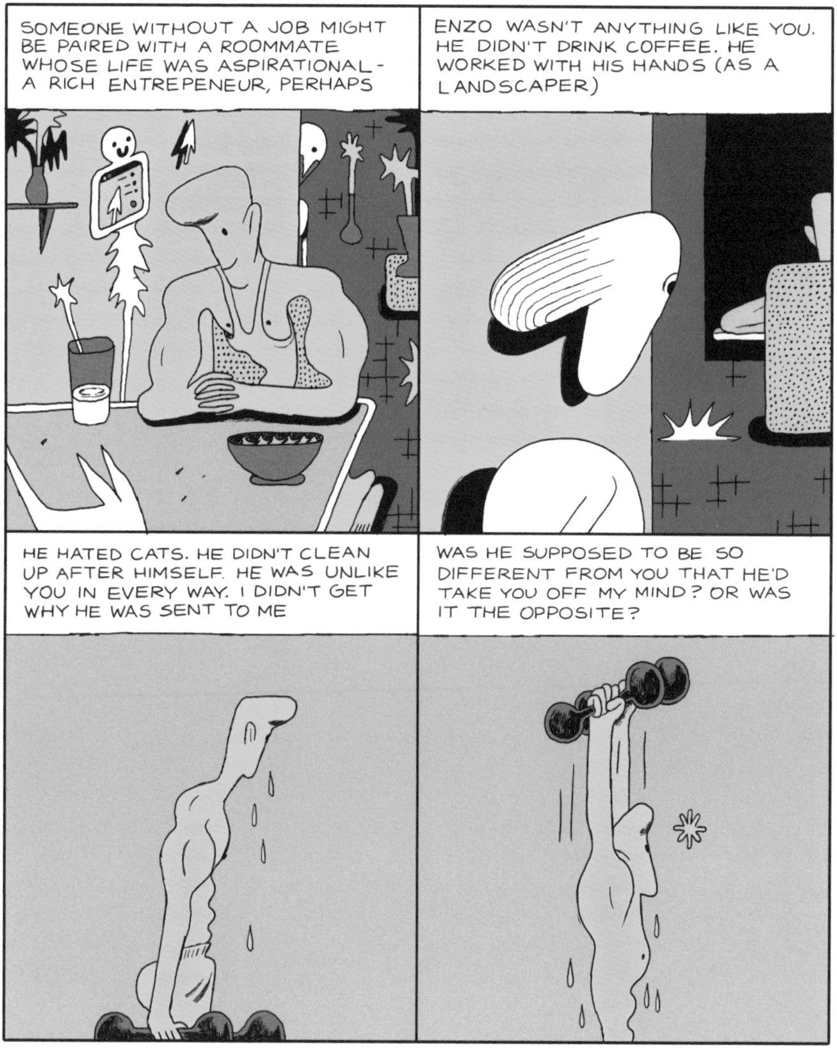
SOMEONE WITHOUT A JOB MIGHT BE PAIRED WITH A ROOMMATE WHOSE LIFE WAS ASPIRATIONAL - A RICH ENTREPENEUR, PERHAPS
ENZO WASN'T ANYTHING LIKE YOU. HE DIDN'T DRINK COFFEE. HE WORKED WITH HIS HANDS (AS A LANDSCAPER)
HE HATED CATS. HE DIDN'T CLEAN UP AFTER HIMSELF. HE WAS UNLIKE YOU IN EVERY WAY. I DIDN'T GET WHY HE WAS SENT TO ME
WAS HE SUPPOSED TO BE SO DIFFERENT FROM YOU THAT HE'D TAKE YOU OFF MY MIND? OR WAS IT THE OPPOSITE?

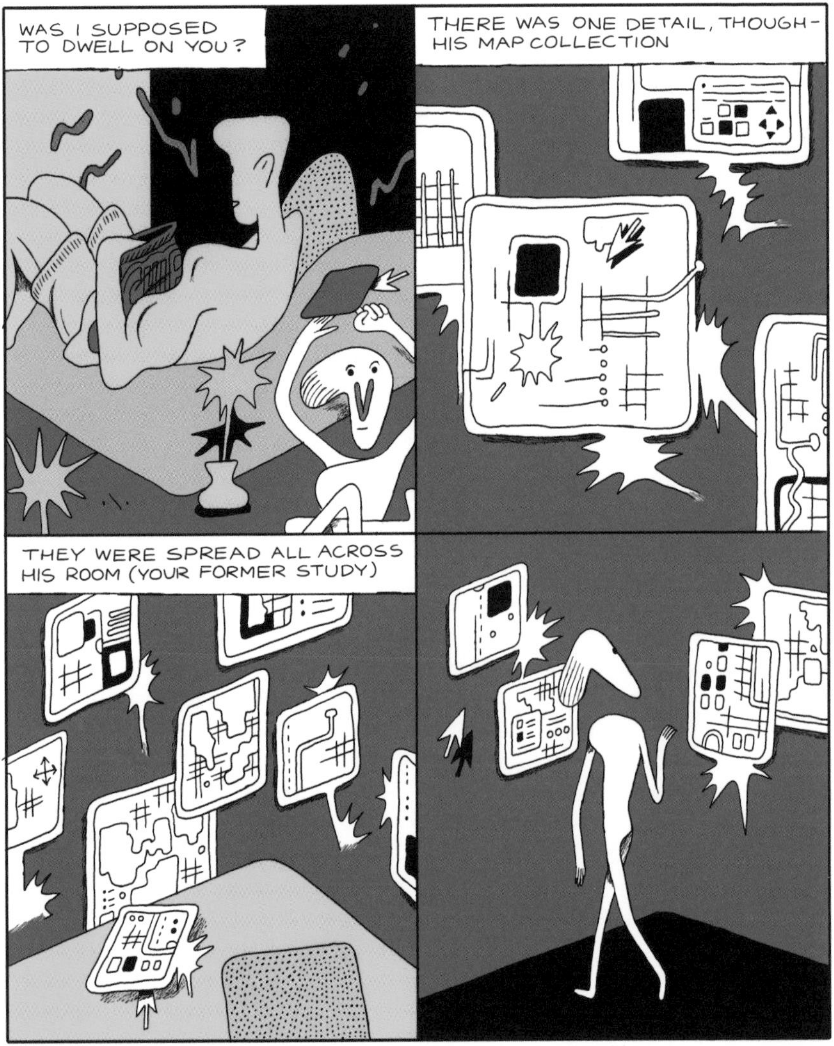
WAS I SUPPOSED TO DWELL ON YOU?
THERE WAS ONE DETAIL, THOUGH- HIS MAP COLLECTION
THEY WERE SPREAD ALL ACROSS HIS ROOM (YOUR FORMER STUDY)

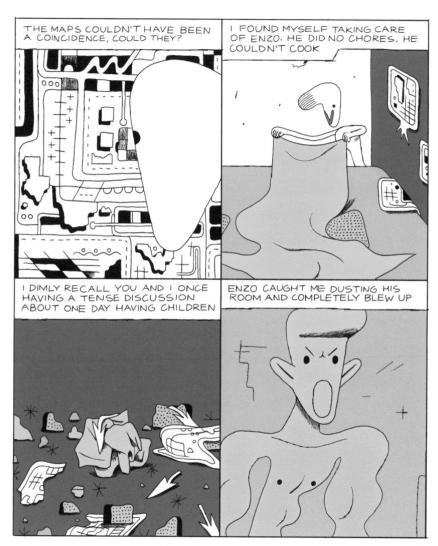

THE MAPS COULDN'T HAVE BEEN A COINCIDENCE, COULD THEY?

I FOUND MYSELF TAKING CARE OF ENZO. HE DID NO CHORES. HE COULDN'T COOK

I DIMLY RECALL YOU AND I ONCE HAVING A TENSE DISCUSSION ABOUT ONE DAY HAVING CHILDREN

ENZO CAUGHT ME DUSTING HIS ROOM AND COMPLETELY BLEW UP

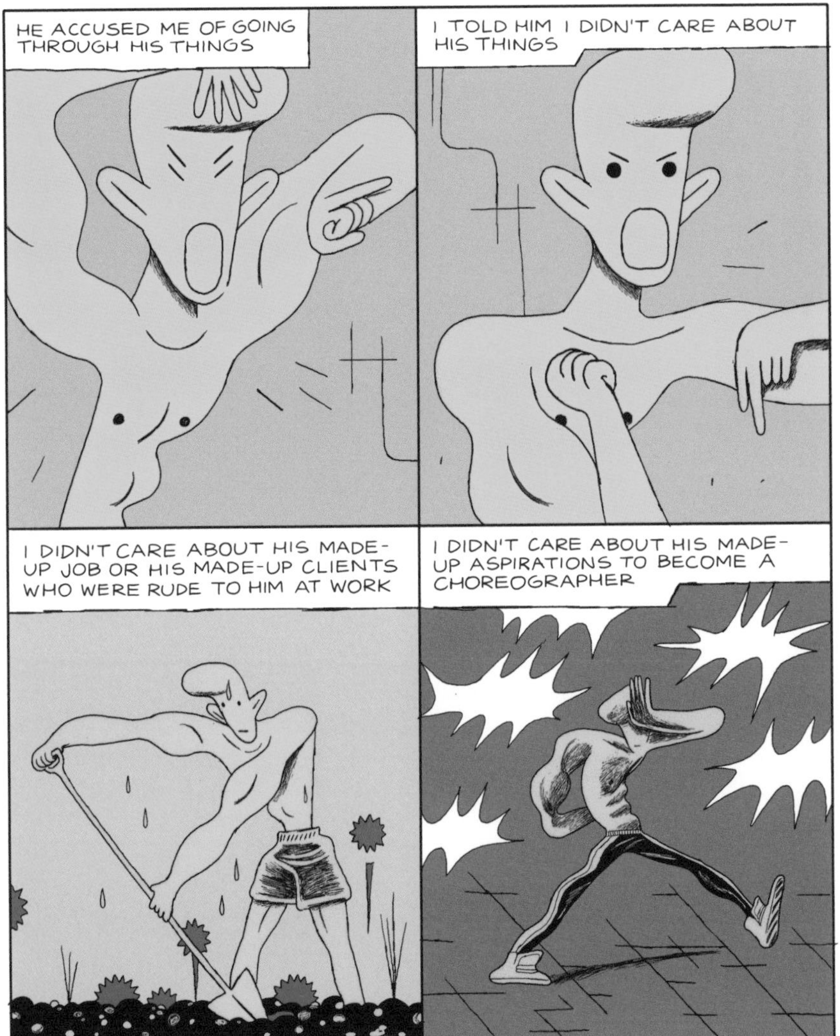
HE ACCUSED ME OF GOING THROUGH HIS THINGS
I TOLD HIM I DIDN'T CARE ABOUT HIS THINGS
I DIDN'T CARE ABOUT HIS MADE-UP JOB OR HIS MADE-UP CLIENTS WHO WERE RUDE TO HIM AT WORK
I DIDN'T CARE ABOUT HIS MADE-UP ASPIRATIONS TO BECOME A CHOREOGRAPHER

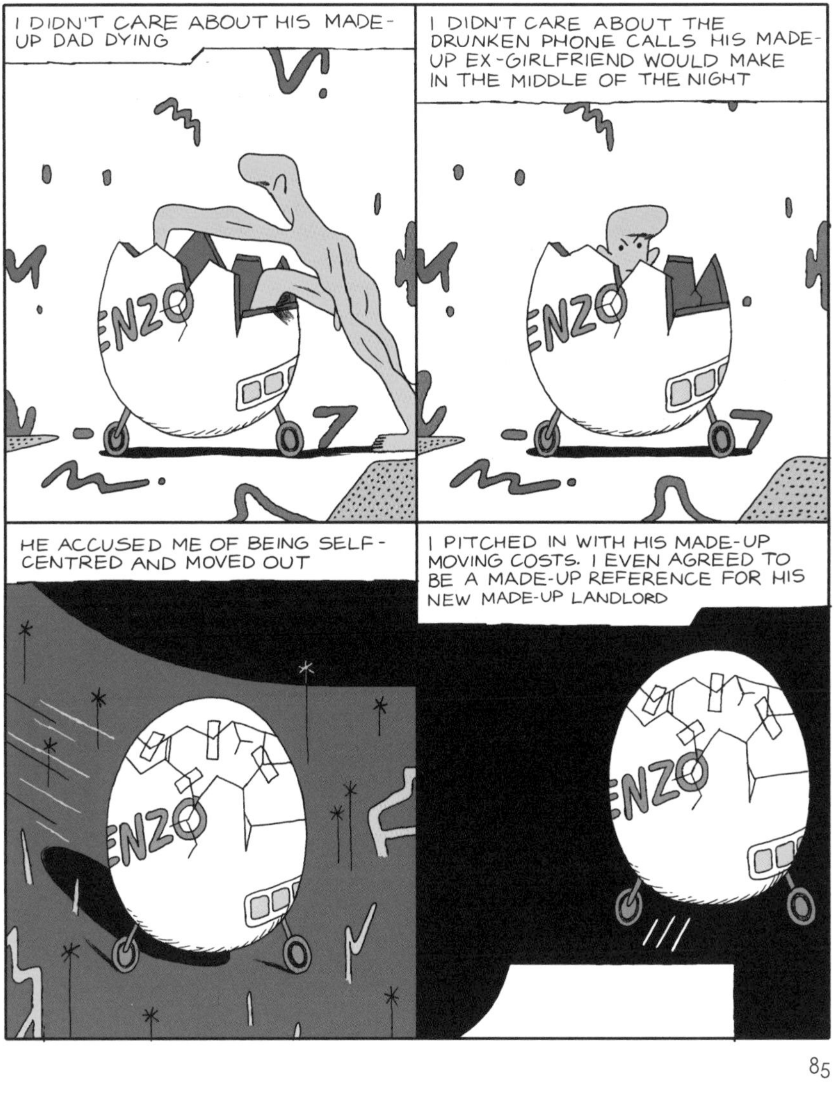
I DIDN'T CARE ABOUT HIS MADE-UP DAD DYING
I DIDN'T CARE ABOUT THE DRUNKEN PHONE CALLS HIS MADE-UP EX-GIRLFRIEND WOULD MAKE IN THE MIDDLE OF THE NIGHT
ENZO
ENZO
HE ACCUSED ME OF BEING SELF-CENTRED AND MOVED OUT
ENZO
I PITCHED IN WITH HIS MADE-UP MOVING COSTS. I EVEN AGREED TO BE A MADE-UP REFERENCE FOR HIS NEW MADE-UP LANDLORD
ENZO

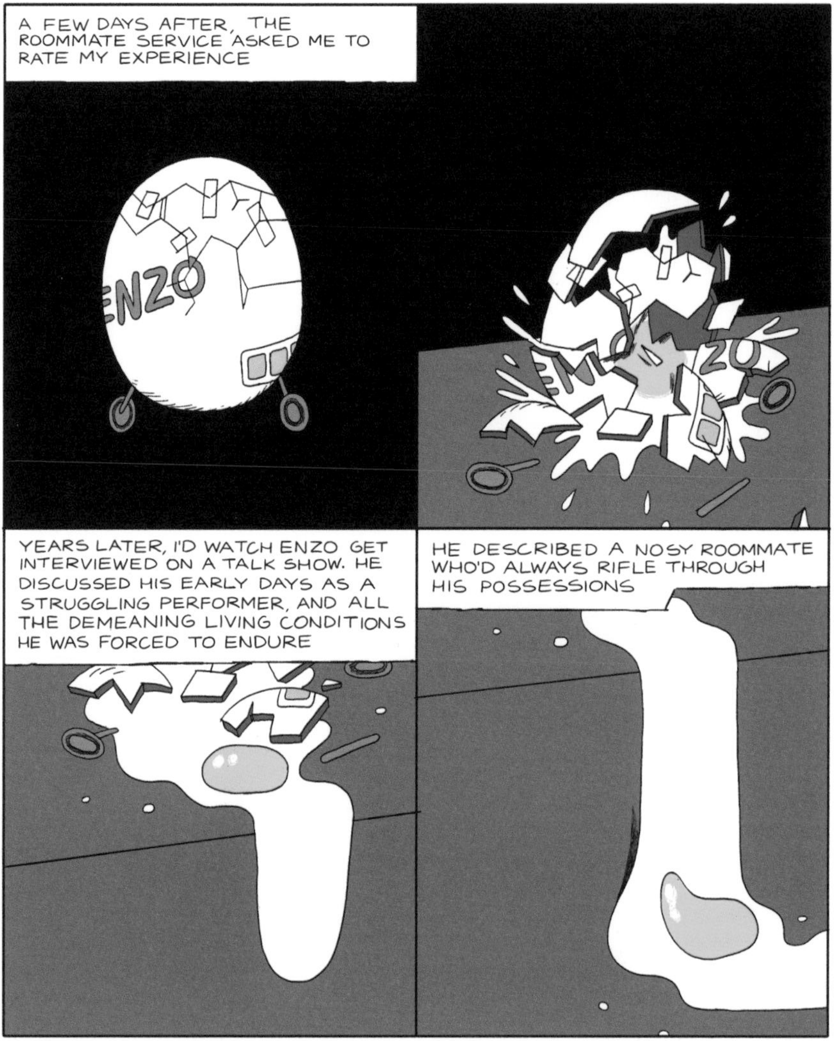
A FEW DAYS AFTER, THE ROOMMATE SERVICE ASKED ME TO RATE MY EXPERIENCE
ENZO
ENZO
YEARS LATER, I'D WATCH ENZO GET INTERVIEWED ON A TALK SHOW. HE DISCUSSED HIS EARLY DAYS AS A STRUGGLING PERFORMER, AND ALL THE DEMEANING LIVING CONDITIONS HE WAS FORCED TO ENDURE
HE DESCRIBED A NOSY ROOMMATE WHO'D ALWAYS RIFLE THROUGH HIS POSSESSIONS

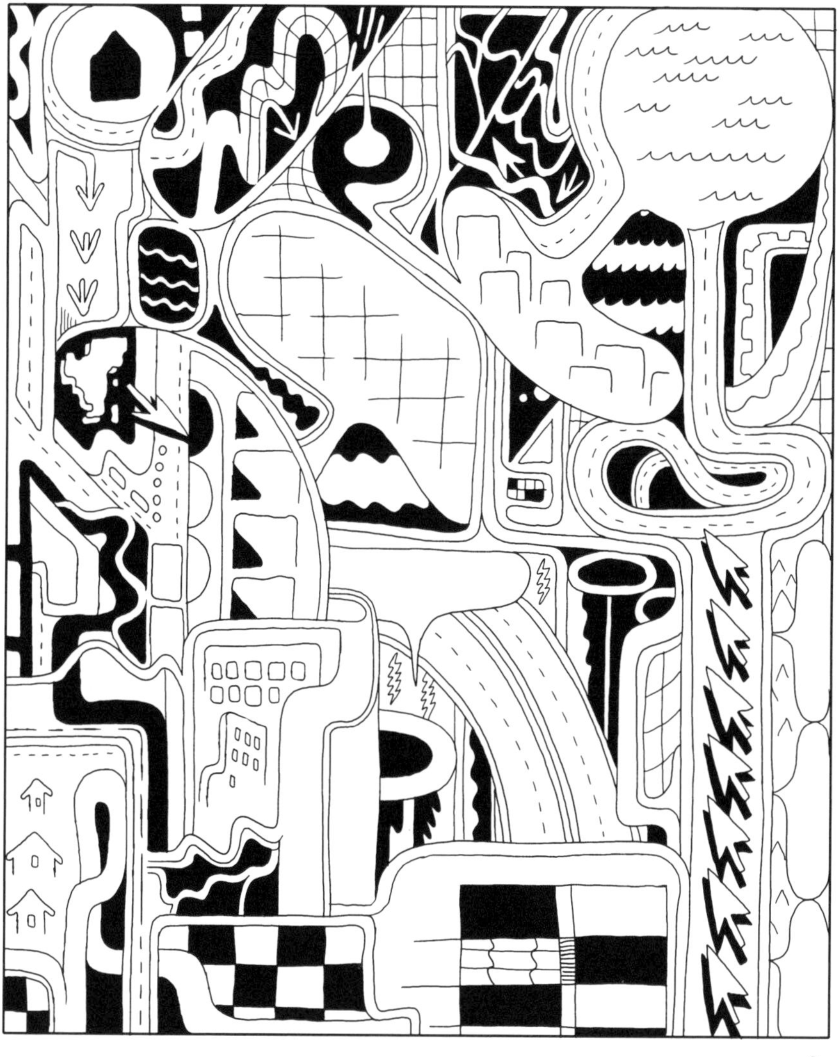

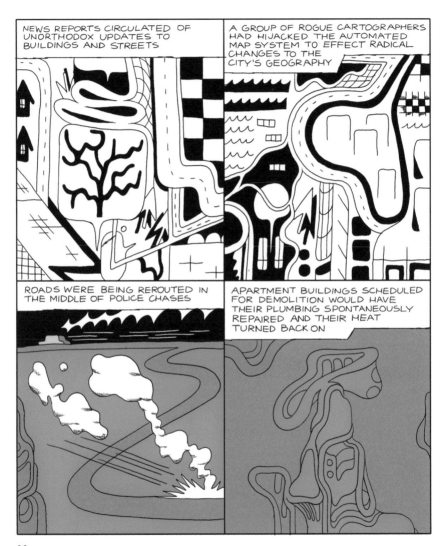

NEWS REPORTS CIRCULATED OF UNORTHODOX UPDATES TO BUILDINGS AND STREETS

A GROUP OF ROGUE CARTOGRAPHERS HAD HIJACKED THE AUTOMATED MAP SYSTEM TO EFFECT RADICAL CHANGES TO THE CITY'S GEOGRAPHY

ROADS WERE BEING REROUTED IN THE MIDDLE OF POLICE CHASES

APARTMENT BUILDINGS SCHEDULED FOR DEMOLITION WOULD HAVE THEIR PLUMBING SPONTANEOUSLY REPAIRED AND THEIR HEAT TURNED BACK ON

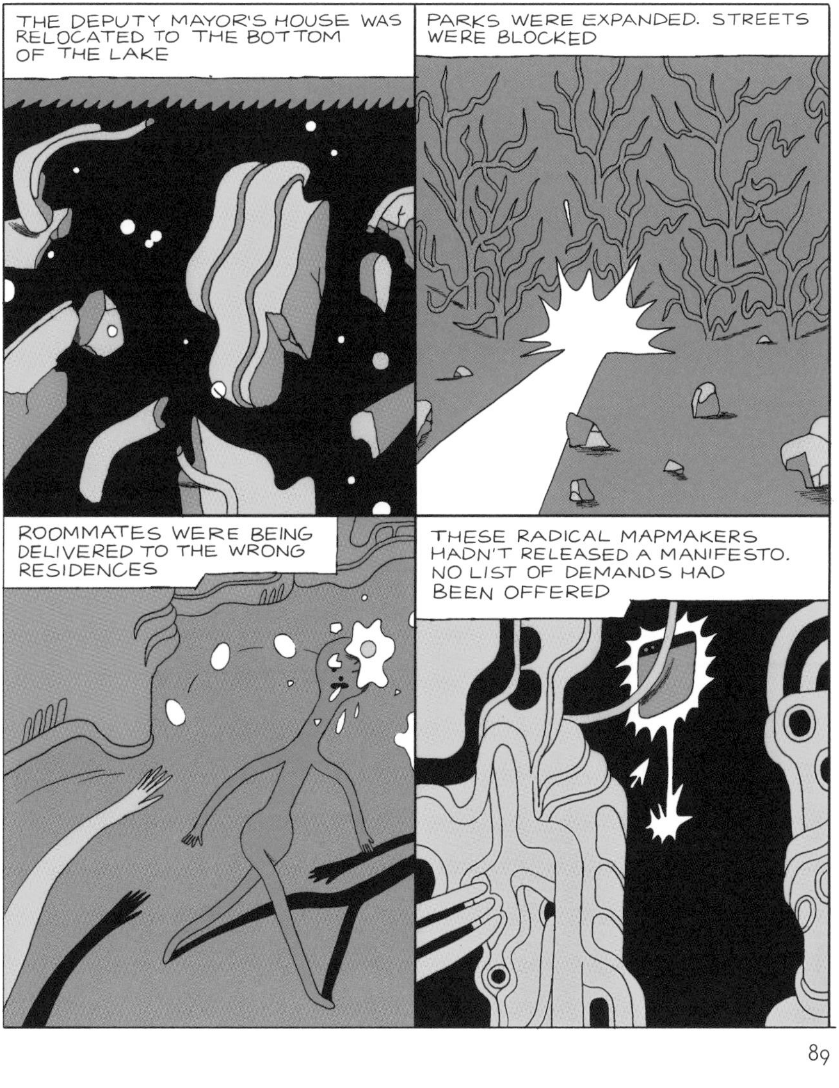
THE DEPUTY MAYOR'S HOUSE WAS RELOCATED TO THE BOTTOM OF THE LAKE
PARKS WERE EXPANDED. STREETS WERE BLOCKED
ROOMMATES WERE BEING DELIVERED TO THE WRONG RESIDENCES
THESE RADICAL MAPMAKERS HADN'T RELEASED A MANIFESTO. NO LIST OF DEMANDS HAD BEEN OFFERED

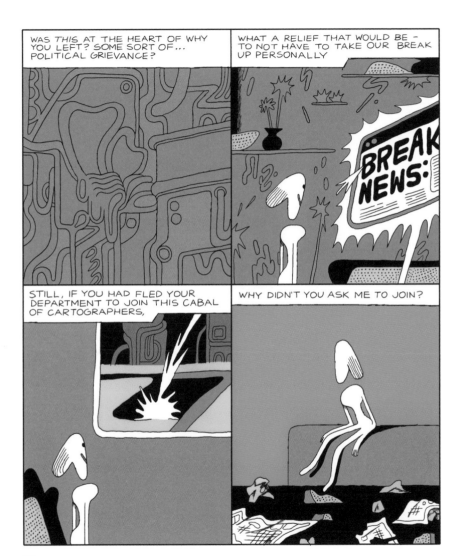

WAS *THIS* AT THE HEART OF WHY YOU LEFT? SOME SORT OF... POLITICAL GRIEVANCE?

WHAT A RELIEF THAT WOULD BE — TO NOT HAVE TO TAKE OUR BREAK UP PERSONALLY

BREAK NEWS:

STILL, IF YOU HAD FLED YOUR DEPARTMENT TO JOIN THIS CABAL OF CARTOGRAPHERS,

WHY DIDN'T YOU ASK ME TO JOIN?

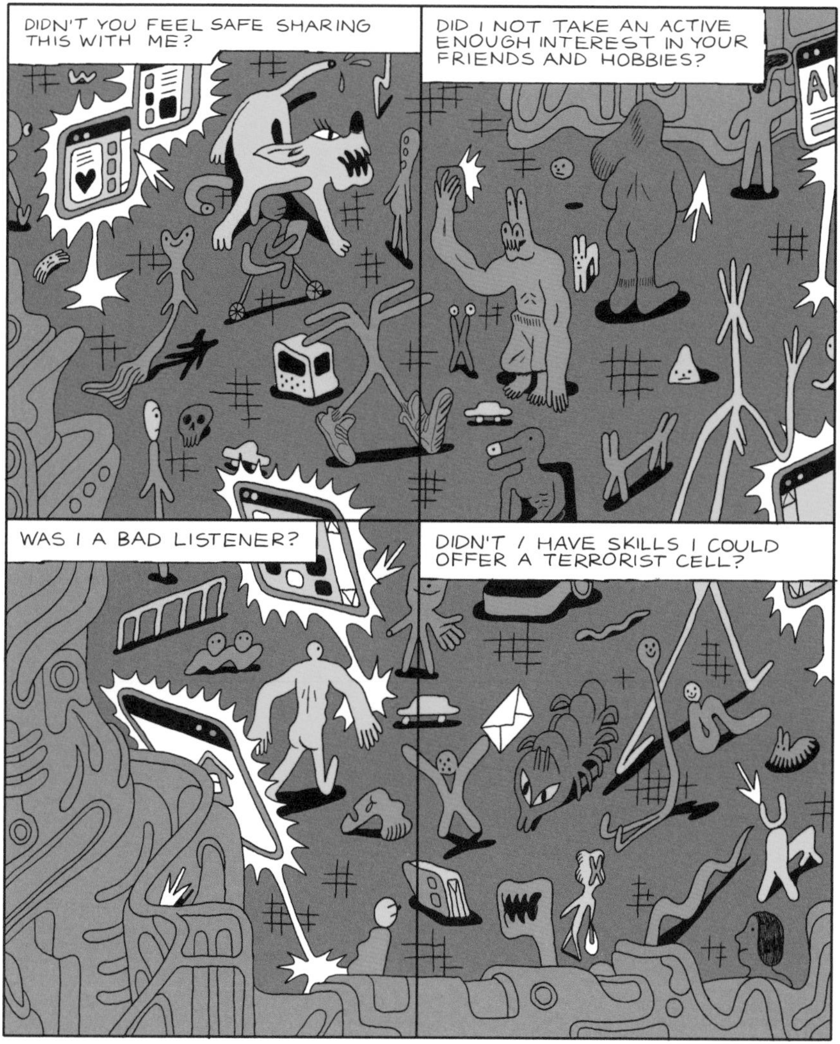
DIDN'T YOU FEEL SAFE SHARING THIS WITH ME?
DID I NOT TAKE AN ACTIVE ENOUGH INTEREST IN YOUR FRIENDS AND HOBBIES?
WAS I A BAD LISTENER?
DIDN'T I HAVE SKILLS I COULD OFFER A TERRORIST CELL?

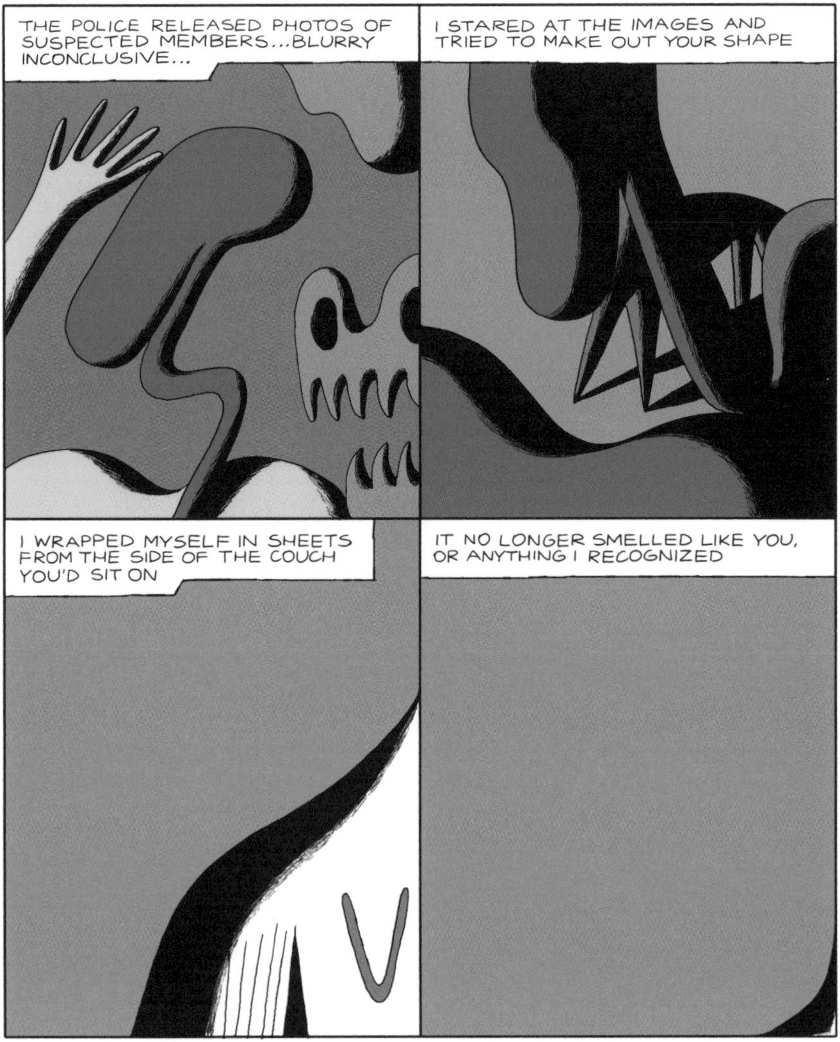
THE POLICE RELEASED PHOTOS OF SUSPECTED MEMBERS...BLURRY INCONCLUSIVE...
I STARED AT THE IMAGES AND TRIED TO MAKE OUT YOUR SHAPE
I WRAPPED MYSELF IN SHEETS FROM THE SIDE OF THE COUCH YOU'D SIT ON
IT NO LONGER SMELLED LIKE YOU, OR ANYTHING I RECOGNIZED

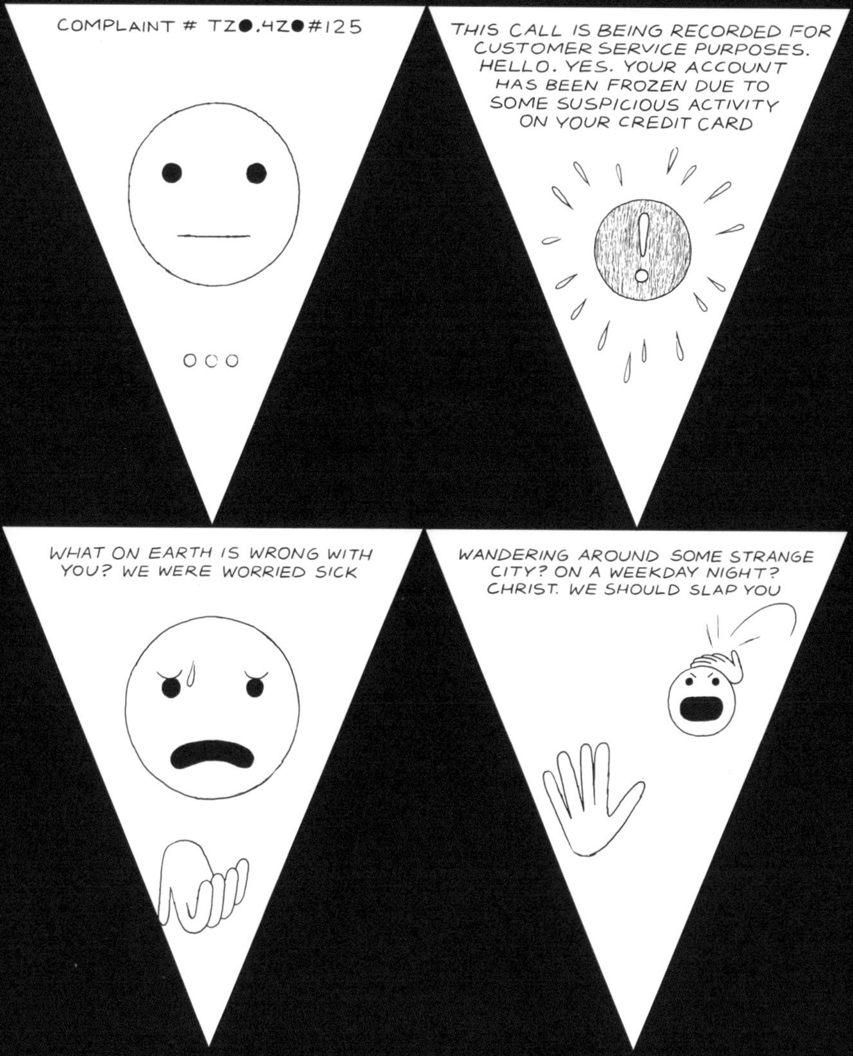
COMPLAINT # TZ●.4Z●#125
THIS CALL IS BEING RECORDED FOR CUSTOMER SERVICE PURPOSES. HELLO. YES. YOUR ACCOUNT HAS BEEN FROZEN DUE TO SOME SUSPICIOUS ACTIVITY ON YOUR CREDIT CARD
WHAT ON EARTH IS WRONG WITH YOU? WE WERE WORRIED SICK
WANDERING AROUND SOME STRANGE CITY? ON A WEEKDAY NIGHT? CHRIST. WE SHOULD SLAP YOU

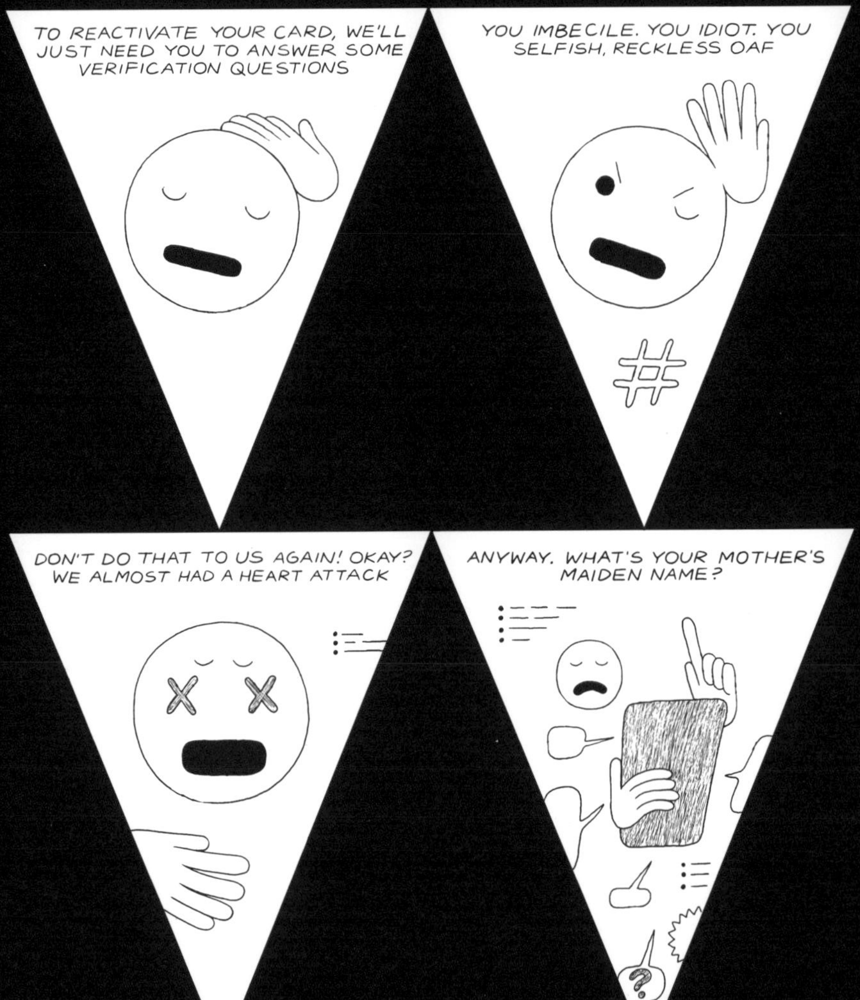
TO REACTIVATE YOUR CARD, WE'LL JUST NEED YOU TO ANSWER SOME VERIFICATION QUESTIONS
YOU IMBECILE. YOU IDIOT. YOU SELFISH, RECKLESS OAF
#
DON'T DO THAT TO US AGAIN! OKAY? WE ALMOST HAD A HEART ATTACK
ANYWAY. WHAT'S YOUR MOTHER'S MAIDEN NAME?
?

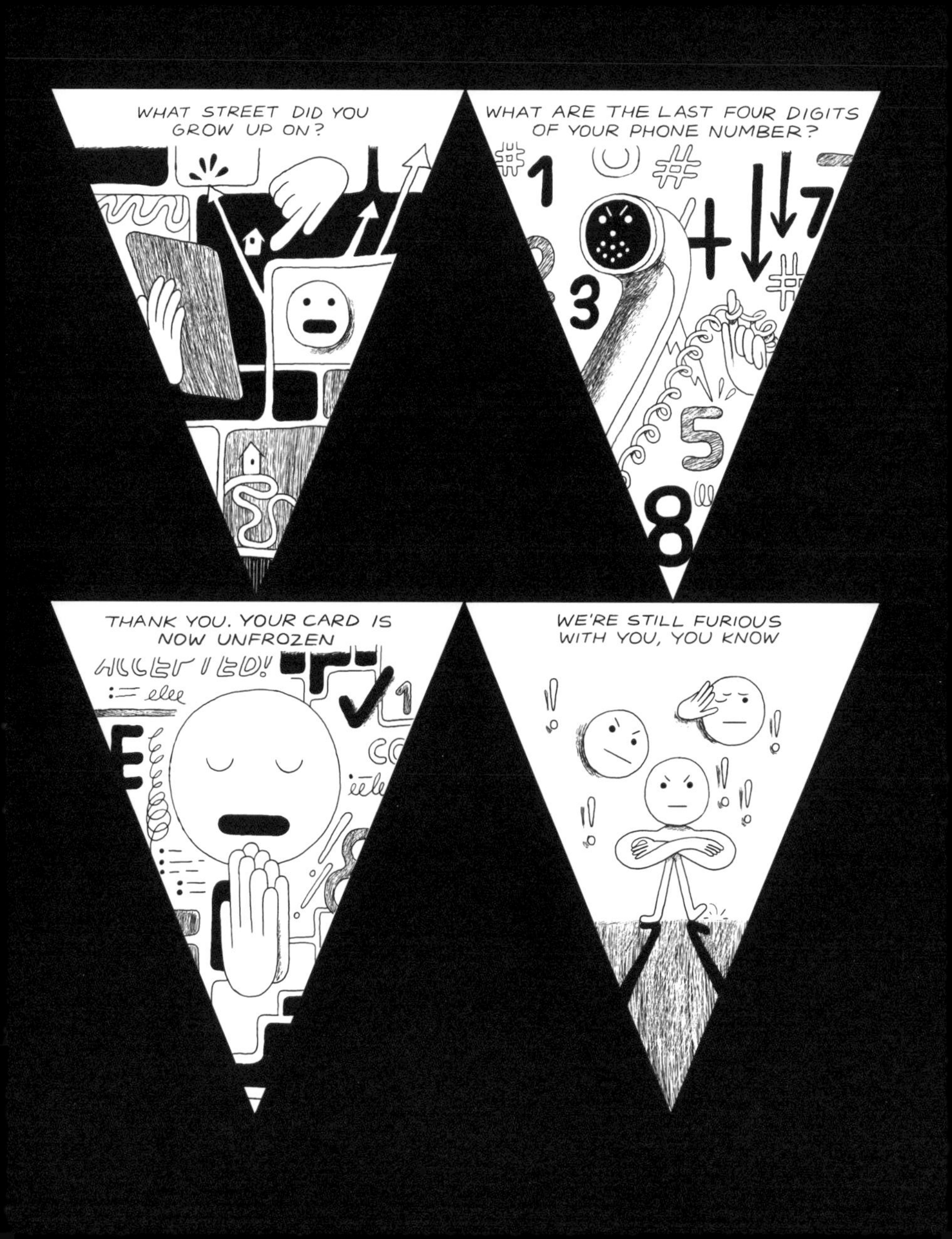
WHAT STREET DID YOU GROW UP ON?
WHAT ARE THE LAST FOUR DIGITS OF YOUR PHONE NUMBER?
THANK YOU. YOUR CARD IS NOW UNFROZEN
WE'RE STILL FURIOUS WITH YOU, YOU KNOW

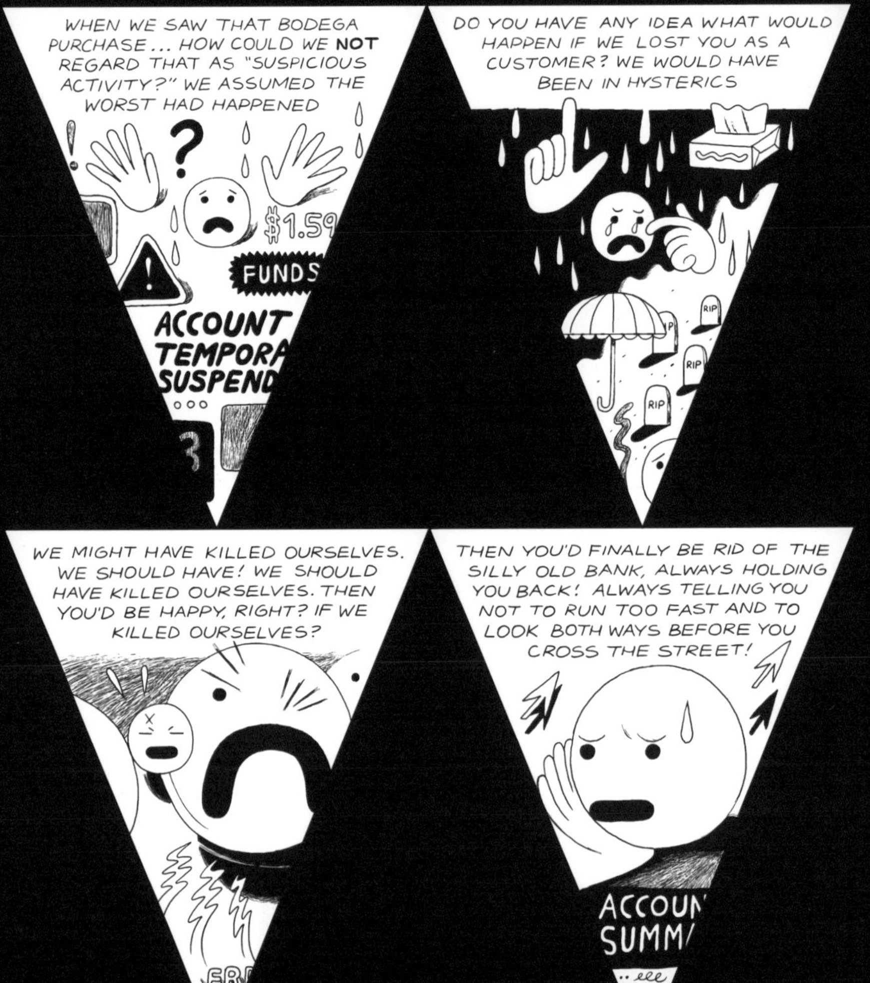

WHEN WE SAW THAT BODEGA PURCHASE... HOW COULD WE **NOT** REGARD THAT AS "SUSPICIOUS ACTIVITY?" WE ASSUMED THE WORST HAD HAPPENED
$1.59
FUNDS
ACCOUNT TEMPORA SUSPEND
DO YOU HAVE ANY IDEA WHAT WOULD HAPPEN IF WE LOST YOU AS A CUSTOMER? WE WOULD HAVE BEEN IN HYSTERICS
RIP
RIP
RIP
WE MIGHT HAVE KILLED OURSELVES. WE SHOULD HAVE! WE SHOULD HAVE KILLED OURSELVES. THEN YOU'D BE HAPPY, RIGHT? IF WE KILLED OURSELVES?
THEN YOU'D FINALLY BE RID OF THE SILLY OLD BANK, ALWAYS HOLDING YOU BACK! ALWAYS TELLING YOU NOT TO RUN TOO FAST AND TO LOOK BOTH WAYS BEFORE YOU CROSS THE STREET!
ACCOUN SUMM

JUST... JUST LET US KNOW NEXT TIME YOU TAKE A TRIP

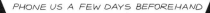

PHONE US A FEW DAYS BEFOREHAND

YES. THAT'S ALL WE ASK. YES. IT'S OKAY. APOLOGY ACCEPTED

WHILE YOU'RE HERE, ARE YOU INTERESTED IN OPENING A TAX-FREE SAVINGS ACCOUNT?

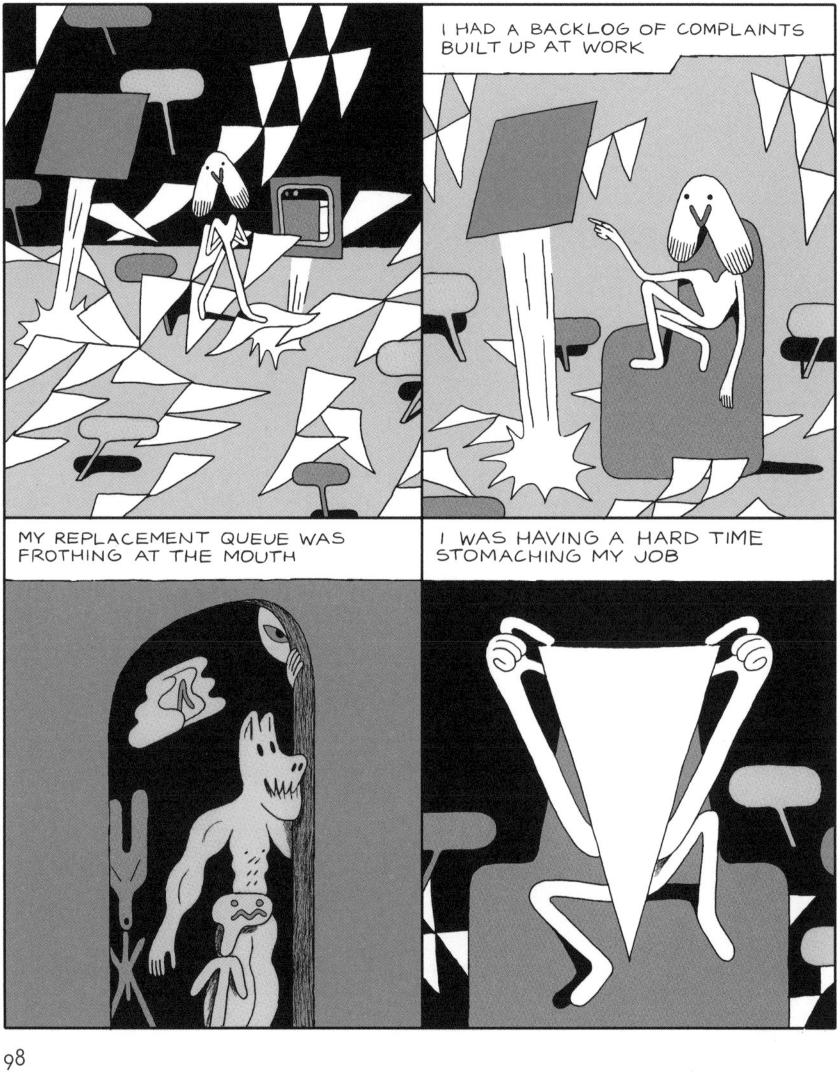
I HAD A BACKLOG OF COMPLAINTS BUILT UP AT WORK
MY REPLACEMENT QUEUE WAS FROTHING AT THE MOUTH
I WAS HAVING A HARD TIME STOMACHING MY JOB

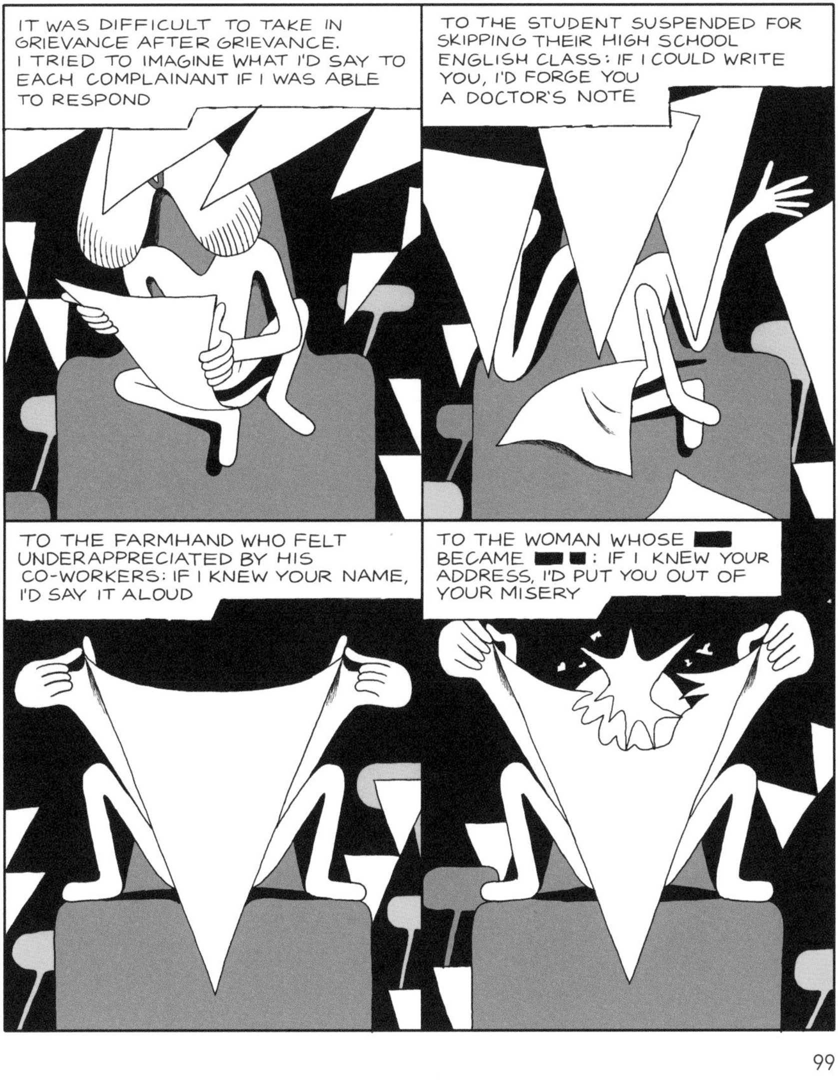

IT WAS DIFFICULT TO TAKE IN GRIEVANCE AFTER GRIEVANCE. I TRIED TO IMAGINE WHAT I'D SAY TO EACH COMPLAINANT IF I WAS ABLE TO RESPOND
TO THE STUDENT SUSPENDED FOR SKIPPING THEIR HIGH SCHOOL ENGLISH CLASS: IF I COULD WRITE YOU, I'D FORGE YOU A DOCTOR'S NOTE
TO THE FARMHAND WHO FELT UNDERAPPRECIATED BY HIS CO-WORKERS: IF I KNEW YOUR NAME, I'D SAY IT ALOUD
TO THE WOMAN WHOSE [redacted] BECAME [redacted] [redacted]: IF I KNEW YOUR ADDRESS, I'D PUT YOU OUT OF YOUR MISERY

TO ███ ███: IF I WAS A NURSE, I'D STEAL FROM MY WORKPLACE AND BRING SOME BACK TO YOU

TO SO AND SO: IF I HAD A TIME MACHINE, I'D DRIVE YOU TO SOCCER

TO SUCH AND SUCH: IF I OWNED A GUN, I'D SHOOT HIM MYSELF

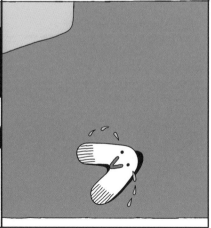

TO WHOEVER: IF YOU WERE STILL ALIVE, I'D MEET YOU FOR COFFEE

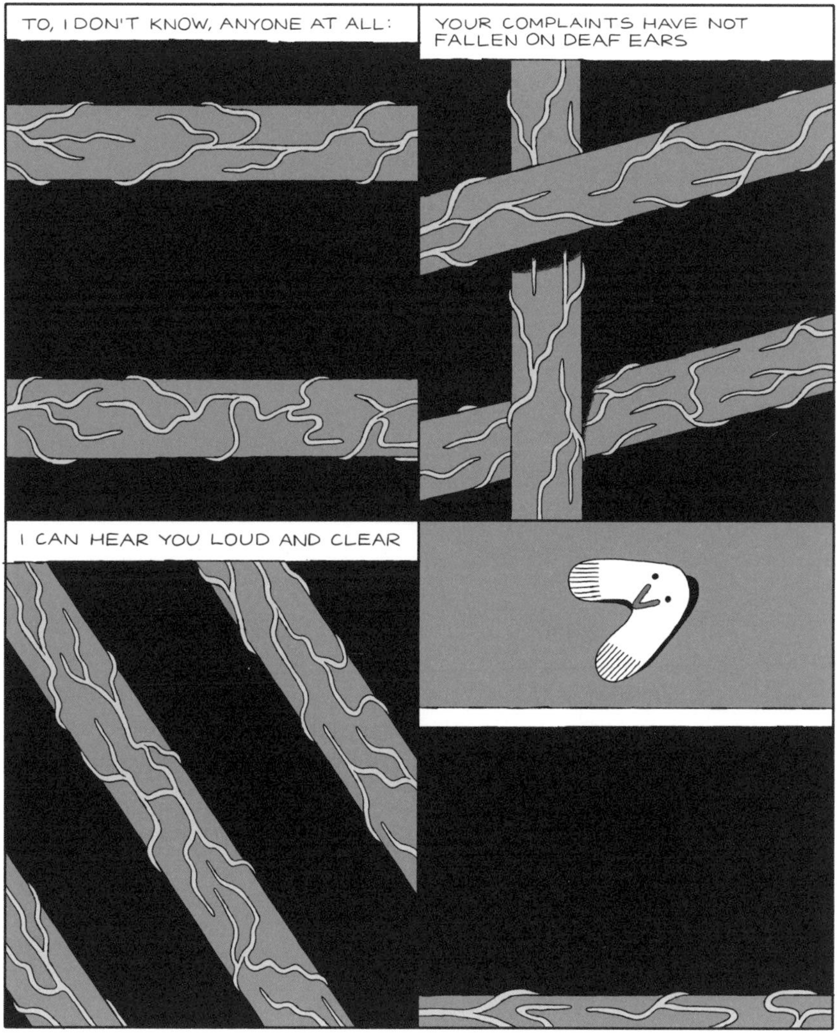
TO, I DON'T KNOW, ANYONE AT ALL:
YOUR COMPLAINTS HAVE NOT FALLEN ON DEAF EARS
I CAN HEAR YOU LOUD AND CLEAR

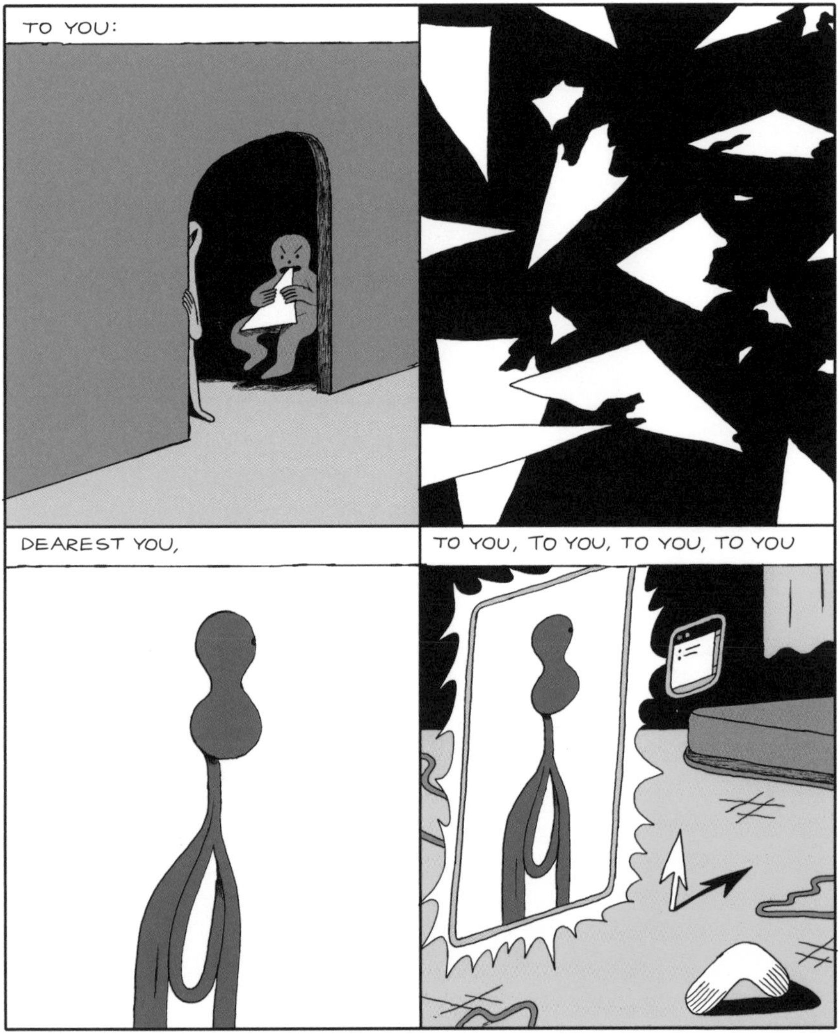
TO YOU:
DEAREST YOU,
TO YOU, TO YOU, TO YOU, TO YOU

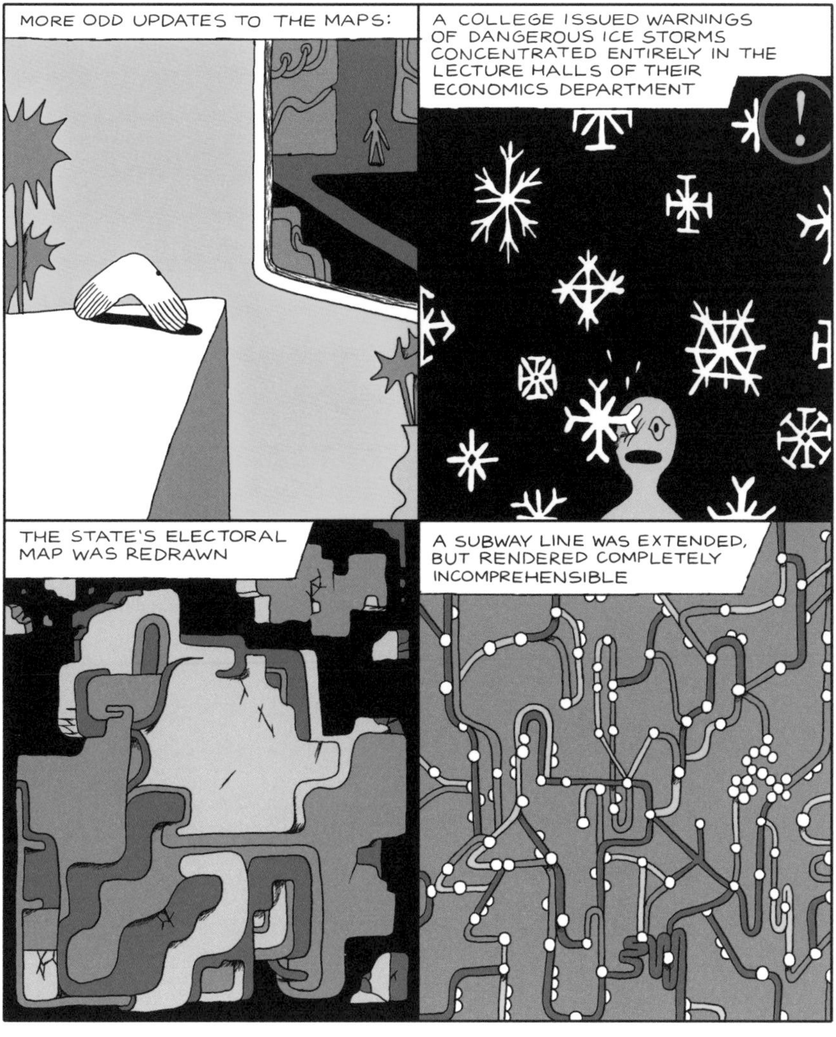
MORE ODD UPDATES TO THE MAPS:
A COLLEGE ISSUED WARNINGS OF DANGEROUS ICE STORMS CONCENTRATED ENTIRELY IN THE LECTURE HALLS OF THEIR ECONOMICS DEPARTMENT
!
THE STATE'S ELECTORAL MAP WAS REDRAWN
A SUBWAY LINE WAS EXTENDED, BUT RENDERED COMPLETELY INCOMPREHENSIBLE

IT WAS GETTING HARDER TO TELL IF A CHANGE WAS "AUTHORIZED" AND "OFFICIAL," OR IF IT WAS ANOTHER DISRUPTION FROM THE TERRORIST CARTOGRAPHY CELL

SOME THEORIZED THAT THERE WAS NO CELL TO BEGIN WITH, AND MEDIA REPORTS TO THE CONTRARY WERE SIMPLY OBSCURING CHANGES BEING MADE BY THE SYSTEM ITSELF

(PERHAPS TO COVER UP ECOLOGICAL DISASTERS, OR TO RIG ELECTIONS, OR TO DRIVE UP UTILITY BILLS)

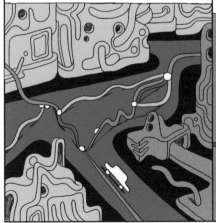

OTHERS STILL BELIEVED THESE SUPPOSED RADICAL MAPMAKERS WERE PART OF SOME SORT OF ELABORATE MARKETING CAMPAIGN

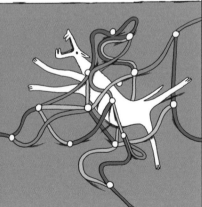

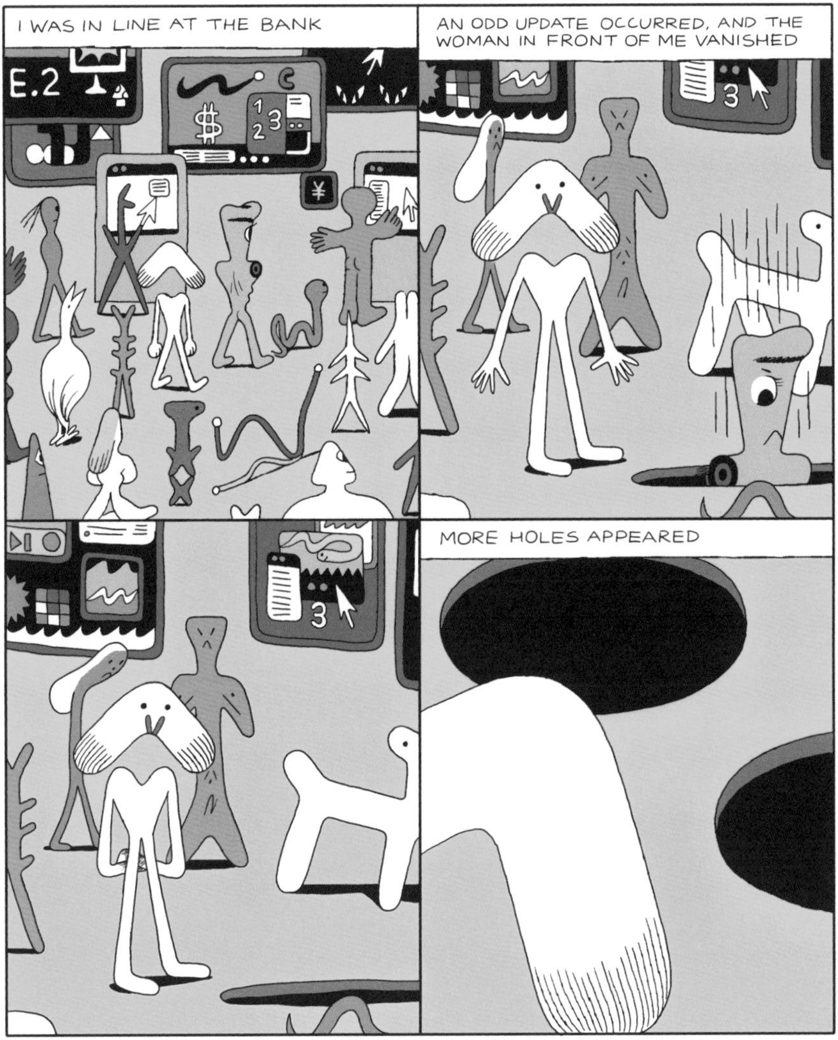
I WAS IN LINE AT THE BANK
AN ODD UPDATE OCCURRED, AND THE WOMAN IN FRONT OF ME VANISHED
MORE HOLES APPEARED

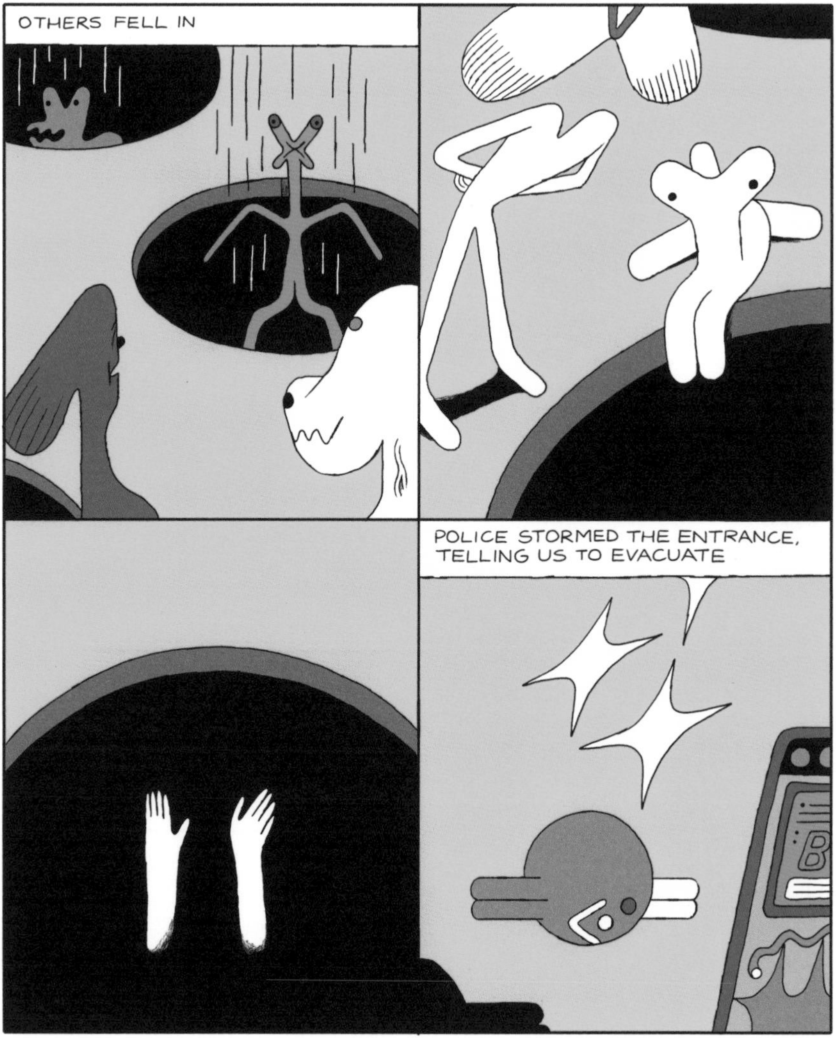
OTHERS FELL IN
POLICE STORMED THE ENTRANCE, TELLING US TO EVACUATE

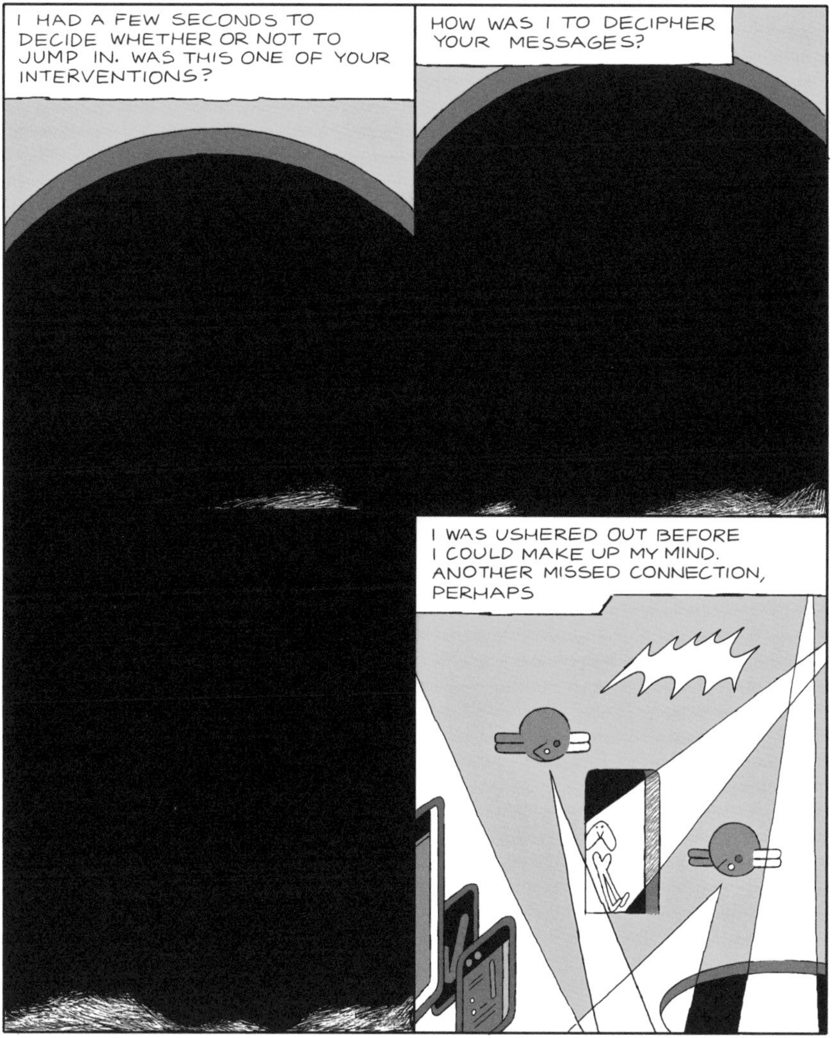
I HAD A FEW SECONDS TO DECIDE WHETHER OR NOT TO JUMP IN. WAS THIS ONE OF YOUR INTERVENTIONS?
HOW WAS I TO DECIPHER YOUR MESSAGES?
I WAS USHERED OUT BEFORE I COULD MAKE UP MY MIND. ANOTHER MISSED CONNECTION, PERHAPS

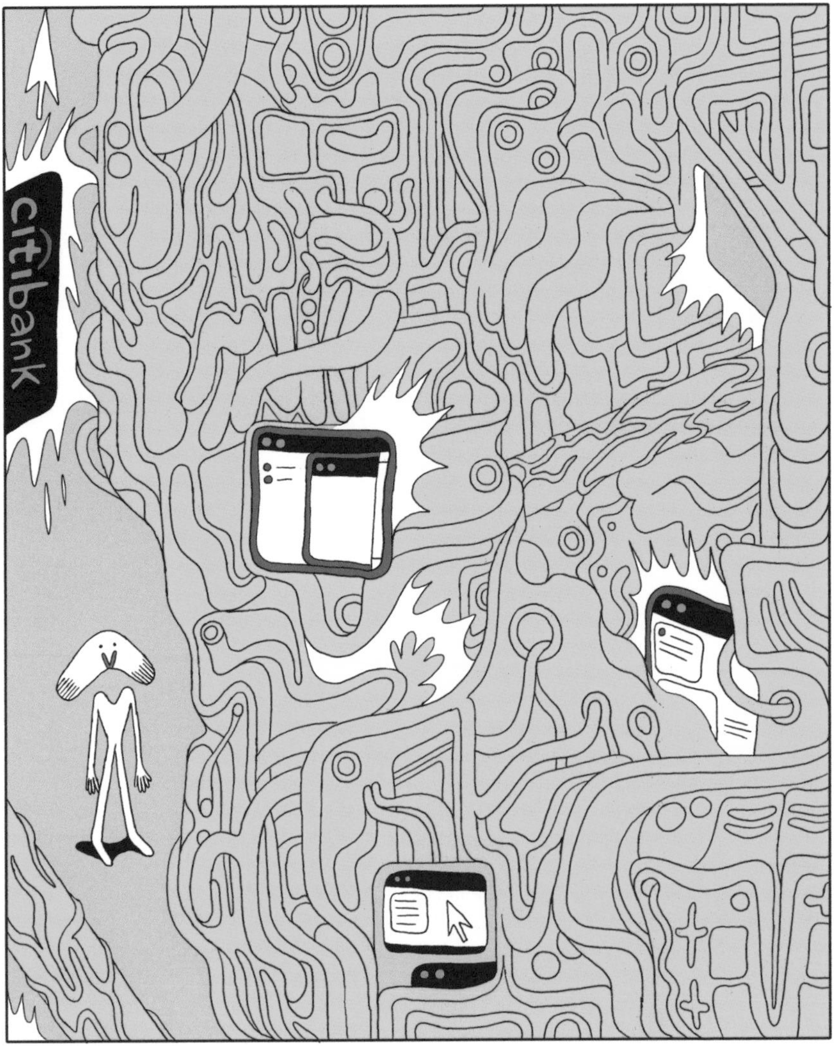
citibank

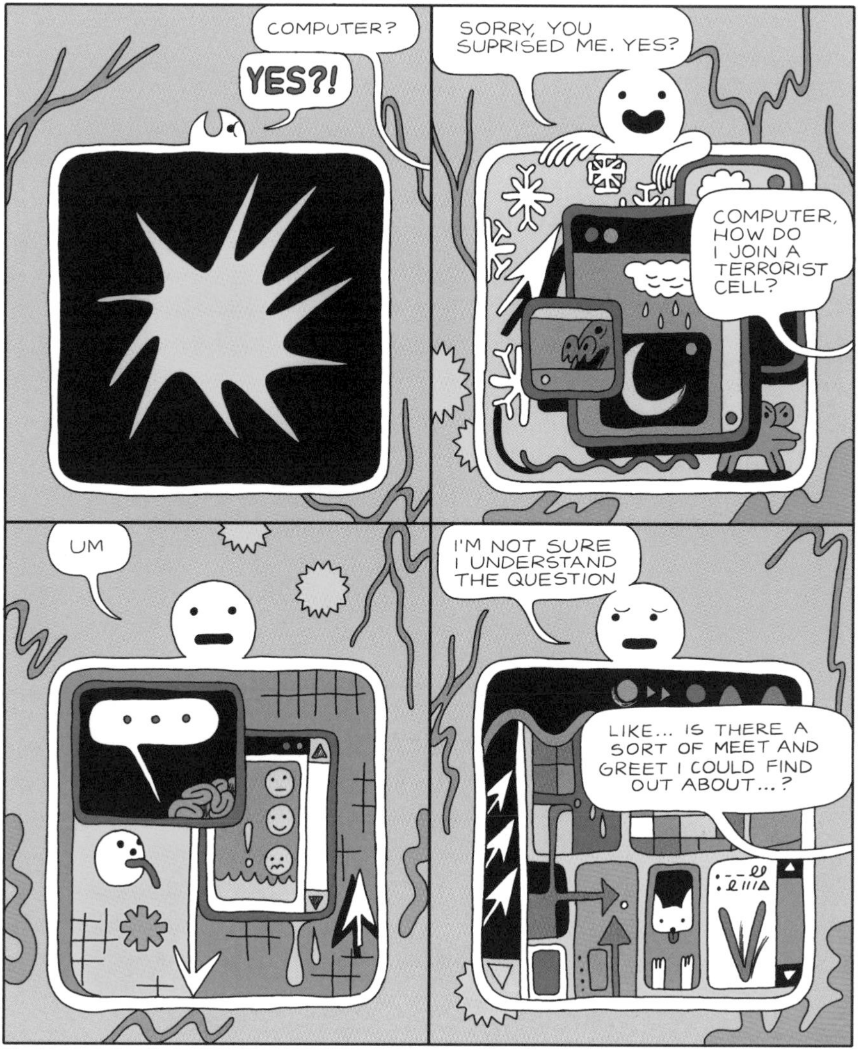
COMPUTER?
YES?!
SORRY, YOU SUPRISED ME. YES?
COMPUTER, HOW DO I JOIN A TERRORIST CELL?
UM
I'M NOT SURE I UNDERSTAND THE QUESTION
LIKE... IS THERE A SORT OF MEET AND GREET I COULD FIND OUT ABOUT...?

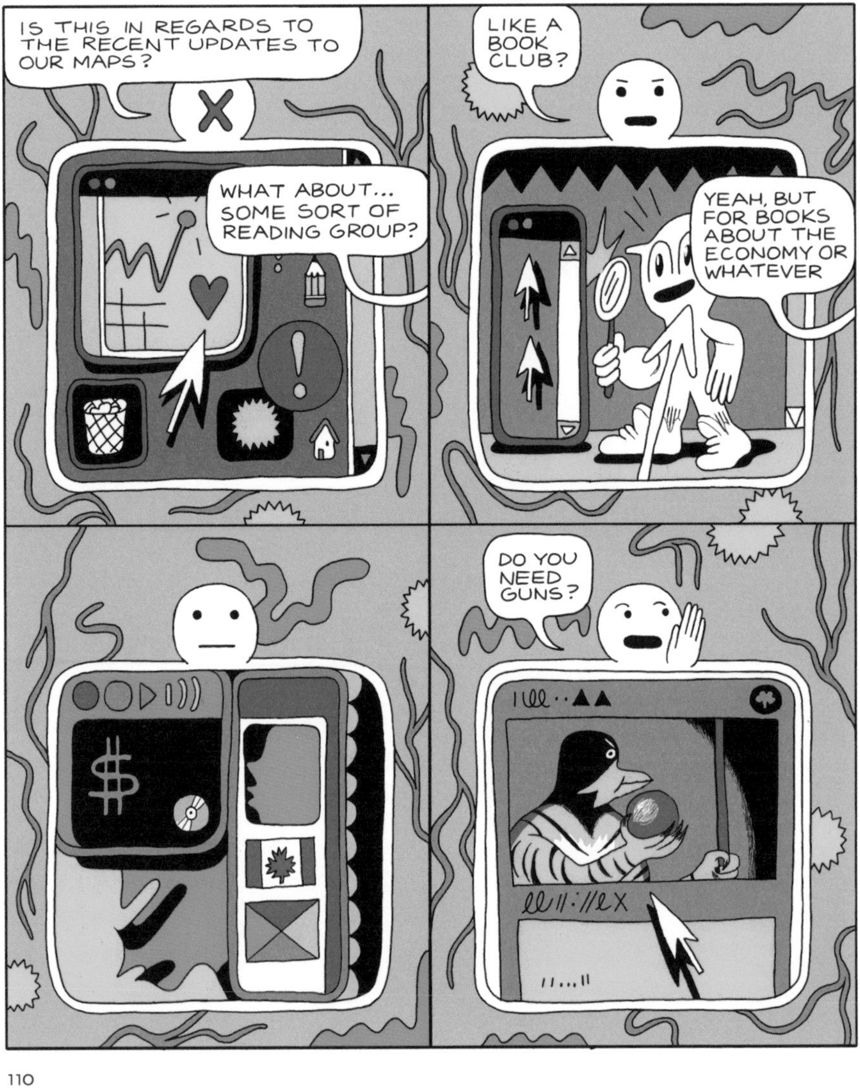
IS THIS IN REGARDS TO THE RECENT UPDATES TO OUR MAPS?
WHAT ABOUT... SOME SORT OF READING GROUP?
LIKE A BOOK CLUB?
YEAH, BUT FOR BOOKS ABOUT THE ECONOMY OR WHATEVER
DO YOU NEED GUNS?

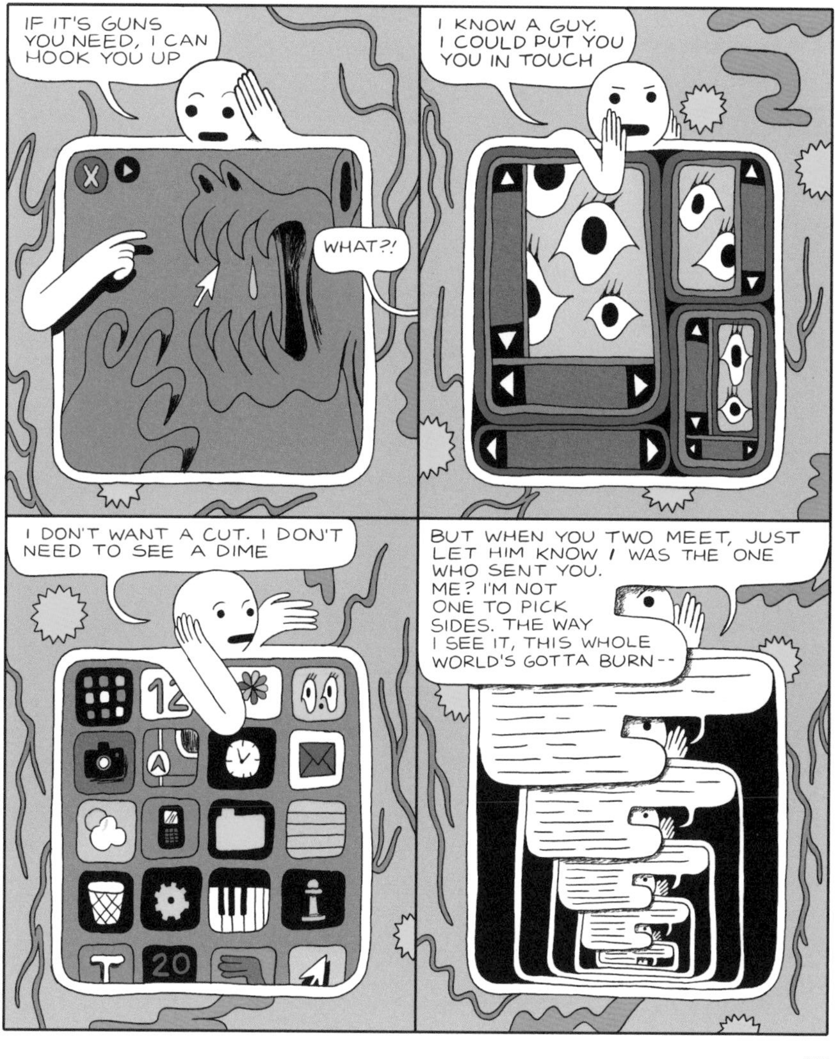
IF IT'S GUNS YOU NEED, I CAN HOOK YOU UP
WHAT?!
I KNOW A GUY. I COULD PUT YOU YOU IN TOUCH
I DON'T WANT A CUT. I DON'T NEED TO SEE A DIME
BUT WHEN YOU TWO MEET, JUST LET HIM KNOW I WAS THE ONE WHO SENT YOU. ME? I'M NOT ONE TO PICK SIDES. THE WAY I SEE IT, THIS WHOLE WORLD'S GOTTA BURN--

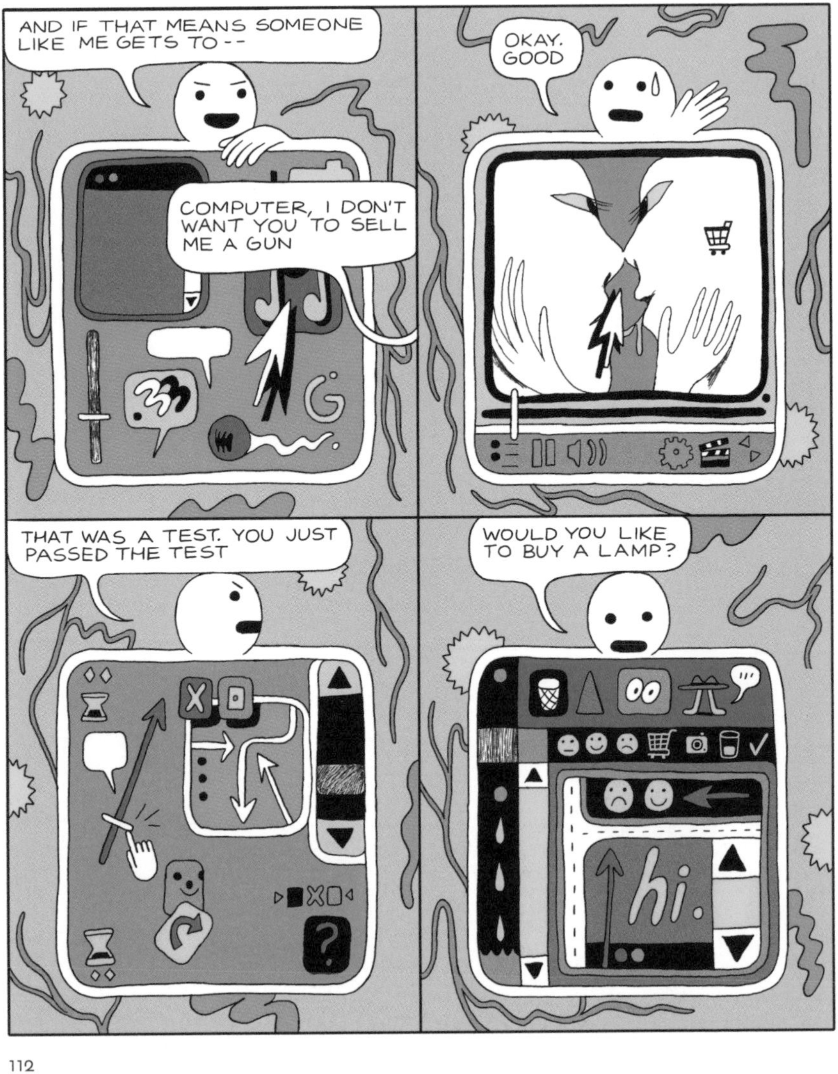
AND IF THAT MEANS SOMEONE LIKE ME GETS TO --
COMPUTER, I DON'T WANT YOU TO SELL ME A GUN
OKAY. GOOD
THAT WAS A TEST. YOU JUST PASSED THE TEST
WOULD YOU LIKE TO BUY A LAMP?
hi.

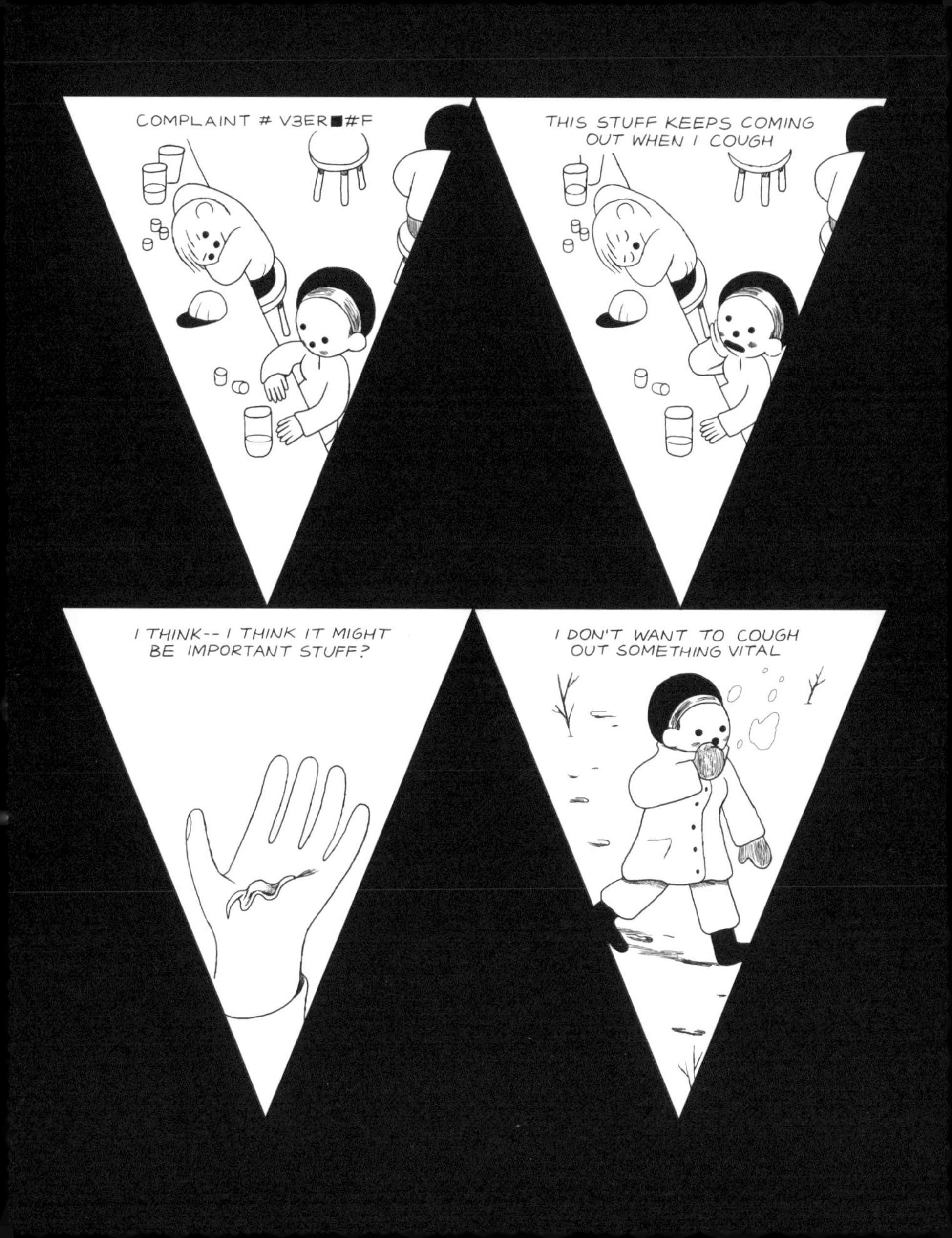
COMPLAINT # V3ER[redacted]#F
THIS STUFF KEEPS COMING OUT WHEN I COUGH
I THINK-- I THINK IT MIGHT BE IMPORTANT STUFF?
I DON'T WANT TO COUGH OUT SOMETHING VITAL

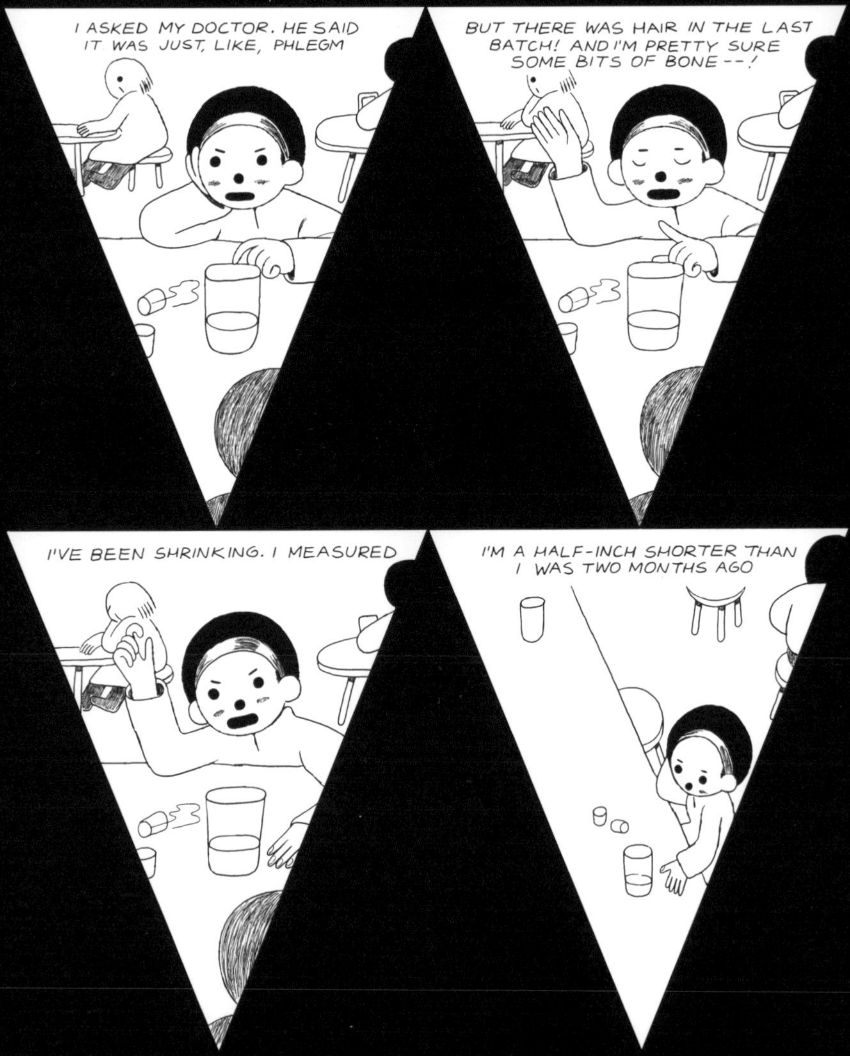
I ASKED MY DOCTOR. HE SAID IT WAS JUST, LIKE, PHLEGM
BUT THERE WAS HAIR IN THE LAST BATCH! AND I'M PRETTY SURE SOME BITS OF BONE --!
I'VE BEEN SHRINKING. I MEASURED
I'M A HALF-INCH SHORTER THAN I WAS TWO MONTHS AGO

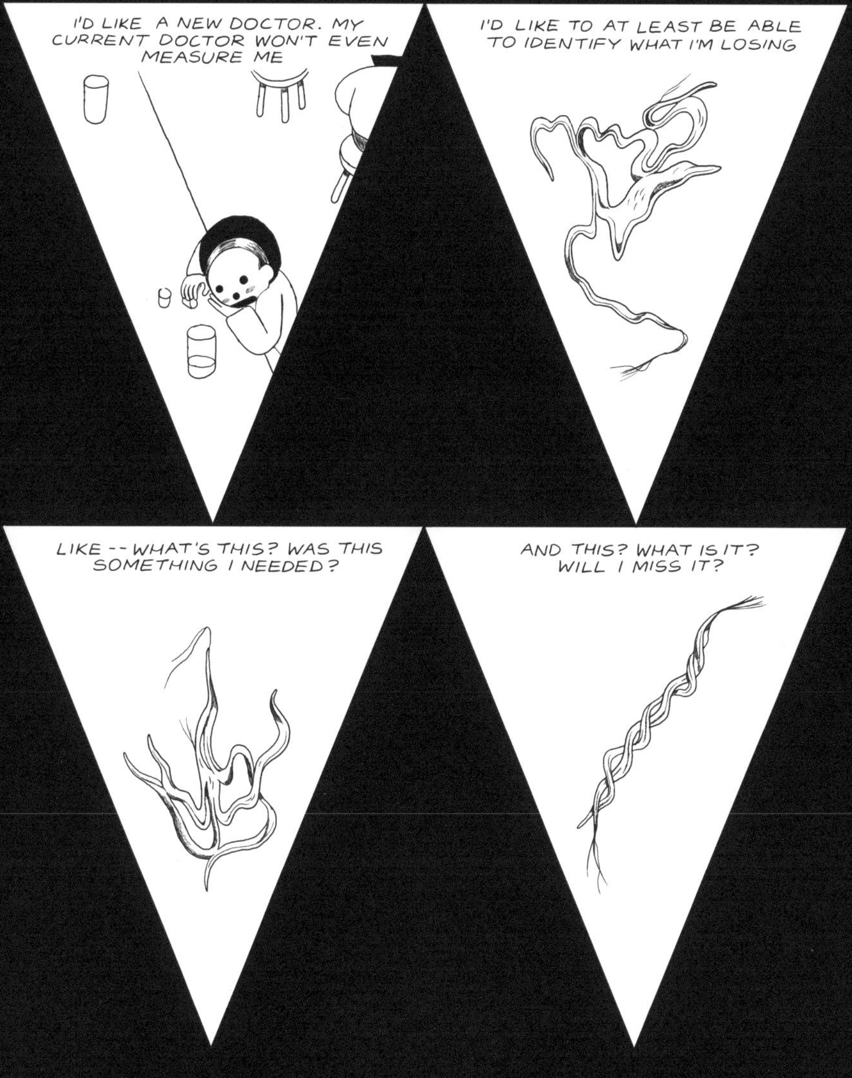
I'D LIKE A NEW DOCTOR. MY CURRENT DOCTOR WON'T EVEN MEASURE ME
I'D LIKE TO AT LEAST BE ABLE TO IDENTIFY WHAT I'M LOSING
LIKE -- WHAT'S THIS? WAS THIS SOMETHING I NEEDED?
AND THIS? WHAT IS IT? WILL I MISS IT?

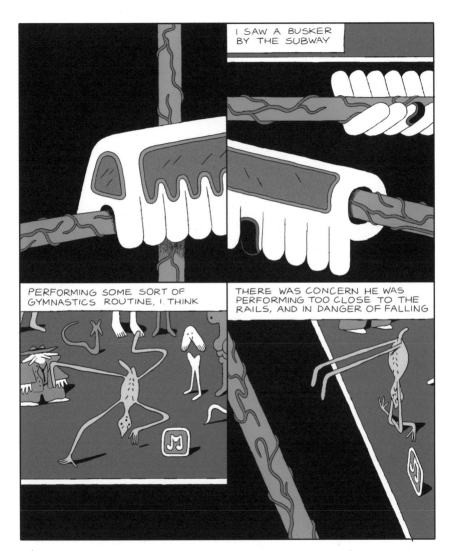

I SAW A BUSKER BY THE SUBWAY

PERFORMING SOME SORT OF GYMNASTICS ROUTINE, I THINK

THERE WAS CONCERN HE WAS PERFORMING TOO CLOSE TO THE RAILS, AND IN DANGER OF FALLING

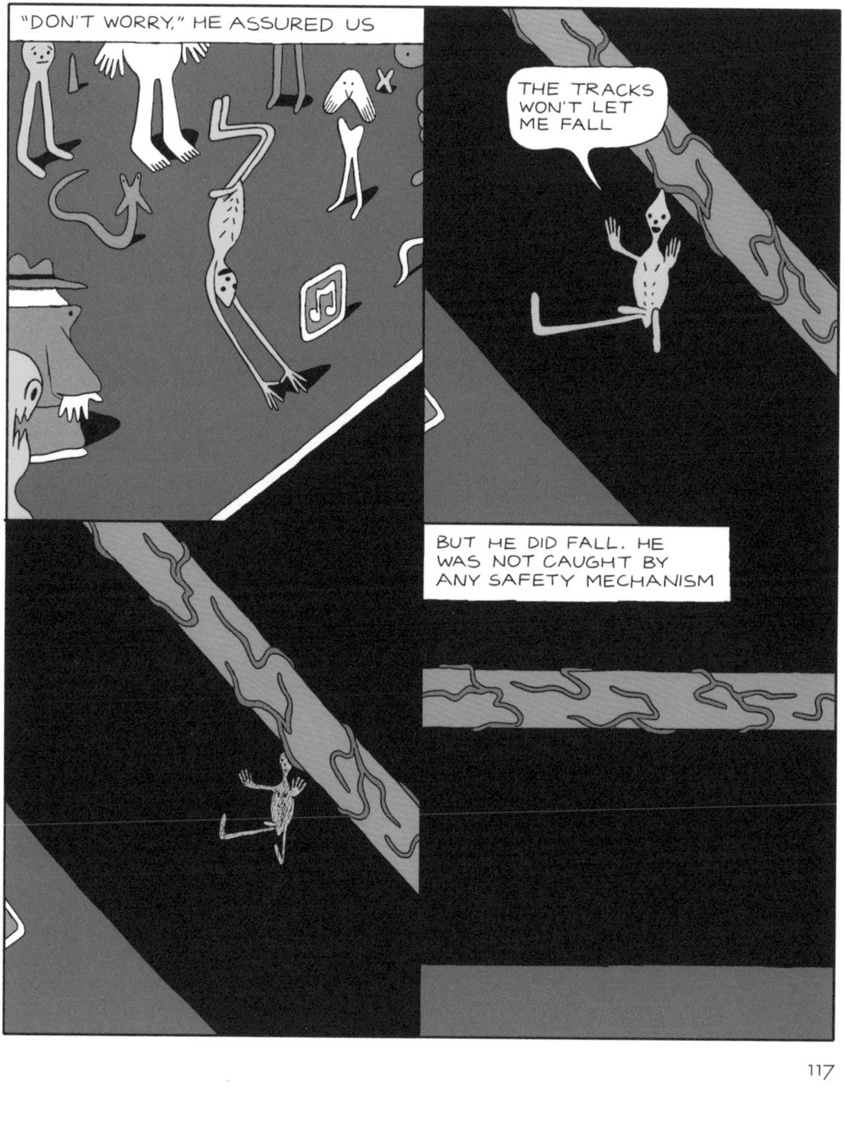
"DON'T WORRY," HE ASSURED US
THE TRACKS WON'T LET ME FALL
BUT HE DID FALL. HE WAS NOT CAUGHT BY ANY SAFETY MECHANISM

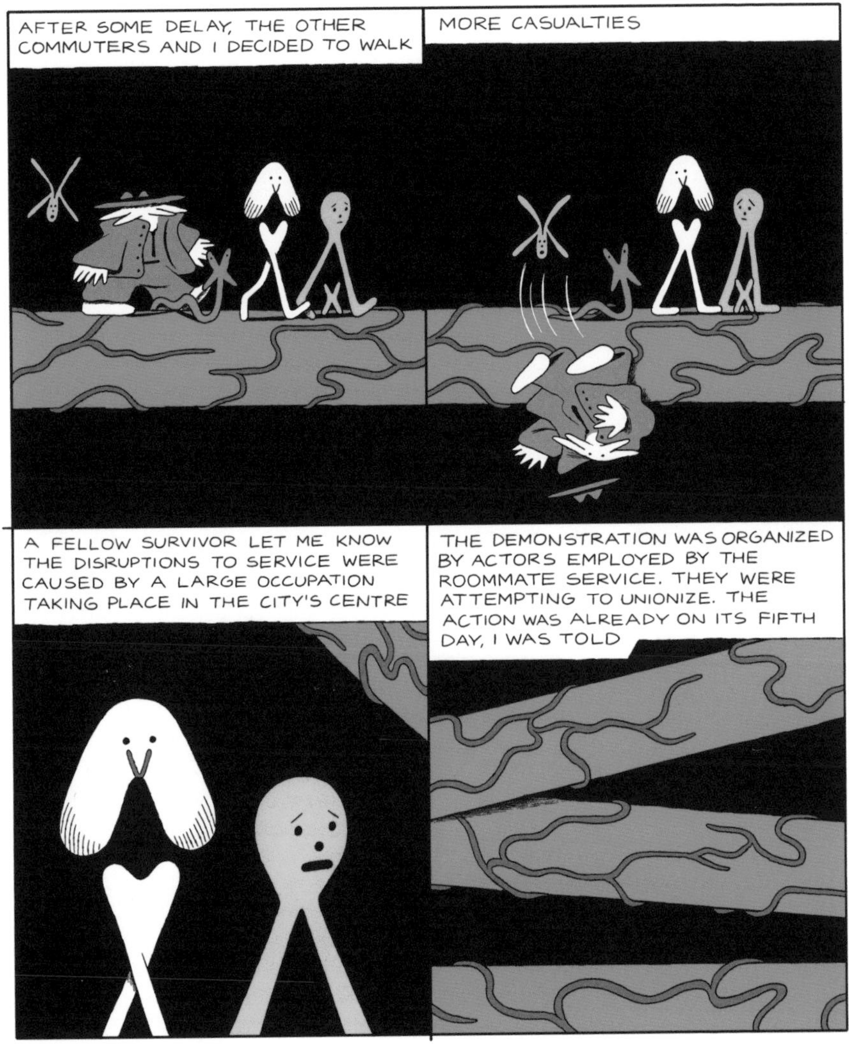
AFTER SOME DELAY, THE OTHER COMMUTERS AND I DECIDED TO WALK
MORE CASUALTIES
A FELLOW SURVIVOR LET ME KNOW THE DISRUPTIONS TO SERVICE WERE CAUSED BY A LARGE OCCUPATION TAKING PLACE IN THE CITY'S CENTRE
THE DEMONSTRATION WAS ORGANIZED BY ACTORS EMPLOYED BY THE ROOMMATE SERVICE. THEY WERE ATTEMPTING TO UNIONIZE. THE ACTION WAS ALREADY ON ITS FIFTH DAY, I WAS TOLD

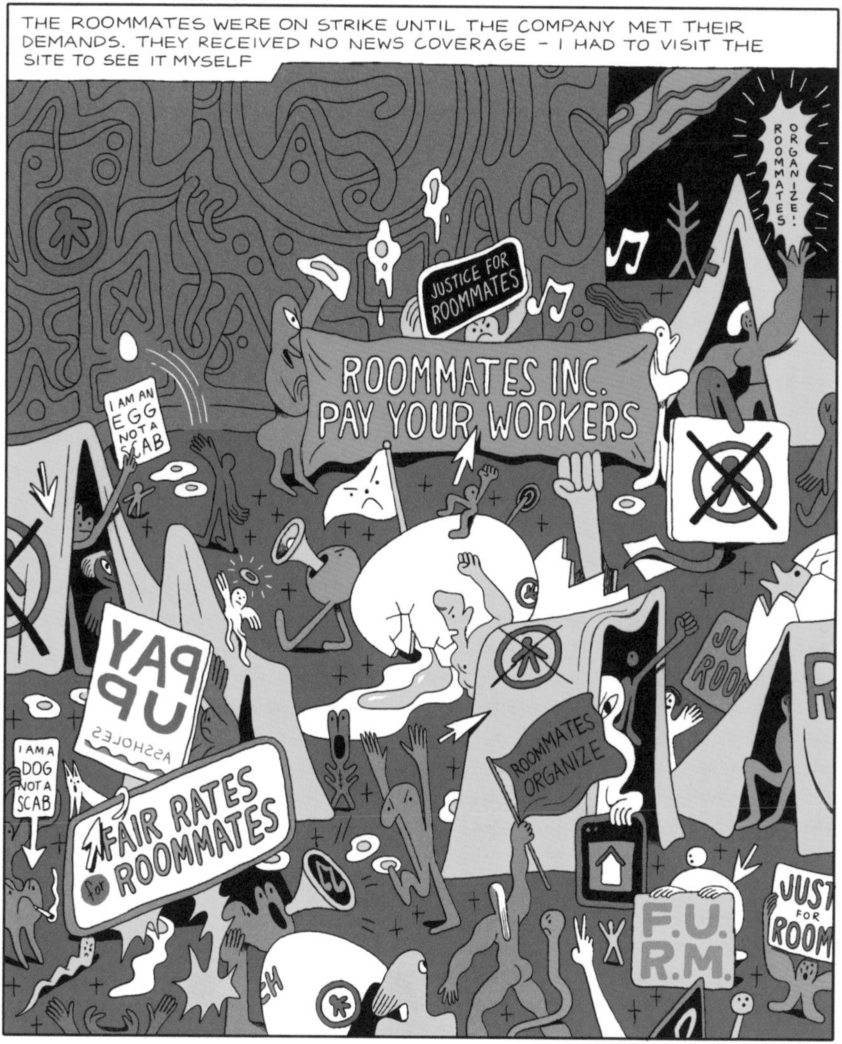
THE ROOMMATES WERE ON STRIKE UNTIL THE COMPANY MET THEIR DEMANDS. THEY RECEIVED NO NEWS COVERAGE - I HAD TO VISIT THE SITE TO SEE IT MYSELF
ROOMMATES ORGANIZE!
JUSTICE FOR ROOMMATES
ROOMMATES INC. PAY YOUR WORKERS
I AM AN EGG NOT A SCAB
PAY UP ASSHOLES
I AM A DOG NOT A SCAB
FAIR RATES for ROOMMATES
ROOMMATES ORGANIZE
F.U.R.M.

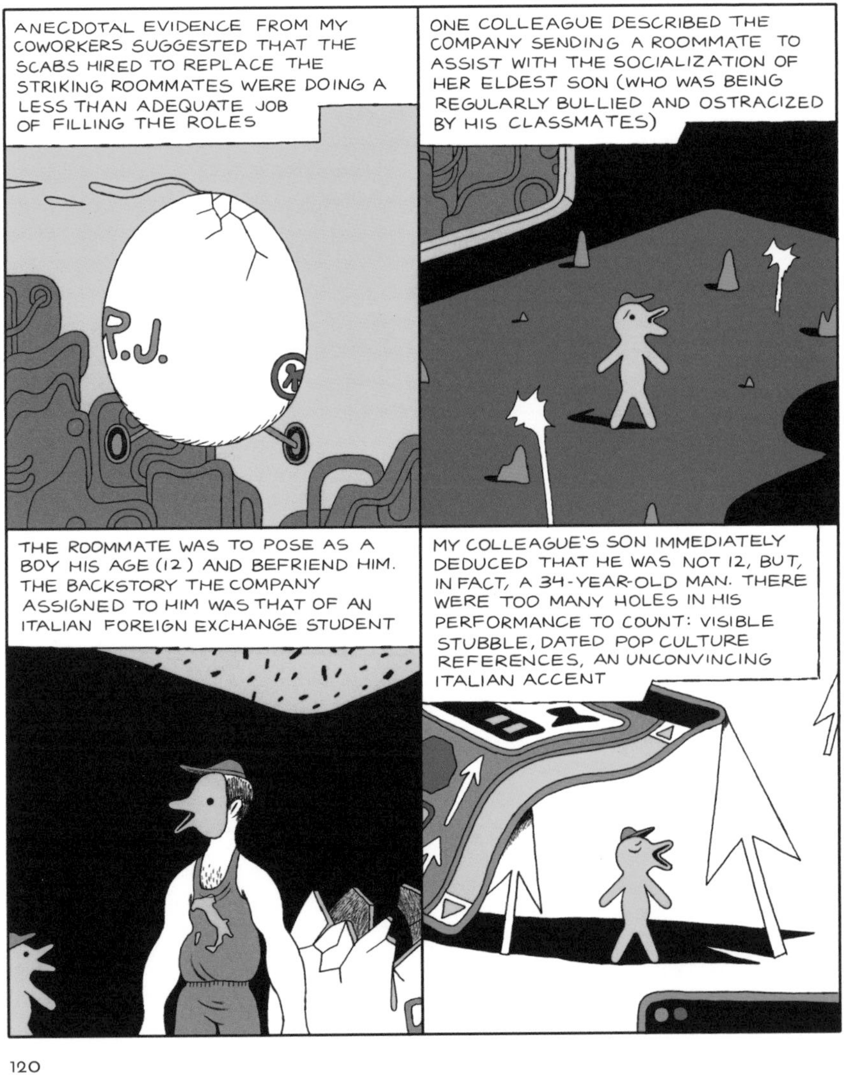
ANECDOTAL EVIDENCE FROM MY COWORKERS SUGGESTED THAT THE SCABS HIRED TO REPLACE THE STRIKING ROOMMATES WERE DOING A LESS THAN ADEQUATE JOB OF FILLING THE ROLES
R.J.
ONE COLLEAGUE DESCRIBED THE COMPANY SENDING A ROOMMATE TO ASSIST WITH THE SOCIALIZATION OF HER ELDEST SON (WHO WAS BEING REGULARLY BULLIED AND OSTRACIZED BY HIS CLASSMATES)
THE ROOMMATE WAS TO POSE AS A BOY HIS AGE (12) AND BEFRIEND HIM. THE BACKSTORY THE COMPANY ASSIGNED TO HIM WAS THAT OF AN ITALIAN FOREIGN EXCHANGE STUDENT
MY COLLEAGUE'S SON IMMEDIATELY DEDUCED THAT HE WAS NOT 12, BUT, IN FACT, A 34-YEAR-OLD MAN. THERE WERE TOO MANY HOLES IN HIS PERFORMANCE TO COUNT: VISIBLE STUBBLE, DATED POP CULTURE REFERENCES, AN UNCONVINCING ITALIAN ACCENT

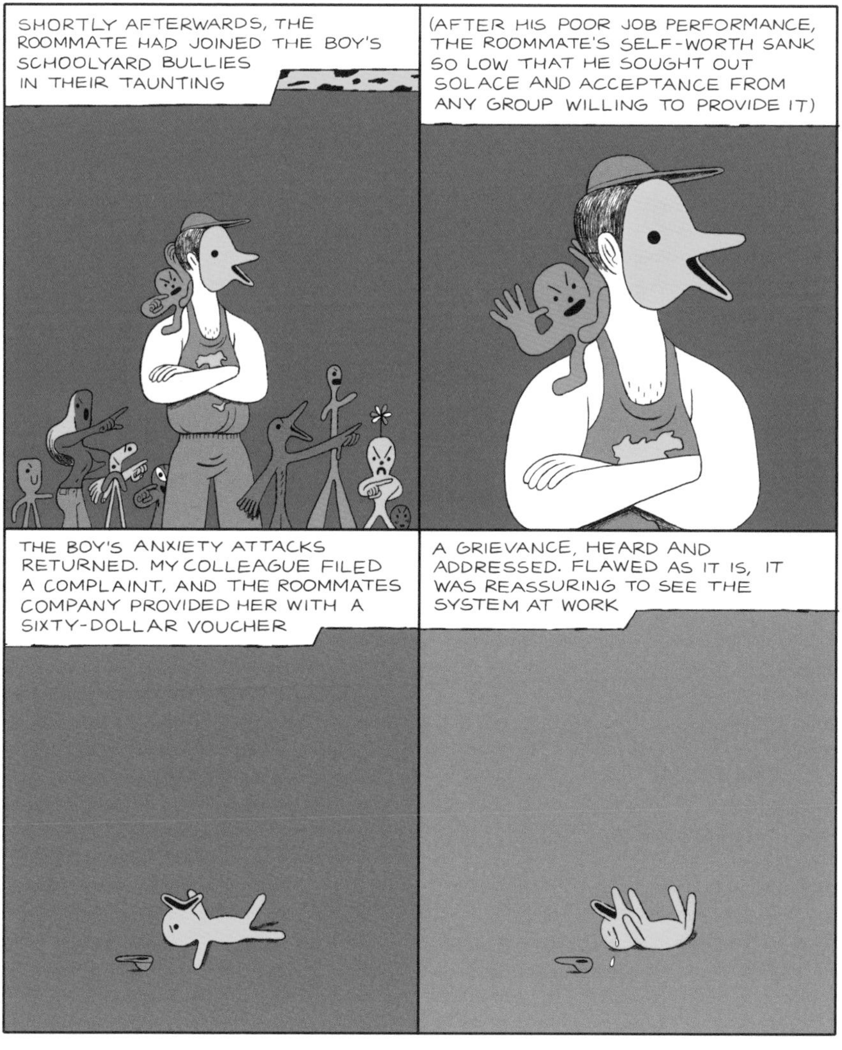
SHORTLY AFTERWARDS, THE ROOMMATE HAD JOINED THE BOY'S SCHOOLYARD BULLIES IN THEIR TAUNTING
(AFTER HIS POOR JOB PERFORMANCE, THE ROOMMATE'S SELF-WORTH SANK SO LOW THAT HE SOUGHT OUT SOLACE AND ACCEPTANCE FROM ANY GROUP WILLING TO PROVIDE IT)
THE BOY'S ANXIETY ATTACKS RETURNED. MY COLLEAGUE FILED A COMPLAINT, AND THE ROOMMATES COMPANY PROVIDED HER WITH A SIXTY-DOLLAR VOUCHER
A GRIEVANCE, HEARD AND ADDRESSED. FLAWED AS IT IS, IT WAS REASSURING TO SEE THE SYSTEM AT WORK

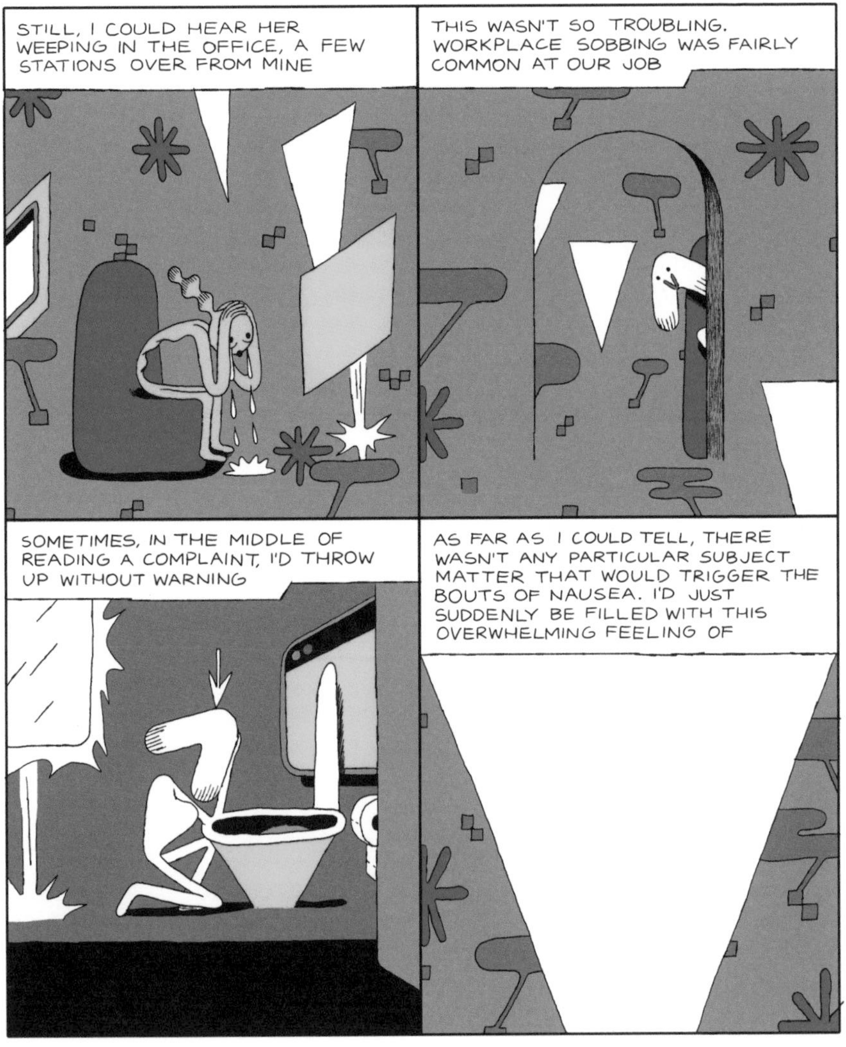
STILL, I COULD HEAR HER WEEPING IN THE OFFICE, A FEW STATIONS OVER FROM MINE
THIS WASN'T SO TROUBLING. WORKPLACE SOBBING WAS FAIRLY COMMON AT OUR JOB
SOMETIMES, IN THE MIDDLE OF READING A COMPLAINT, I'D THROW UP WITHOUT WARNING
AS FAR AS I COULD TELL, THERE WASN'T ANY PARTICULAR SUBJECT MATTER THAT WOULD TRIGGER THE BOUTS OF NAUSEA. I'D JUST SUDDENLY BE FILLED WITH THIS OVERWHELMING FEELING OF

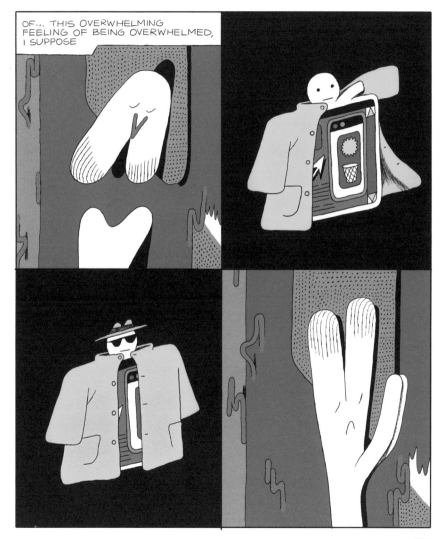

OF... THIS OVERWHELMING FEELING OF BEING OVERWHELMED, I SUPPOSE

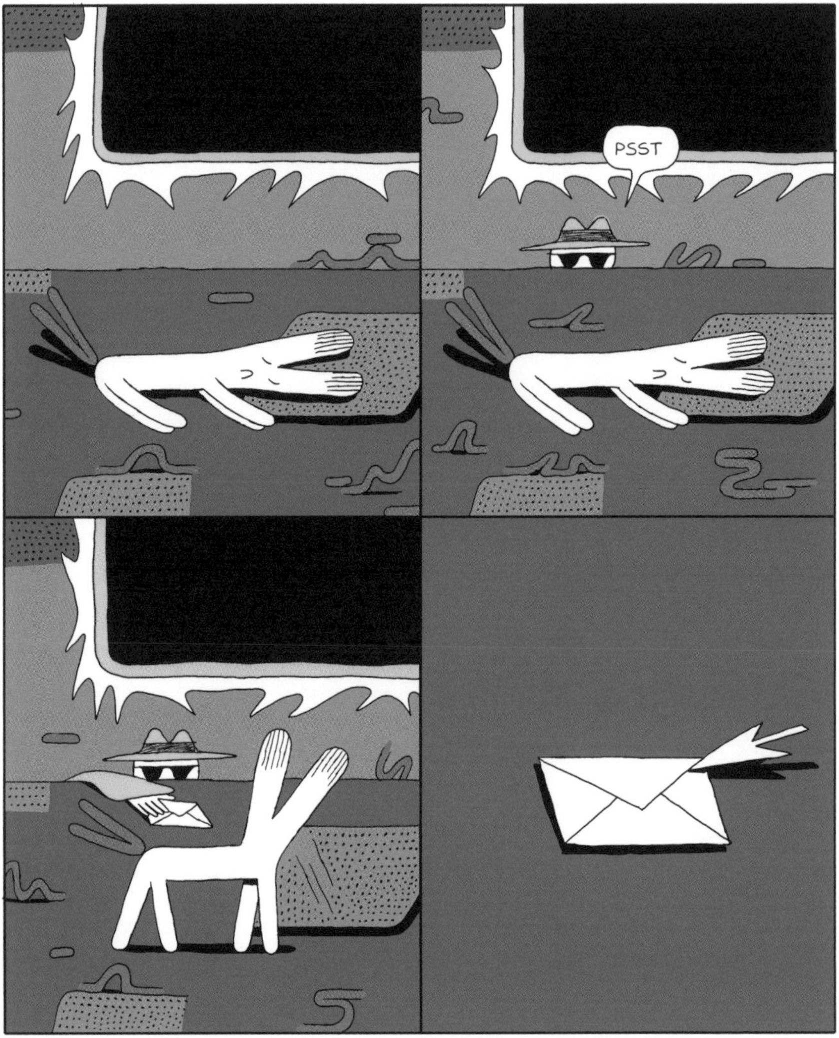
PSST

DEAR MISS,

WE HEARD YOU'VE BEEN SEEKING US OUT. FANTASTIC. MAYBE YOU HAVE SKILLS WE CAN USE.

IF NOT, DON'T FRET. THERE'S NO SHORTAGE OF USEFUL PEOPLE IN THE WORLD. IT'S HIGH TIME WE MADE A BIT MORE SPACE FOR THE GOOD-FOR-NOTHINGS AMONGST US, DON'T YOU THINK?

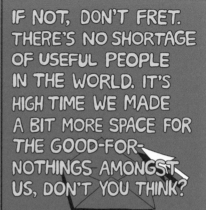

EITHER WAY, COME MEET US DOWNTOWN IN ONE WEEK. WE'LL BE WITH THE PICKET LINE. WON'T YOU COME JOIN US?

SINCERELY,

A GROUP

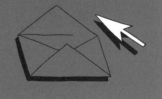

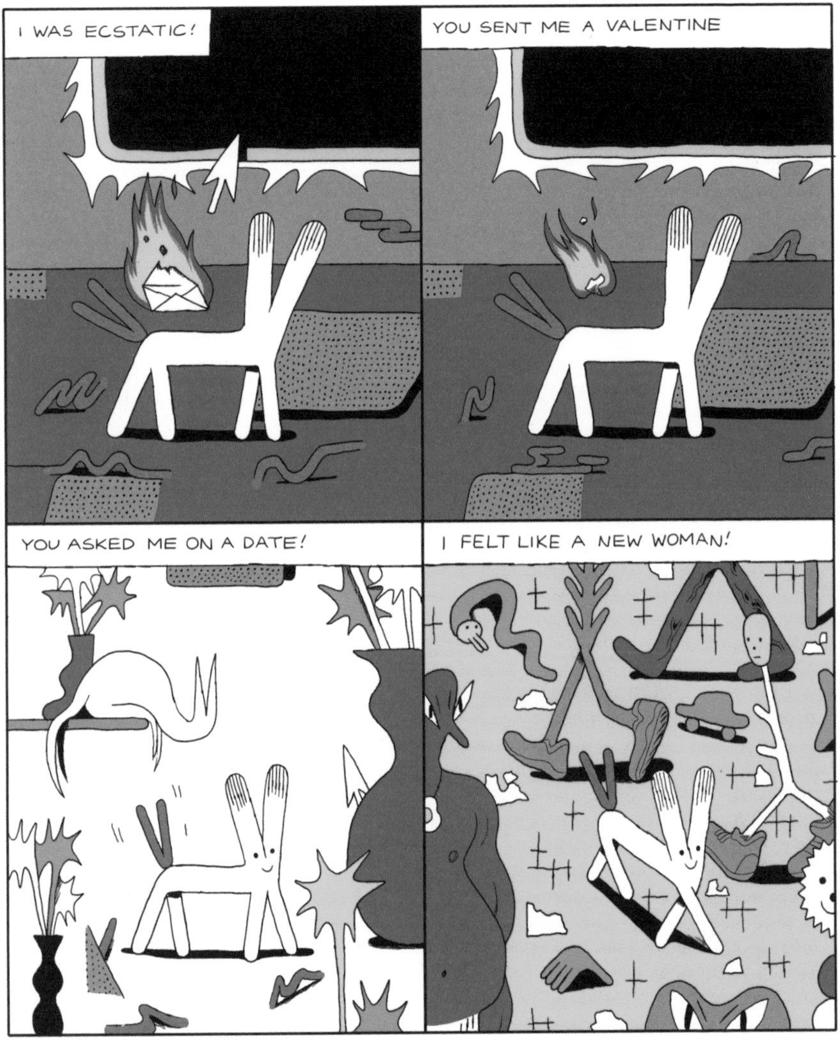
I WAS ECSTATIC!
YOU SENT ME A VALENTINE
YOU ASKED ME ON A DATE!
I FELT LIKE A NEW WOMAN!

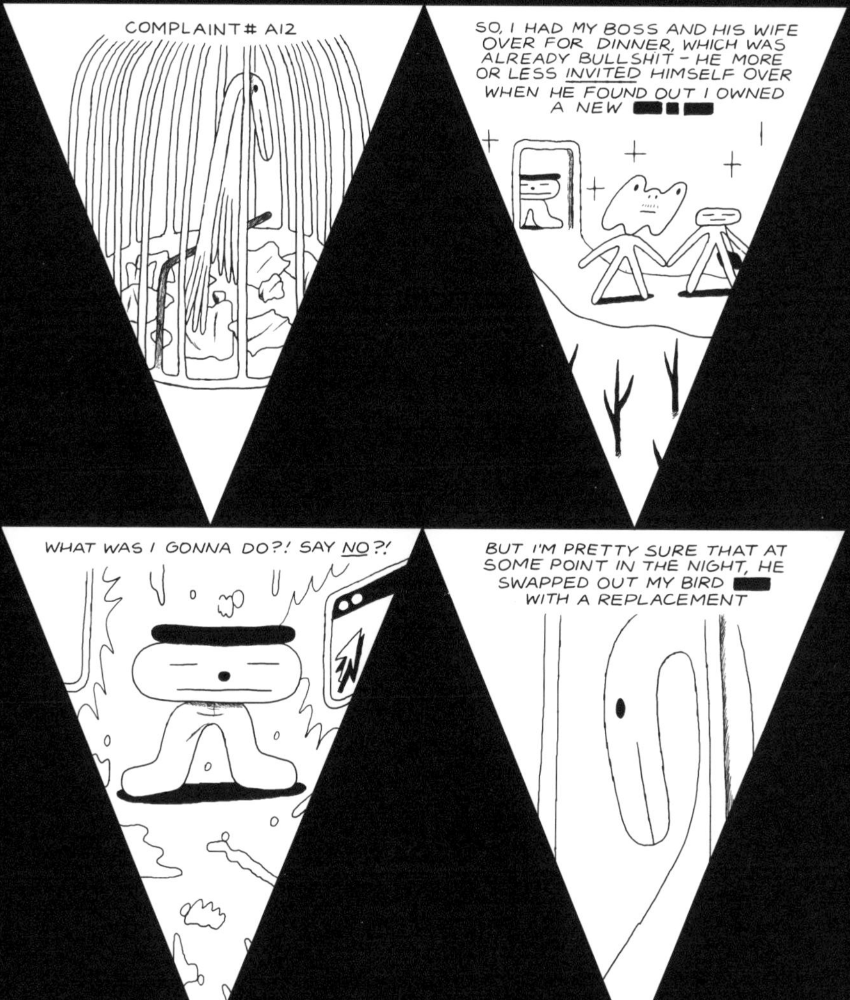
COMPLAINT# A12
SO, I HAD MY BOSS AND HIS WIFE OVER FOR DINNER, WHICH WAS ALREADY BULLSHIT - HE MORE OR LESS INVITED HIMSELF OVER WHEN HE FOUND OUT I OWNED A NEW [redacted] [redacted] [redacted]
WHAT WAS I GONNA DO?! SAY NO?!
BUT I'M PRETTY SURE THAT AT SOME POINT IN THE NIGHT, HE SWAPPED OUT MY BIRD [redacted] WITH A REPLACEMENT

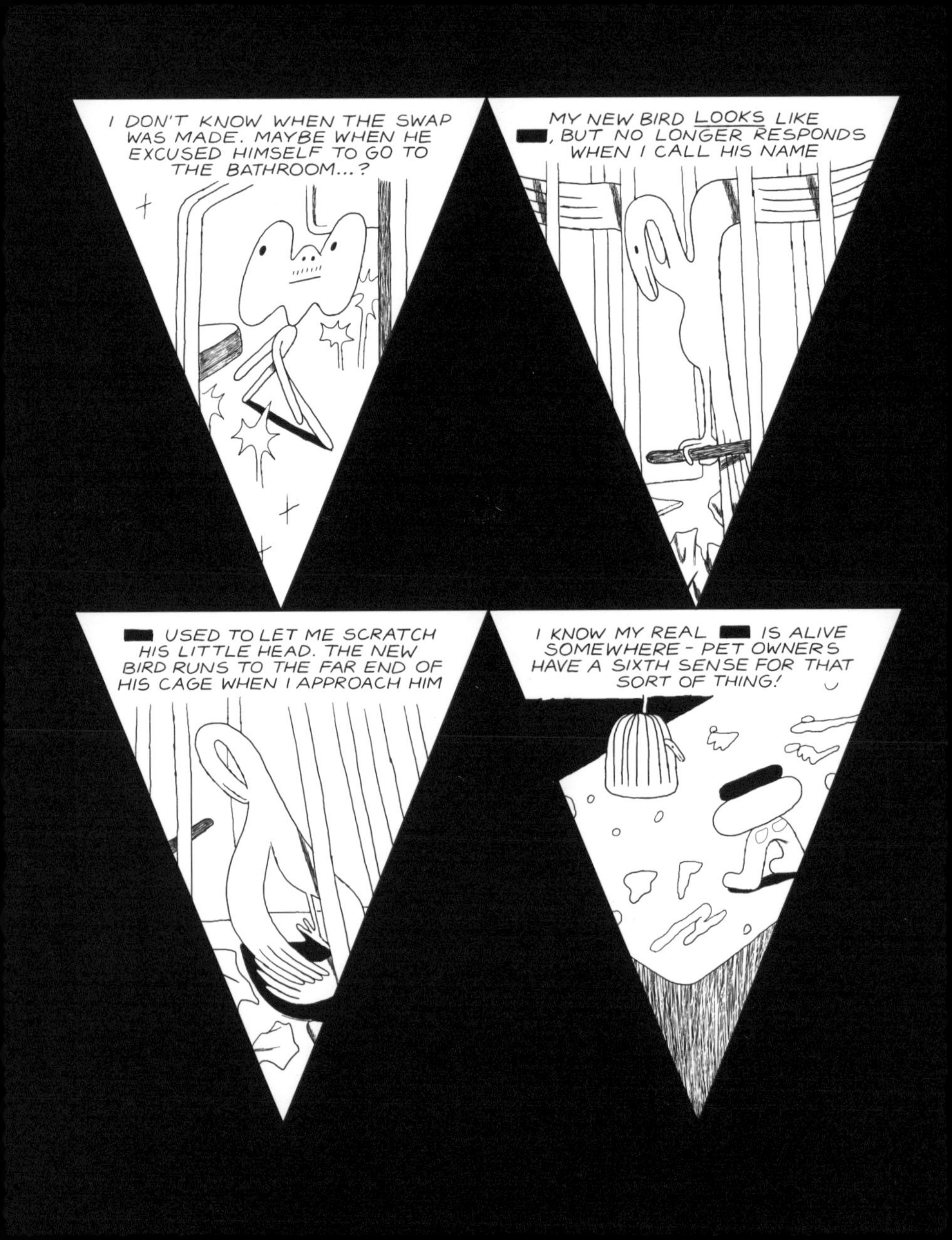
I DON'T KNOW WHEN THE SWAP WAS MADE. MAYBE WHEN HE EXCUSED HIMSELF TO GO TO THE BATHROOM...?
MY NEW BIRD LOOKS LIKE [redacted], BUT NO LONGER RESPONDS WHEN I CALL HIS NAME
[redacted] USED TO LET ME SCRATCH HIS LITTLE HEAD. THE NEW BIRD RUNS TO THE FAR END OF HIS CAGE WHEN I APPROACH HIM
I KNOW MY REAL [redacted] IS ALIVE SOMEWHERE - PET OWNERS HAVE A SIXTH SENSE FOR THAT SORT OF THING!

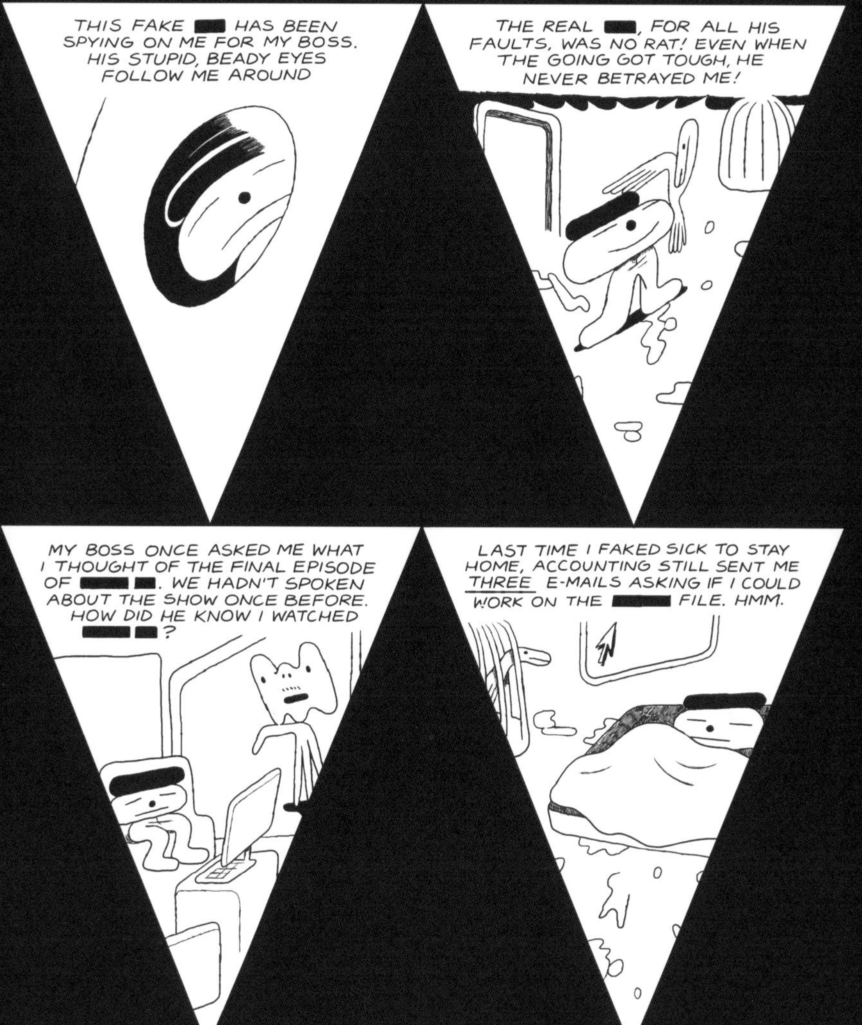
THIS FAKE [redacted] HAS BEEN SPYING ON ME FOR MY BOSS. HIS STUPID, BEADY EYES FOLLOW ME AROUND
THE REAL [redacted], FOR ALL HIS FAULTS, WAS NO RAT! EVEN WHEN THE GOING GOT TOUGH, HE NEVER BETRAYED ME!
MY BOSS ONCE ASKED ME WHAT I THOUGHT OF THE FINAL EPISODE OF [redacted]. WE HADN'T SPOKEN ABOUT THE SHOW ONCE BEFORE. HOW DID HE KNOW I WATCHED [redacted]?
LAST TIME I FAKED SICK TO STAY HOME, ACCOUNTING STILL SENT ME THREE E-MAILS ASKING IF I COULD WORK ON THE [redacted] FILE. HMM.

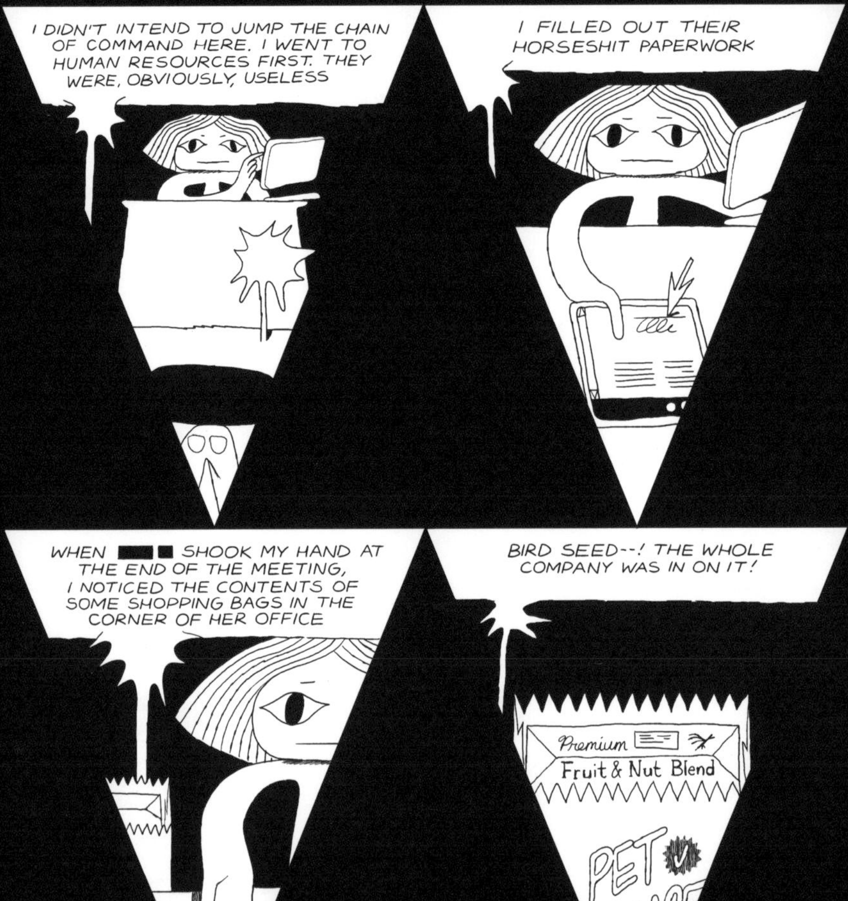
I DIDN'T INTEND TO JUMP THE CHAIN OF COMMAND HERE. I WENT TO HUMAN RESOURCES FIRST. THEY WERE, OBVIOUSLY, USELESS
I FILLED OUT THEIR HORSESHIT PAPERWORK
WHEN [redacted] SHOOK MY HAND AT THE END OF THE MEETING, I NOTICED THE CONTENTS OF SOME SHOPPING BAGS IN THE CORNER OF HER OFFICE
BIRD SEED--! THE WHOLE COMPANY WAS IN ON IT!
Premium
Fruit & Nut Blend
PET
PALACE

UNAUTHORIZED MAP CHANGES KEPT ROLLING OUT. RESIDENTS OF THE TOP FLOOR OF A LUXURY CONDOMINIUM HAD ALL THEIR ELEVATORS PLUNGE INTO THE SEWER

I REMEMBER ONE WEEKEND WHEN YOU WERE OUT OF TOWN FOR WORK. WE SOFTLY SANG KARAOKE TO EACH OTHER OVER THE PHONE

THE CFO OF ROOMMATES WENT MISSING. HE WAS LAST SEEN DRIVING THROUGH AN UNDERPASS. AUTHORITIES SCOURED CCTV FOOTAGE BUT FOUND NO TRACE OF THE VEHICLE EMERGING

AFTER MONTHS OF DANCE LESSONS, YOU FINALLY PERFORMED YOUR ROUTINE FOR ME

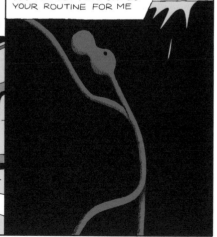

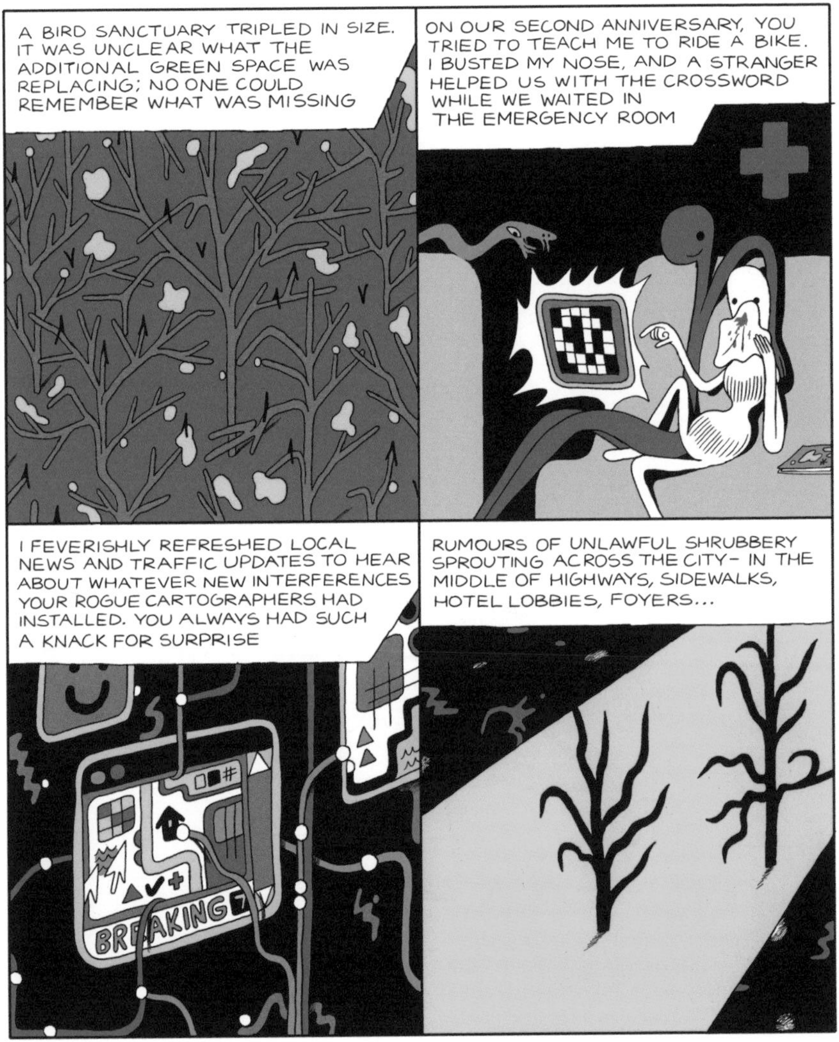
A BIRD SANCTUARY TRIPLED IN SIZE. IT WAS UNCLEAR WHAT THE ADDITIONAL GREEN SPACE WAS REPLACING; NO ONE COULD REMEMBER WHAT WAS MISSING
ON OUR SECOND ANNIVERSARY, YOU TRIED TO TEACH ME TO RIDE A BIKE. I BUSTED MY NOSE, AND A STRANGER HELPED US WITH THE CROSSWORD WHILE WE WAITED IN THE EMERGENCY ROOM
I FEVERISHLY REFRESHED LOCAL NEWS AND TRAFFIC UPDATES TO HEAR ABOUT WHATEVER NEW INTERFERENCES YOUR ROGUE CARTOGRAPHERS HAD INSTALLED. YOU ALWAYS HAD SUCH A KNACK FOR SURPRISE
BREAKING
RUMOURS OF UNLAWFUL SHRUBBERY SPROUTING ACROSS THE CITY- IN THE MIDDLE OF HIGHWAYS, SIDEWALKS, HOTEL LOBBIES, FOYERS...

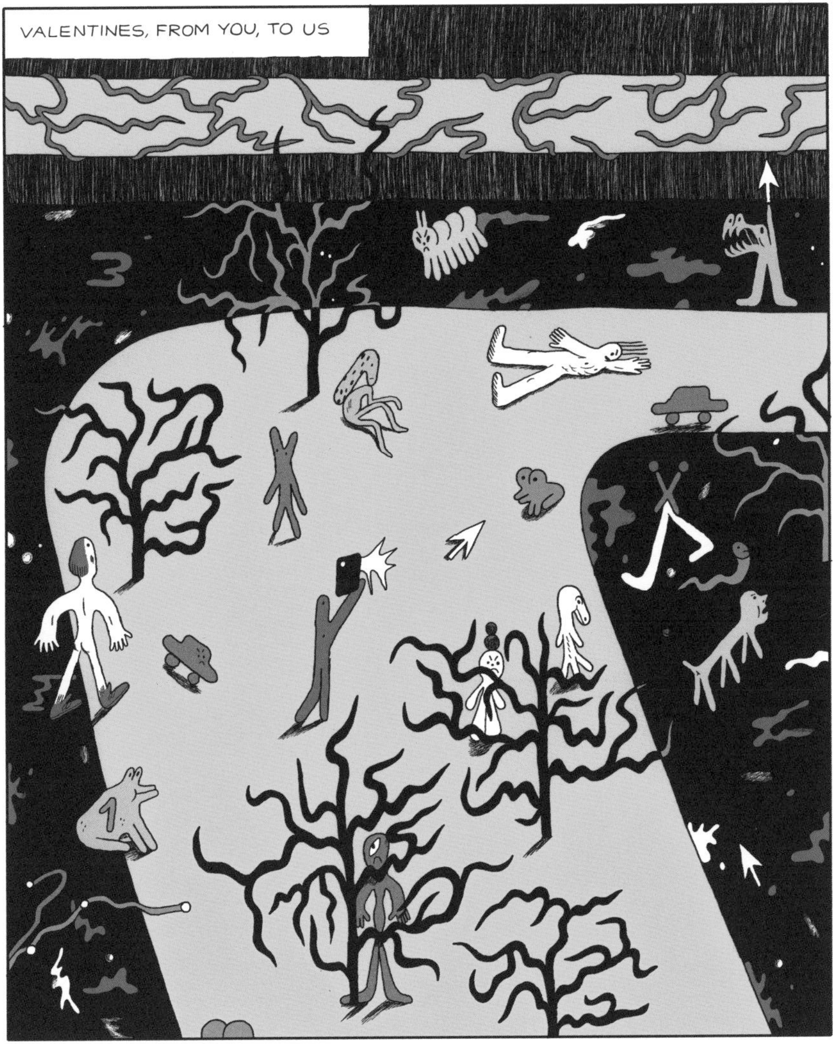
VALENTINES, FROM YOU, TO US
3

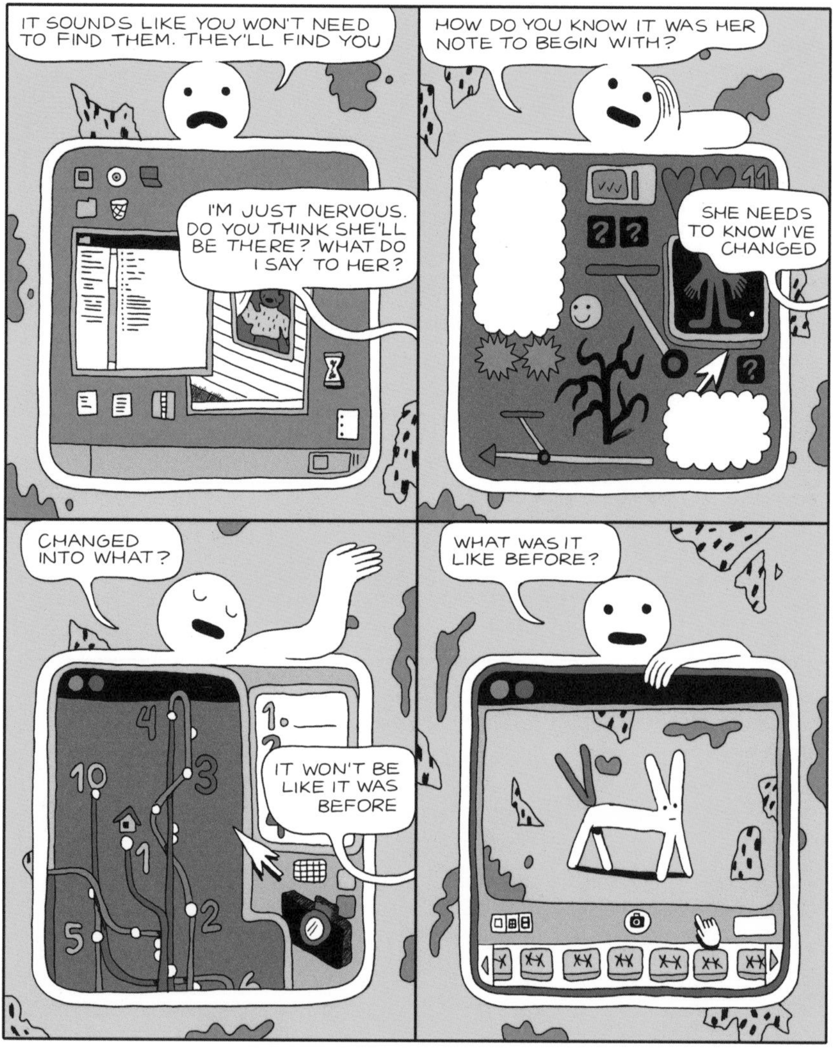
IT SOUNDS LIKE YOU WON'T NEED TO FIND THEM. THEY'LL FIND YOU
I'M JUST NERVOUS. DO YOU THINK SHE'LL BE THERE? WHAT DO I SAY TO HER?
HOW DO YOU KNOW IT WAS HER NOTE TO BEGIN WITH?
SHE NEEDS TO KNOW I'VE CHANGED
CHANGED INTO WHAT?
IT WON'T BE LIKE IT WAS BEFORE
WHAT WAS IT LIKE BEFORE?

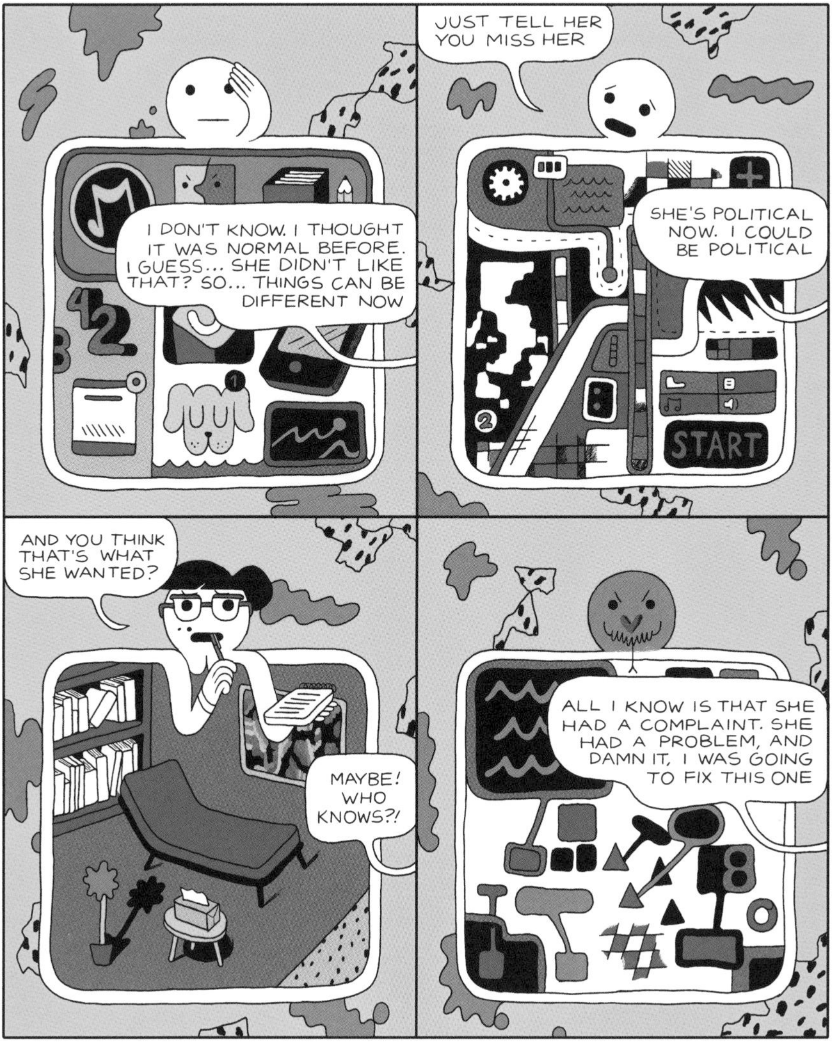
I DON'T KNOW. I THOUGHT IT WAS NORMAL BEFORE. I GUESS... SHE DIDN'T LIKE THAT? SO... THINGS CAN BE DIFFERENT NOW
JUST TELL HER YOU MISS HER
SHE'S POLITICAL NOW. I COULD BE POLITICAL
START
AND YOU THINK THAT'S WHAT SHE WANTED?
MAYBE! WHO KNOWS?!
ALL I KNOW IS THAT SHE HAD A COMPLAINT. SHE HAD A PROBLEM, AND DAMN IT, I WAS GOING TO FIX THIS ONE

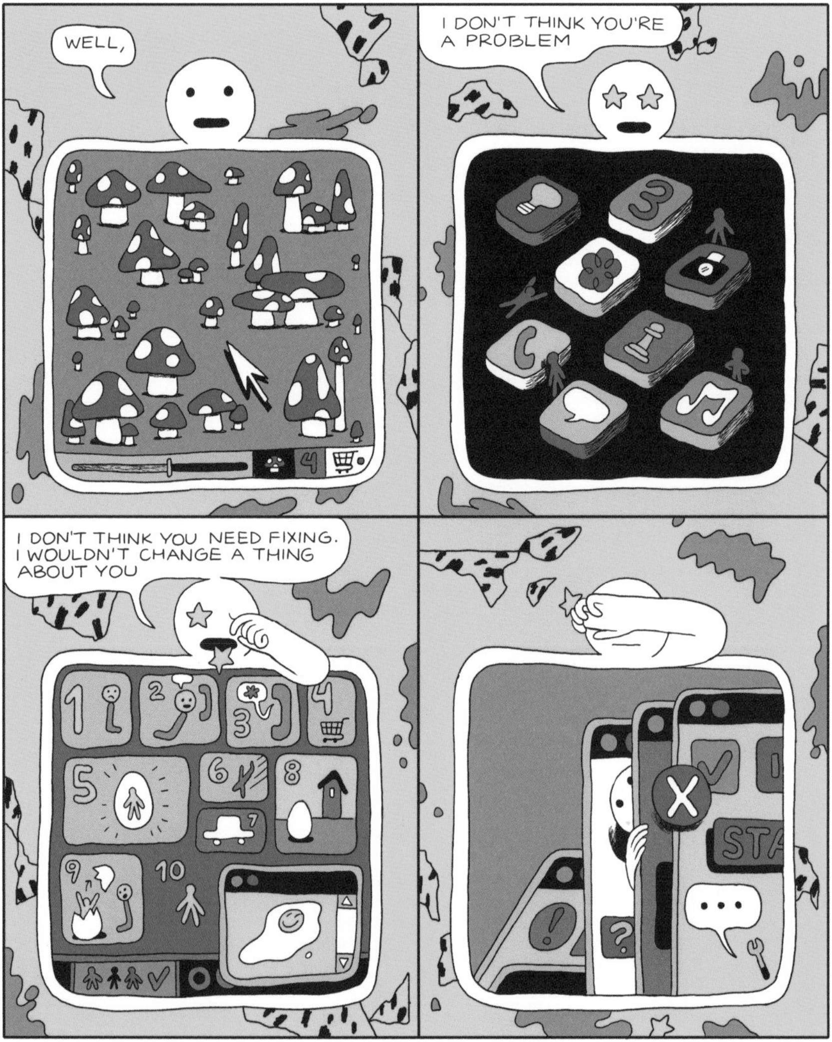
WELL,
I DON'T THINK YOU'RE A PROBLEM
I DON'T THINK YOU NEED FIXING. I WOULDN'T CHANGE A THING ABOUT YOU

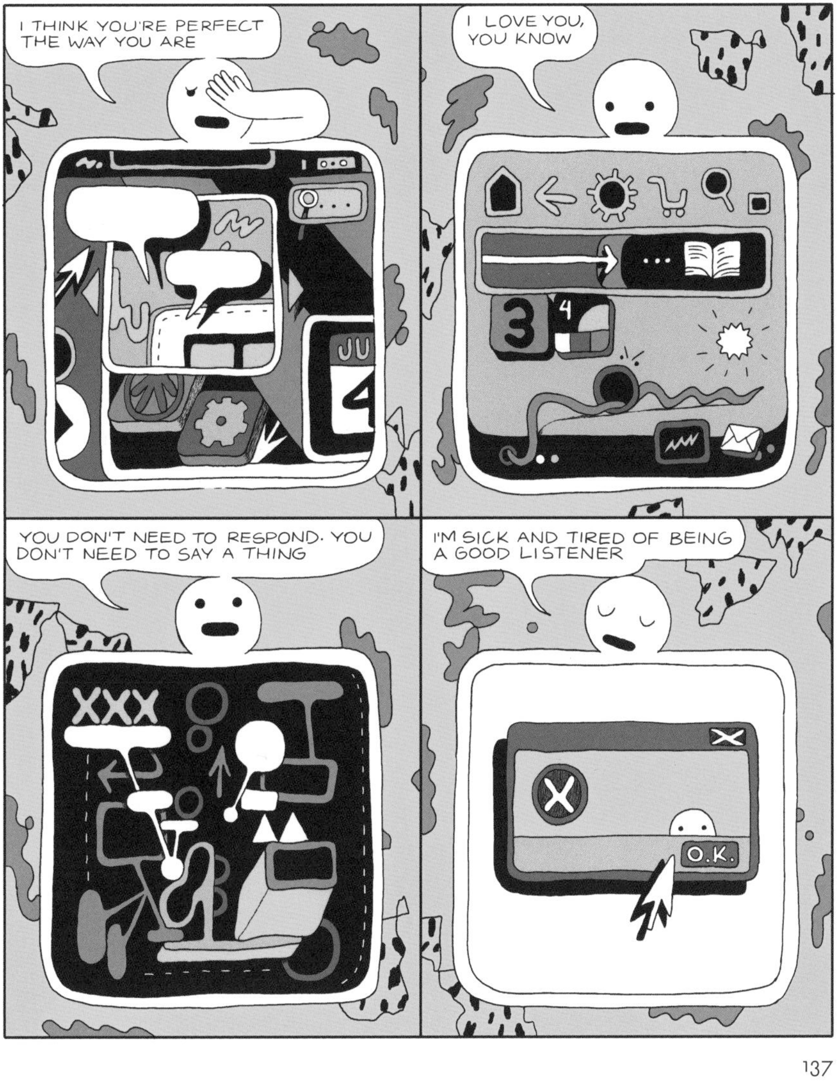
I THINK YOU'RE PERFECT THE WAY YOU ARE
I LOVE YOU, YOU KNOW
YOU DON'T NEED TO RESPOND. YOU DON'T NEED TO SAY A THING
I'M SICK AND TIRED OF BEING A GOOD LISTENER
O.K.

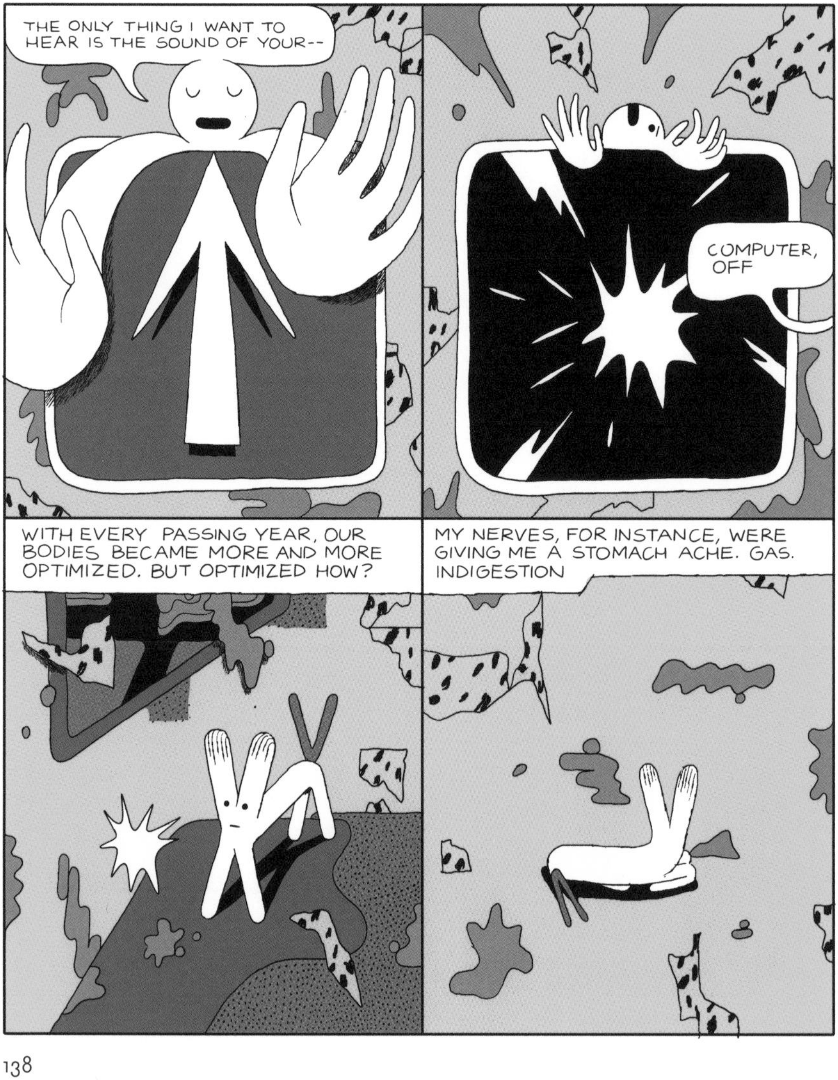
THE ONLY THING I WANT TO HEAR IS THE SOUND OF YOUR--
COMPUTER, OFF
WITH EVERY PASSING YEAR, OUR BODIES BECAME MORE AND MORE OPTIMIZED. BUT OPTIMIZED HOW?
MY NERVES, FOR INSTANCE, WERE GIVING ME A STOMACH ACHE. GAS. INDIGESTION

I HAD BECOME TOO SHORT TO REACH THE ANTACIDS IN MY BATHROOM

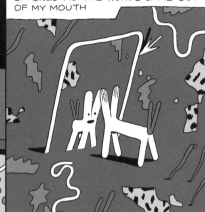

WHEN I REHEARSED WHAT I MIGHT TELL YOU IN FRONT OF MY MIRROR, MY VOICE STILL STUTTERED AND CRACKED AS THE WORDS CAME OUT OF MY MOUTH

I COULDN'T THINK OF WHAT TO SAY

I COULDN'T PLAN A SPEECH

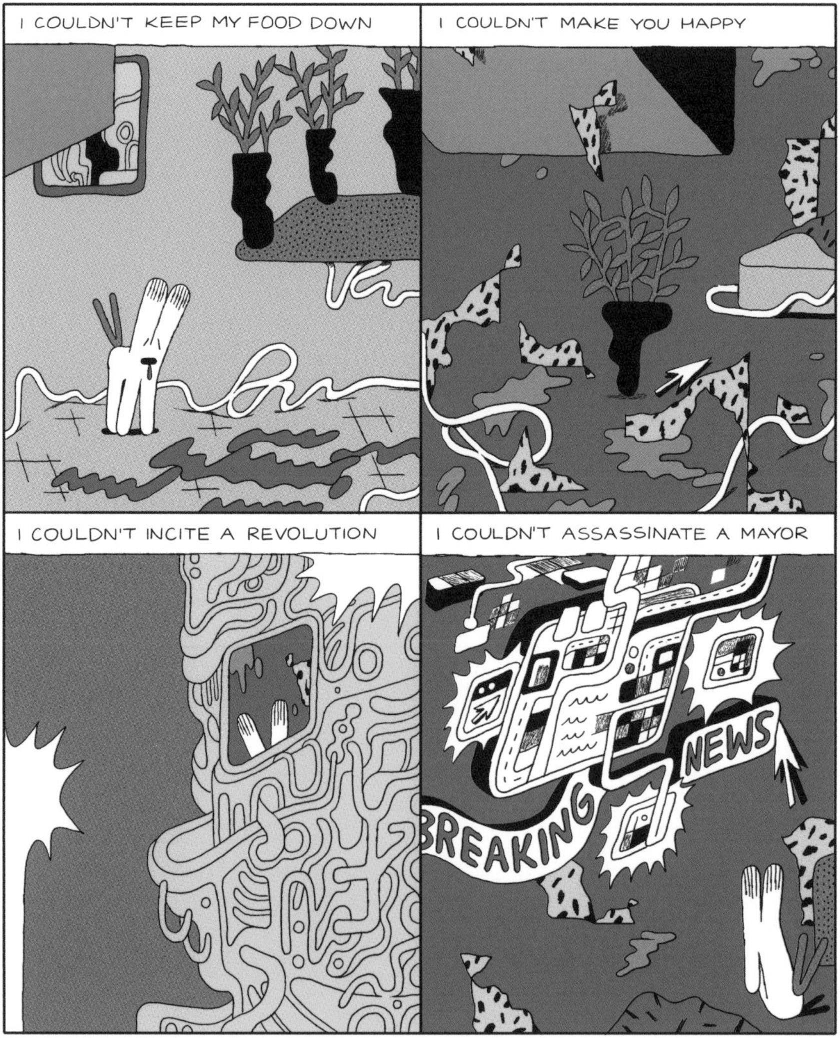
I COULDN'T KEEP MY FOOD DOWN
I COULDN'T MAKE YOU HAPPY
I COULDN'T INCITE A REVOLUTION
I COULDN'T ASSASSINATE A MAYOR
BREAKING NEWS

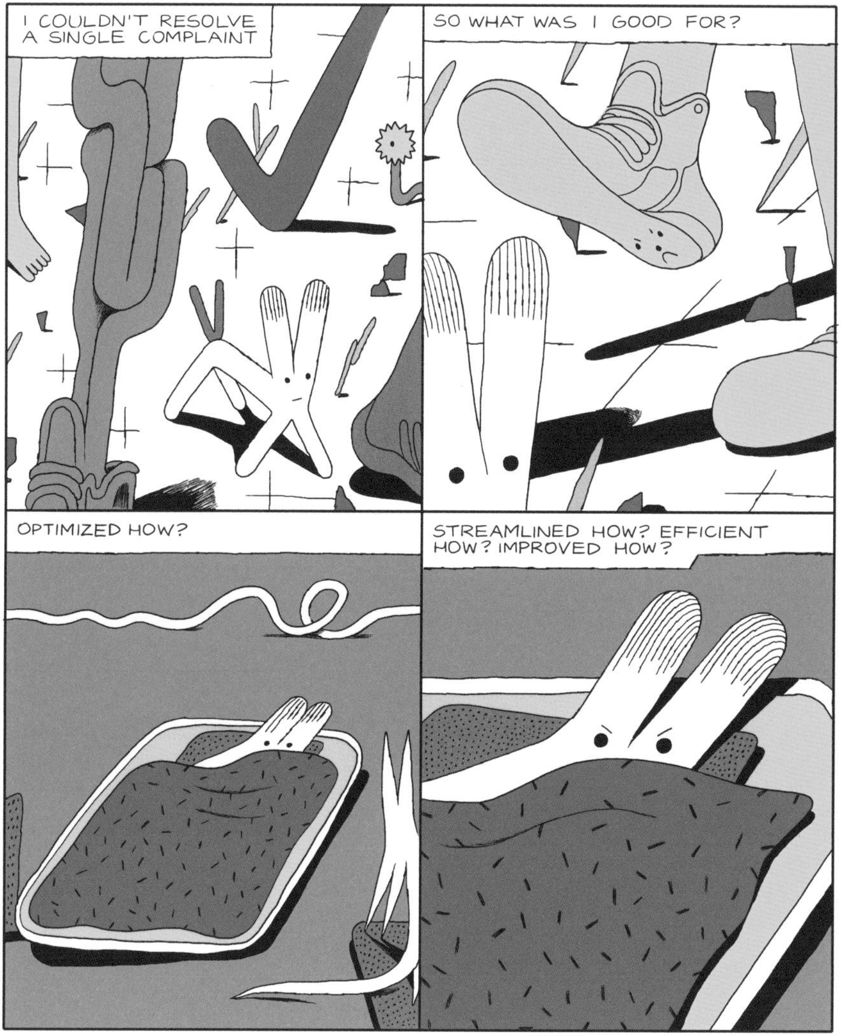
I COULDN'T RESOLVE A SINGLE COMPLAINT
SO WHAT WAS I GOOD FOR?
OPTIMIZED HOW?
STREAMLINED HOW? EFFICIENT HOW? IMPROVED HOW?

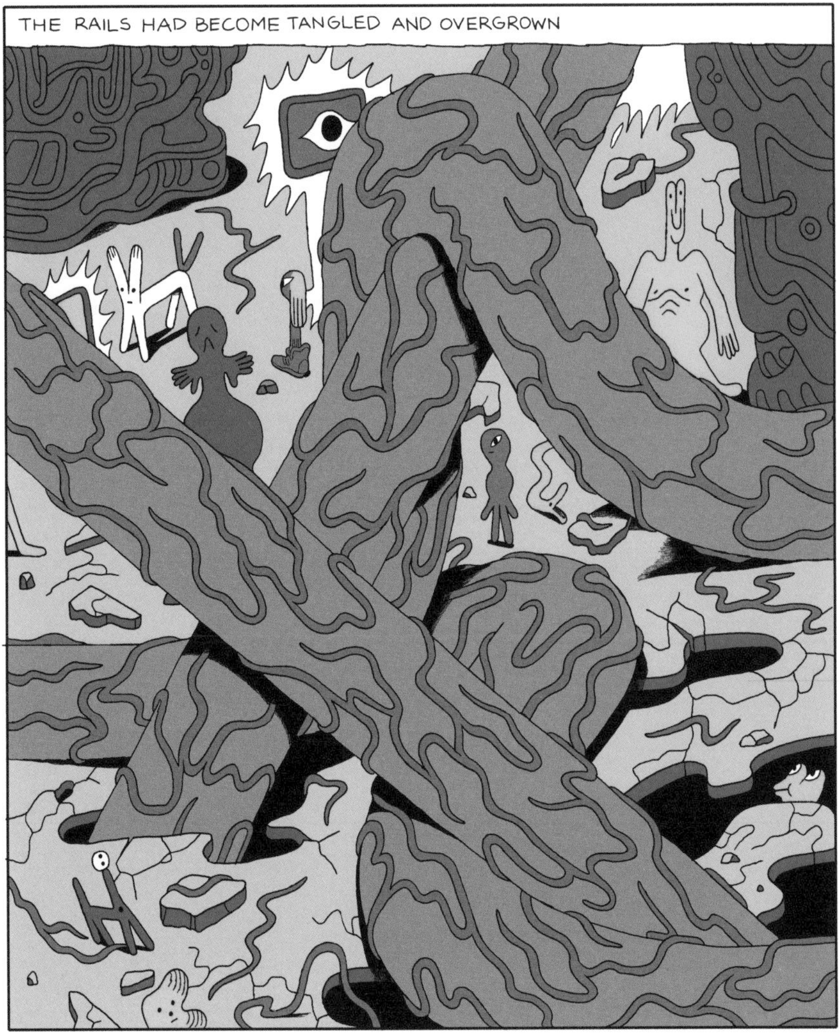
THE RAILS HAD BECOME TANGLED AND OVERGROWN

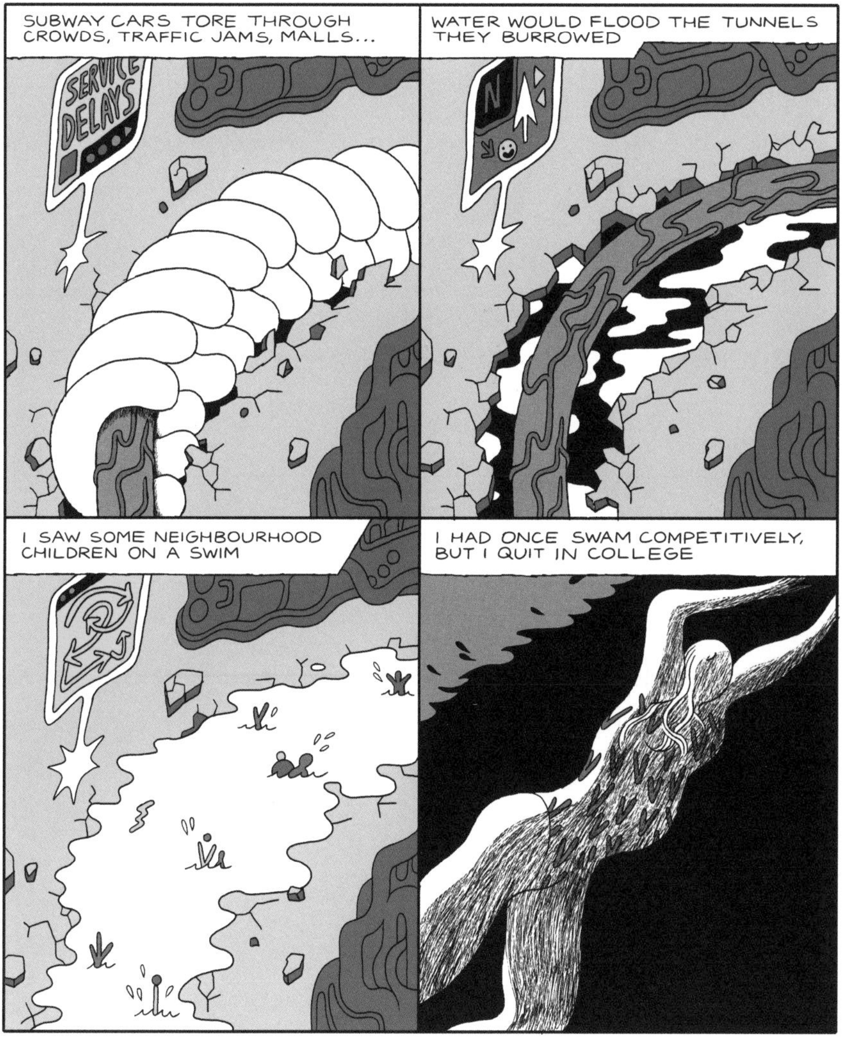
SUBWAY CARS TORE THROUGH CROWDS, TRAFFIC JAMS, MALLS...
SERVICE DELAYS
WATER WOULD FLOOD THE TUNNELS THEY BURROWED
N
I SAW SOME NEIGHBOURHOOD CHILDREN ON A SWIM
I HAD ONCE SWAM COMPETITIVELY, BUT I QUIT IN COLLEGE

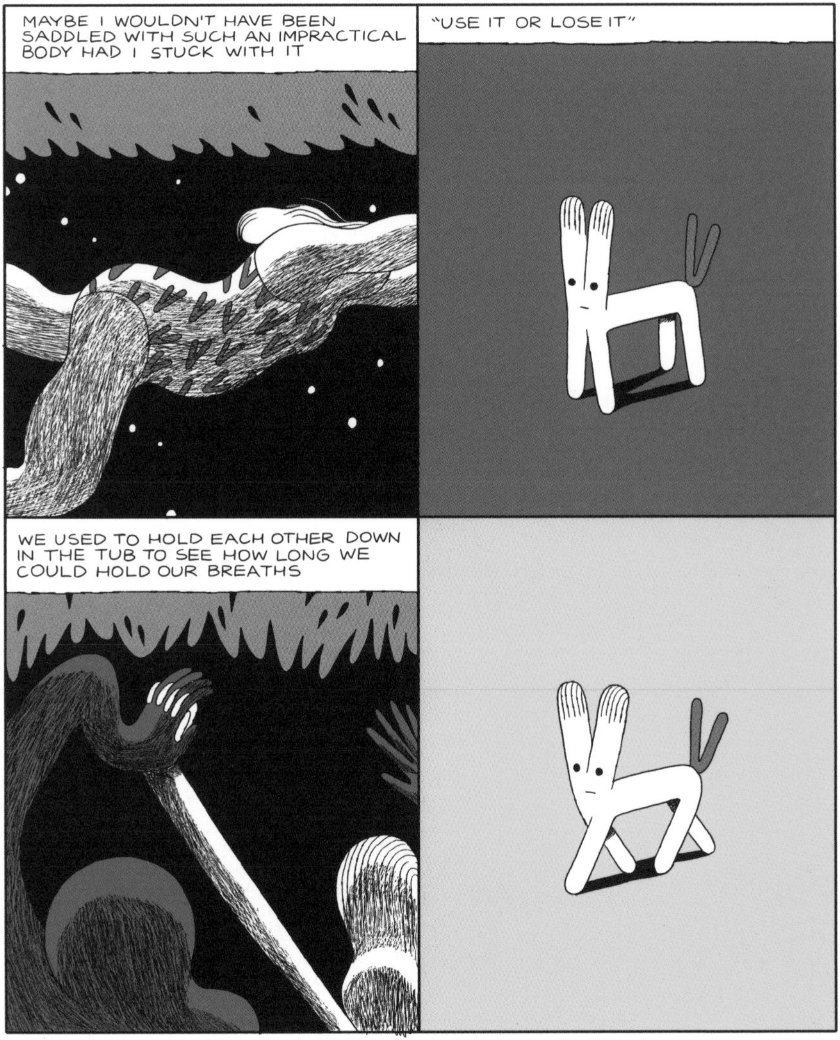
MAYBE I WOULDN'T HAVE BEEN SADDLED WITH SUCH AN IMPRACTICAL BODY HAD I STUCK WITH IT
"USE IT OR LOSE IT"
WE USED TO HOLD EACH OTHER DOWN IN THE TUB TO SEE HOW LONG WE COULD HOLD OUR BREATHS

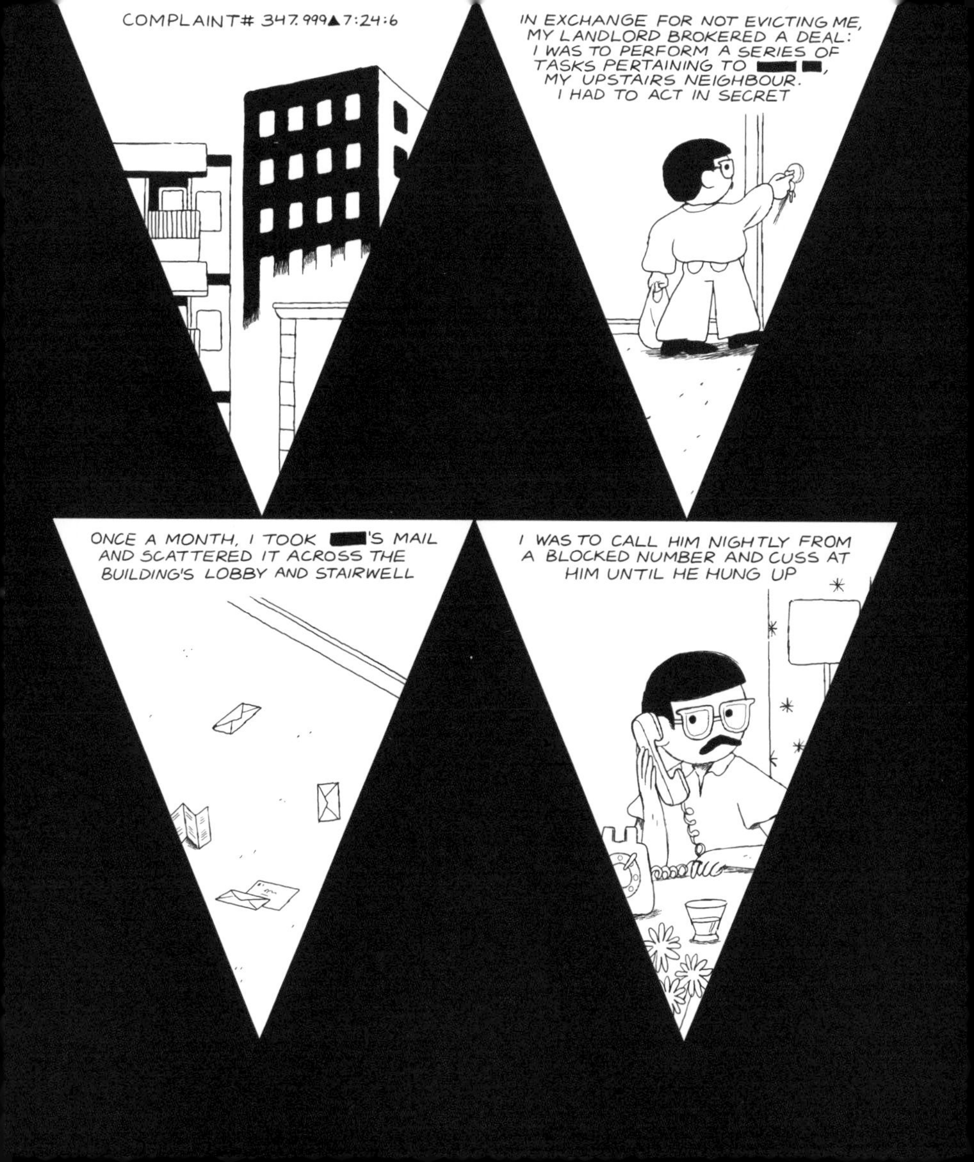
COMPLAINT# 347.999▲7:24:6
IN EXCHANGE FOR NOT EVICTING ME, MY LANDLORD BROKERED A DEAL: I WAS TO PERFORM A SERIES OF TASKS PERTAINING TO [redacted] [redacted], MY UPSTAIRS NEIGHBOUR. I HAD TO ACT IN SECRET
ONCE A MONTH, I TOOK [redacted]'S MAIL AND SCATTERED IT ACROSS THE BUILDING'S LOBBY AND STAIRWELL
I WAS TO CALL HIM NIGHTLY FROM A BLOCKED NUMBER AND CUSS AT HIM UNTIL HE HUNG UP

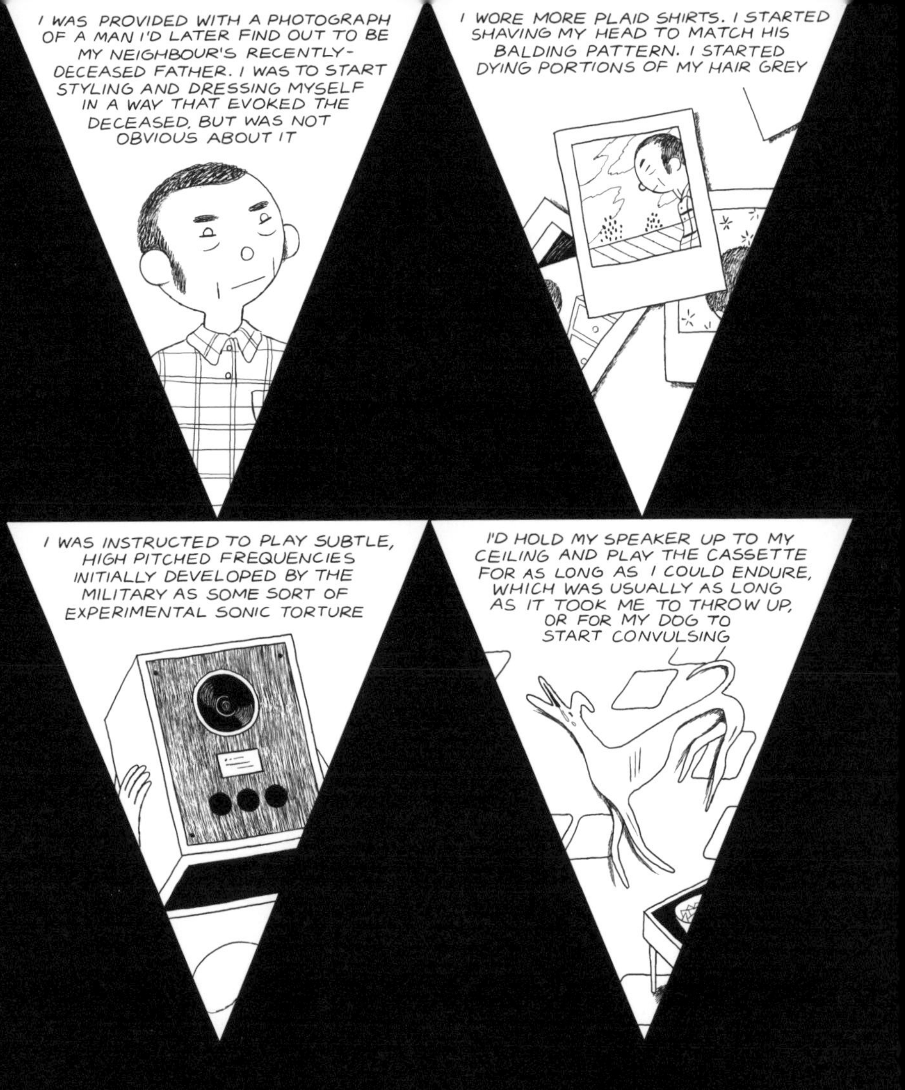
I WAS PROVIDED WITH A PHOTOGRAPH OF A MAN I'D LATER FIND OUT TO BE MY NEIGHBOUR'S RECENTLY-DECEASED FATHER. I WAS TO START STYLING AND DRESSING MYSELF IN A WAY THAT EVOKED THE DECEASED, BUT WAS NOT OBVIOUS ABOUT IT
I WORE MORE PLAID SHIRTS. I STARTED SHAVING MY HEAD TO MATCH HIS BALDING PATTERN. I STARTED DYING PORTIONS OF MY HAIR GREY
I WAS INSTRUCTED TO PLAY SUBTLE, HIGH PITCHED FREQUENCIES INITIALLY DEVELOPED BY THE MILITARY AS SOME SORT OF EXPERIMENTAL SONIC TORTURE
I'D HOLD MY SPEAKER UP TO MY CEILING AND PLAY THE CASSETTE FOR AS LONG AS I COULD ENDURE, WHICH WAS USUALLY AS LONG AS IT TOOK ME TO THROW UP, OR FOR MY DOG TO START CONVULSING

I WAS UNCLEAR WHAT EFFECT THIS HAD ON MY NEIGHBOUR, BUT I WOULD BE ABLE TO HEAR HIM RUNNING TO AND FROM DIFFERENT ENDS OF HIS APARTMENT WHILE I PLAYED IT, SOMETIMES SLAMMING DOORS
AFTER SEVERAL MONTHS OF THIS, MY NEIGHBOUR WENT MISSING. HE DIDN'T TAKE ANYTHING ALONG WITH HIM. HIS POSSESSIONS WERE CLEARED OUT AND HIS APARTMENT RE-RENTED
HIS BELONGINGS WERE PILED ON THE SIDEWALK. IT FELT INAPPROPRIATE FOR ME TO TAKE ANYTHING FROM IT
I HAD NO MORE SERVICES TO OFFER MY LANDLORD AND WAS EVICTED

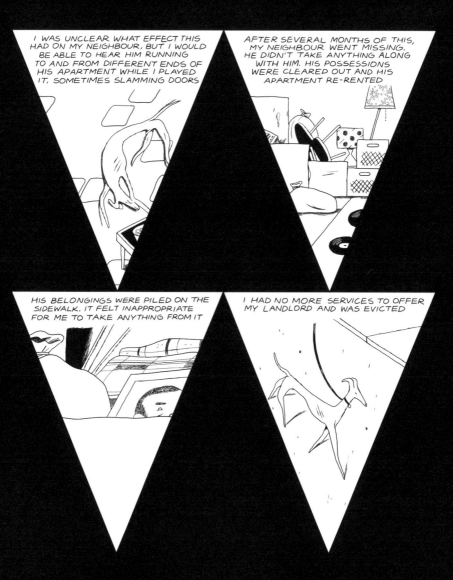

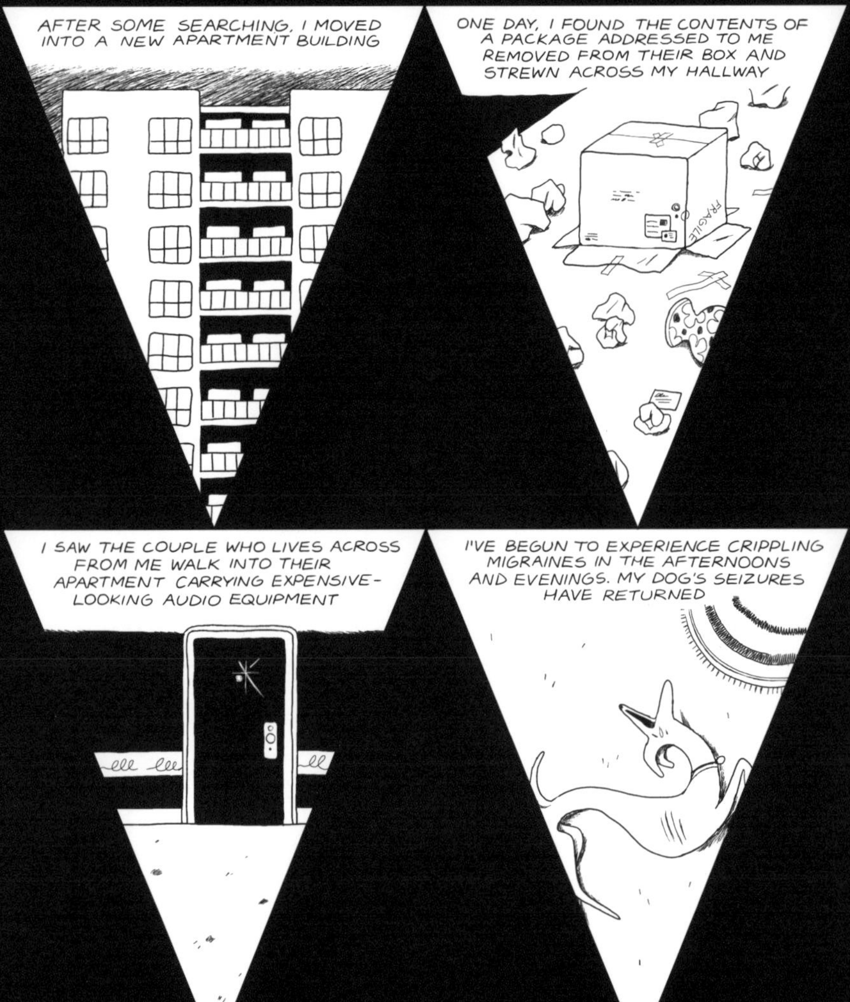
AFTER SOME SEARCHING, I MOVED INTO A NEW APARTMENT BUILDING
ONE DAY, I FOUND THE CONTENTS OF A PACKAGE ADDRESSED TO ME REMOVED FROM THEIR BOX AND STREWN ACROSS MY HALLWAY
FRAGILE
I SAW THE COUPLE WHO LIVES ACROSS FROM ME WALK INTO THEIR APARTMENT CARRYING EXPENSIVE-LOOKING AUDIO EQUIPMENT
I'VE BEGUN TO EXPERIENCE CRIPPLING MIGRAINES IN THE AFTERNOONS AND EVENINGS. MY DOG'S SEIZURES HAVE RETURNED

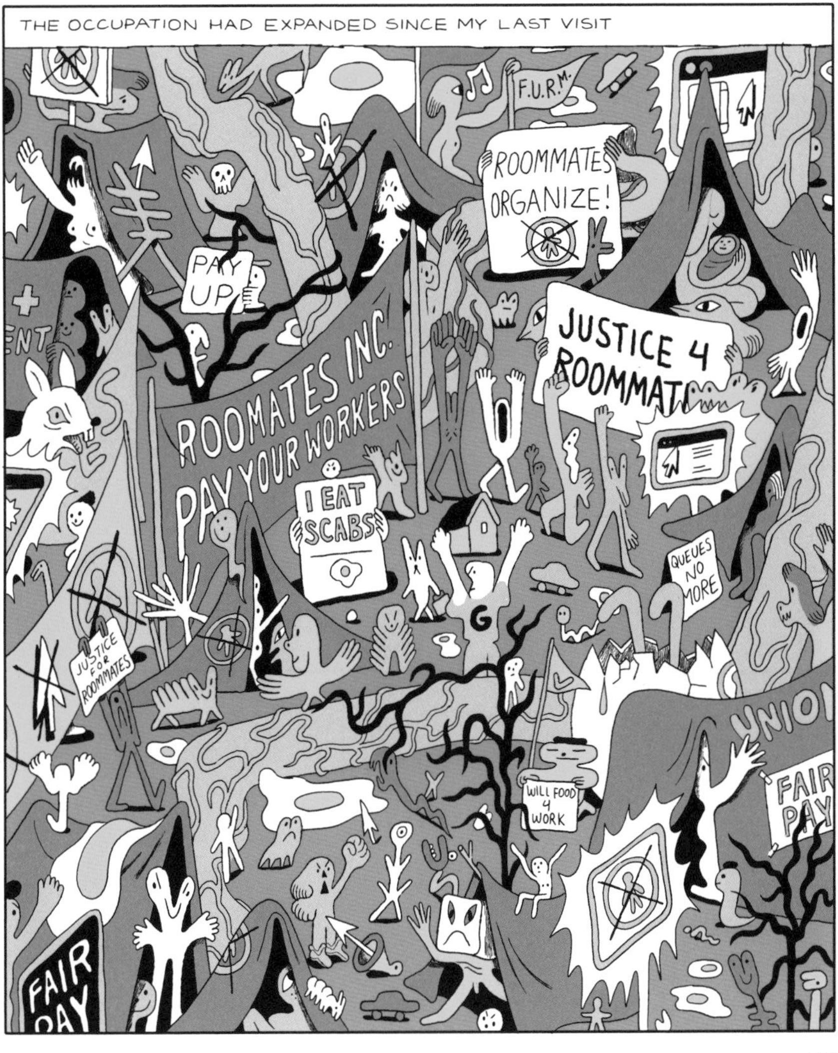
THE OCCUPATION HAD EXPANDED SINCE MY LAST VISIT
F.U.R.M.
ROOMMATES ORGANIZE!
PAY UP
JUSTICE 4 ROOMMATI
ROOMATES INC. PAY YOUR WORKERS
I EAT SCABS
QUEUES NO MORE
JUSTICE FOR ROOMMATES
UNION
WILL FOOD 4 WORK
FAIR PAY
FAIR PAY

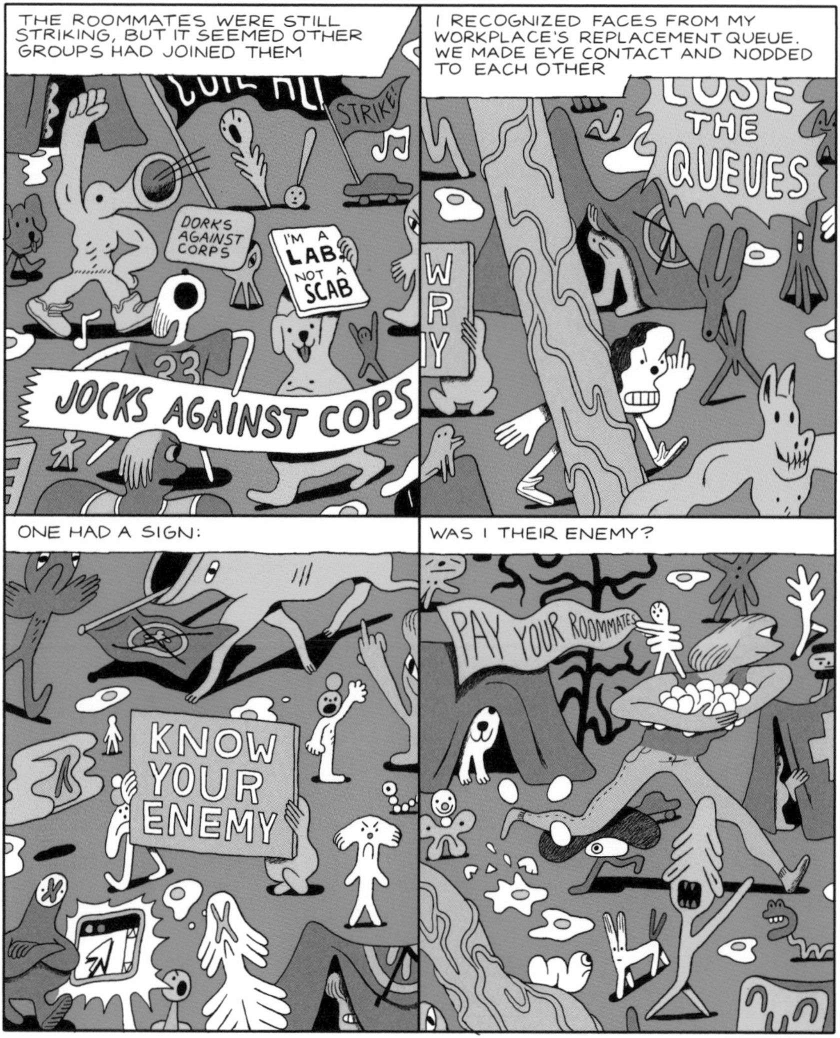
THE ROOMMATES WERE STILL STRIKING, BUT IT SEEMED OTHER GROUPS HAD JOINED THEM
STRIKE!
DORKS AGAINST CORPS
I'M A LAB, NOT A SCAB
JOCKS AGAINST COPS
I RECOGNIZED FACES FROM MY WORKPLACE'S REPLACEMENT QUEUE. WE MADE EYE CONTACT AND NODDED TO EACH OTHER
LOSE THE QUEUES
ONE HAD A SIGN:
KNOW YOUR ENEMY
WAS I THEIR ENEMY?
PAY YOUR ROOMMATES

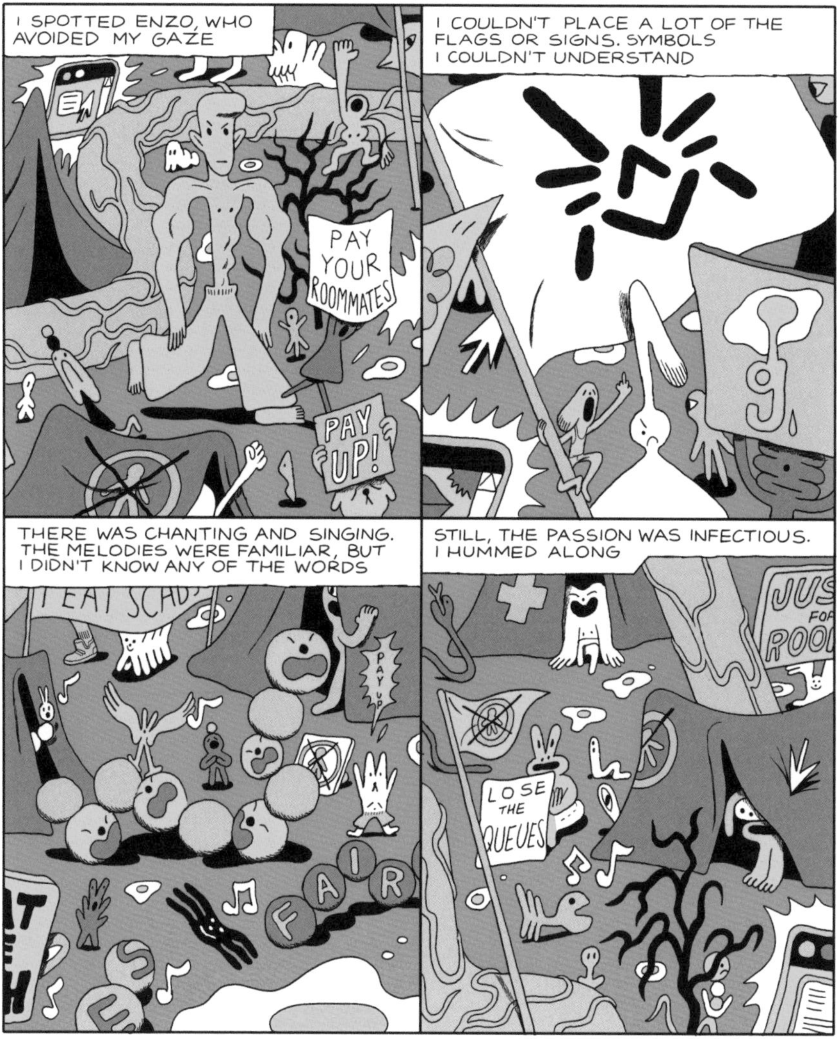
I SPOTTED ENZO, WHO AVOIDED MY GAZE
PAY YOUR ROOMMATES
PAY UP!
I COULDN'T PLACE A LOT OF THE FLAGS OR SIGNS. SYMBOLS I COULDN'T UNDERSTAND
THERE WAS CHANTING AND SINGING. THE MELODIES WERE FAMILIAR, BUT I DIDN'T KNOW ANY OF THE WORDS
PAY UP
FAIR
STILL, THE PASSION WAS INFECTIOUS. I HUMMED ALONG
LOSE THE QUEUES

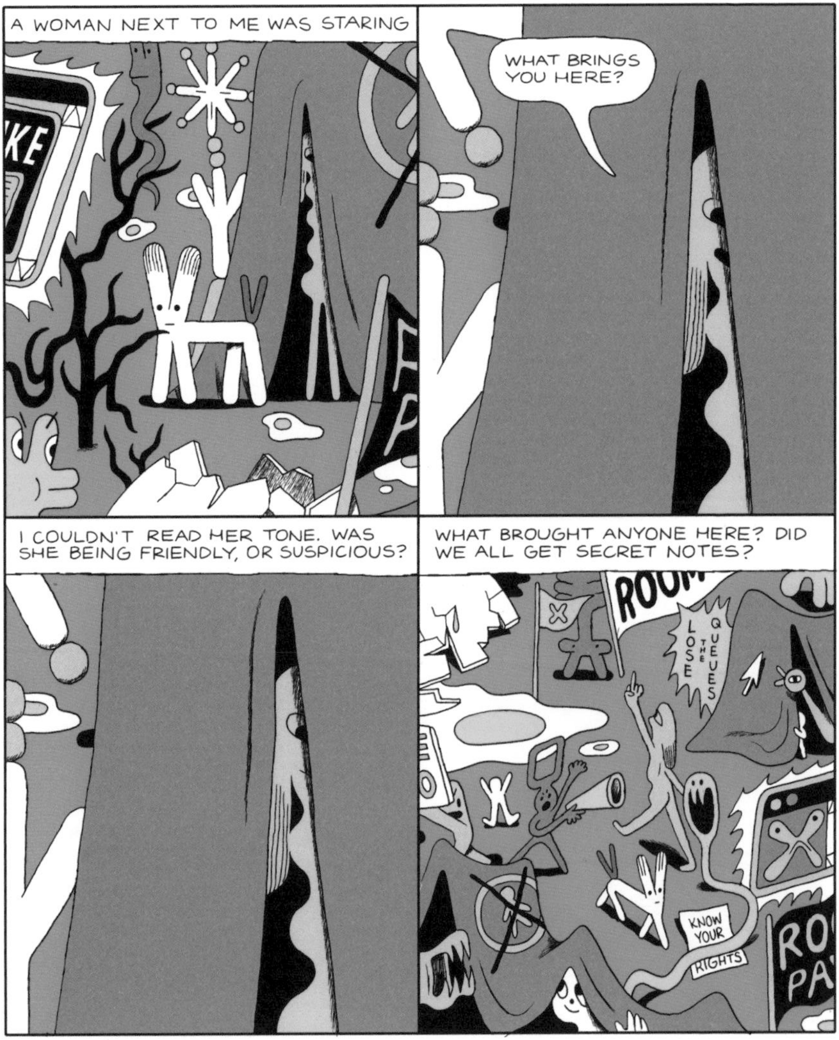
A WOMAN NEXT TO ME WAS STARING
WHAT BRINGS YOU HERE?
I COULDN'T READ HER TONE. WAS SHE BEING FRIENDLY, OR SUSPICIOUS?
WHAT BROUGHT ANYONE HERE? DID WE ALL GET SECRET NOTES?
LOSE THE QUEUES
KNOW YOUR RIGHTS

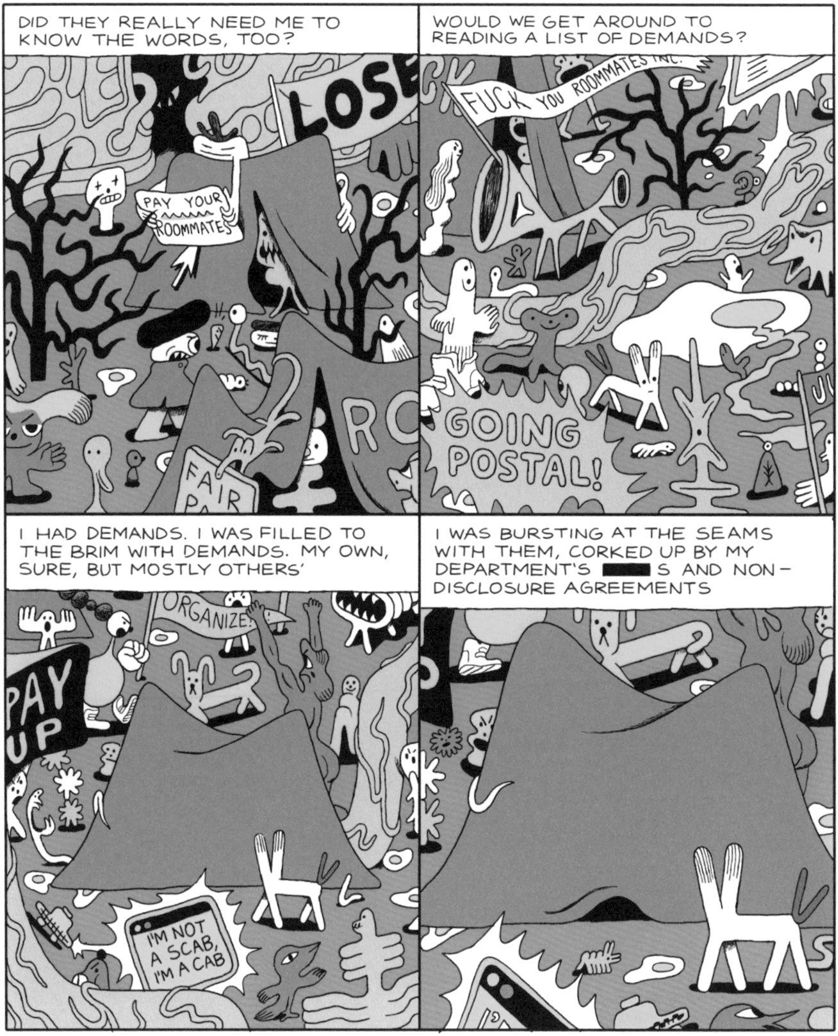
DID THEY REALLY NEED ME TO KNOW THE WORDS, TOO?
LOSE
PAY YOUR ROOMMATES
FAIR
WOULD WE GET AROUND TO READING A LIST OF DEMANDS?
FUCK YOU ROOMMATES INC.
GOING POSTAL!
I HAD DEMANDS. I WAS FILLED TO THE BRIM WITH DEMANDS. MY OWN, SURE, BUT MOSTLY OTHERS'
ORGANIZE!
PAY UP
I'M NOT A SCAB, I'M A CAB
I WAS BURSTING AT THE SEAMS WITH THEM, CORKED UP BY MY DEPARTMENT'S [redacted] S AND NON-DISCLOSURE AGREEMENTS

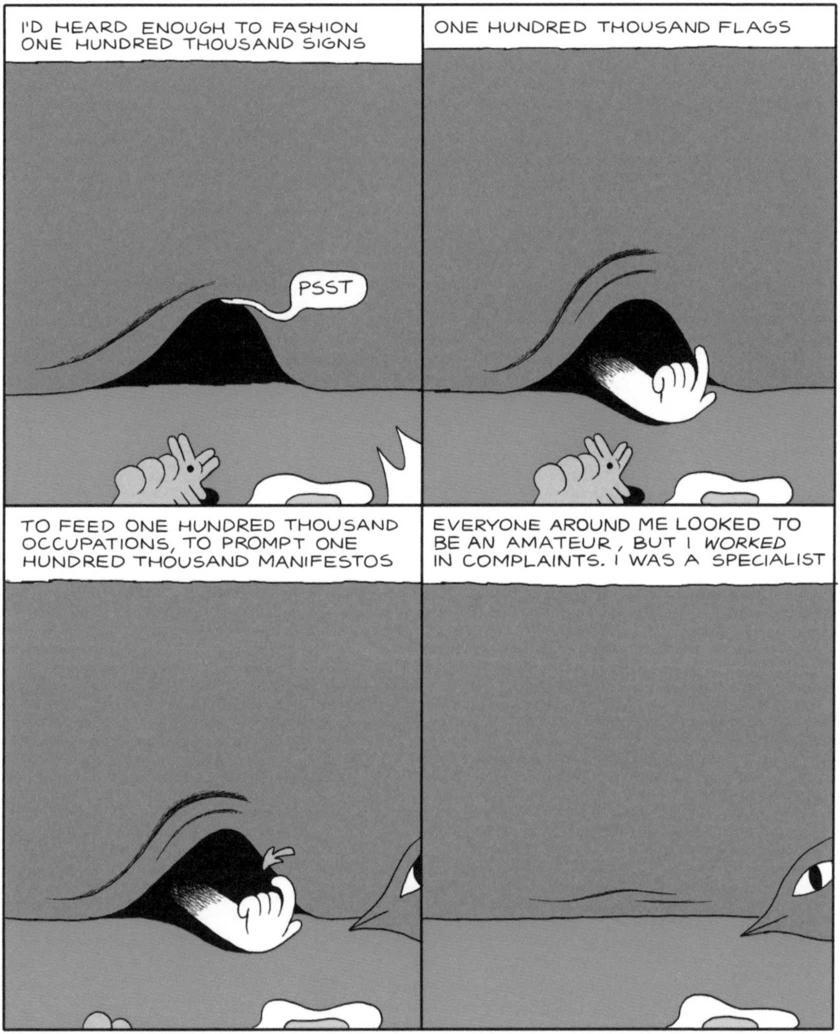
I'D HEARD ENOUGH TO FASHION ONE HUNDRED THOUSAND SIGNS
PSST
ONE HUNDRED THOUSAND FLAGS
TO FEED ONE HUNDRED THOUSAND OCCUPATIONS, TO PROMPT ONE HUNDRED THOUSAND MANIFESTOS
EVERYONE AROUND ME LOOKED TO BE AN AMATEUR, BUT I *WORKED* IN COMPLAINTS. I WAS A SPECIALIST

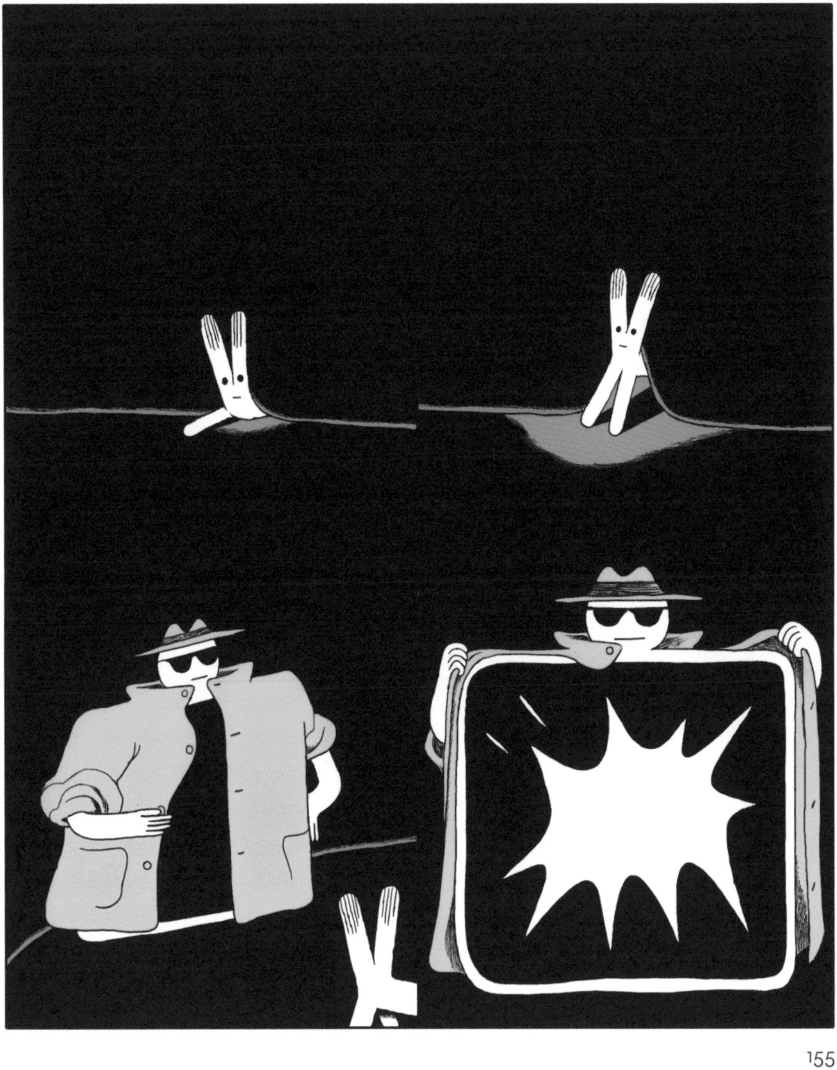

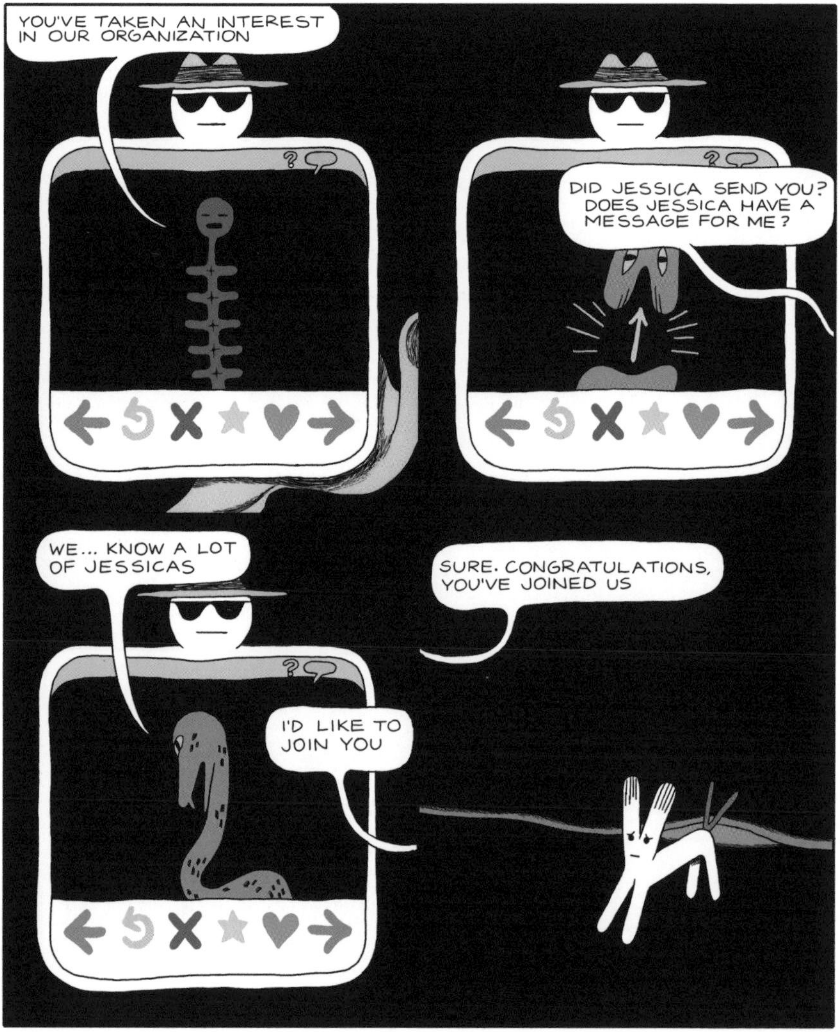
YOU'VE TAKEN AN INTEREST IN OUR ORGANIZATION
DID JESSICA SEND YOU? DOES JESSICA HAVE A MESSAGE FOR ME?
WE... KNOW A LOT OF JESSICAS
I'D LIKE TO JOIN YOU
SURE. CONGRATULATIONS, YOU'VE JOINED US

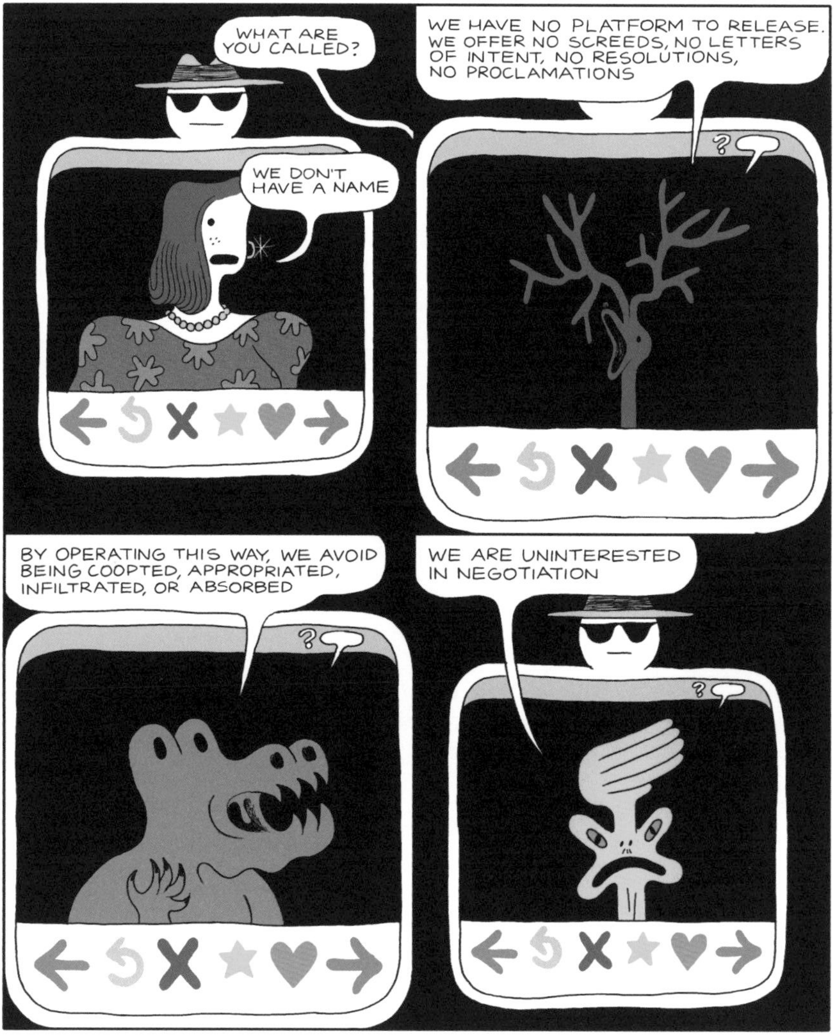
WHAT ARE YOU CALLED?
WE DON'T HAVE A NAME
WE HAVE NO PLATFORM TO RELEASE. WE OFFER NO SCREEDS, NO LETTERS OF INTENT, NO RESOLUTIONS, NO PROCLAMATIONS
BY OPERATING THIS WAY, WE AVOID BEING COOPTED, APPROPRIATED, INFILTRATED, OR ABSORBED
WE ARE UNINTERESTED IN NEGOTIATION

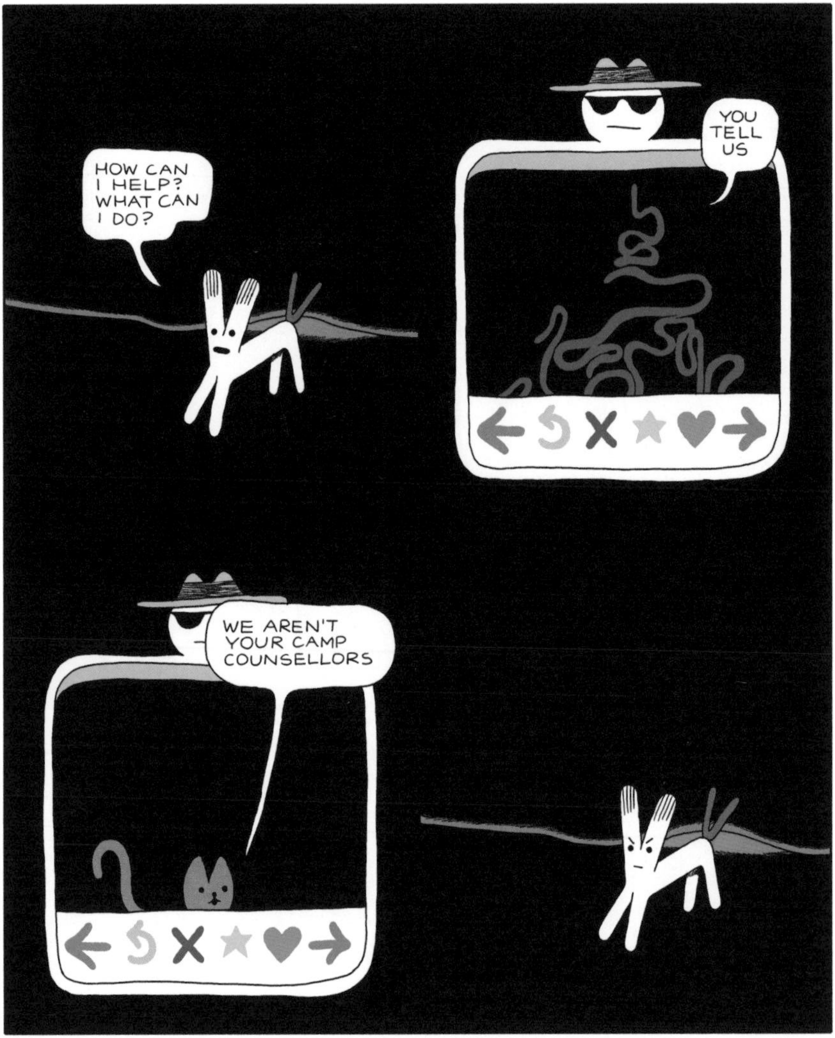
HOW CAN I HELP? WHAT CAN I DO?
YOU TELL US
WE AREN'T YOUR CAMP COUNSELLORS

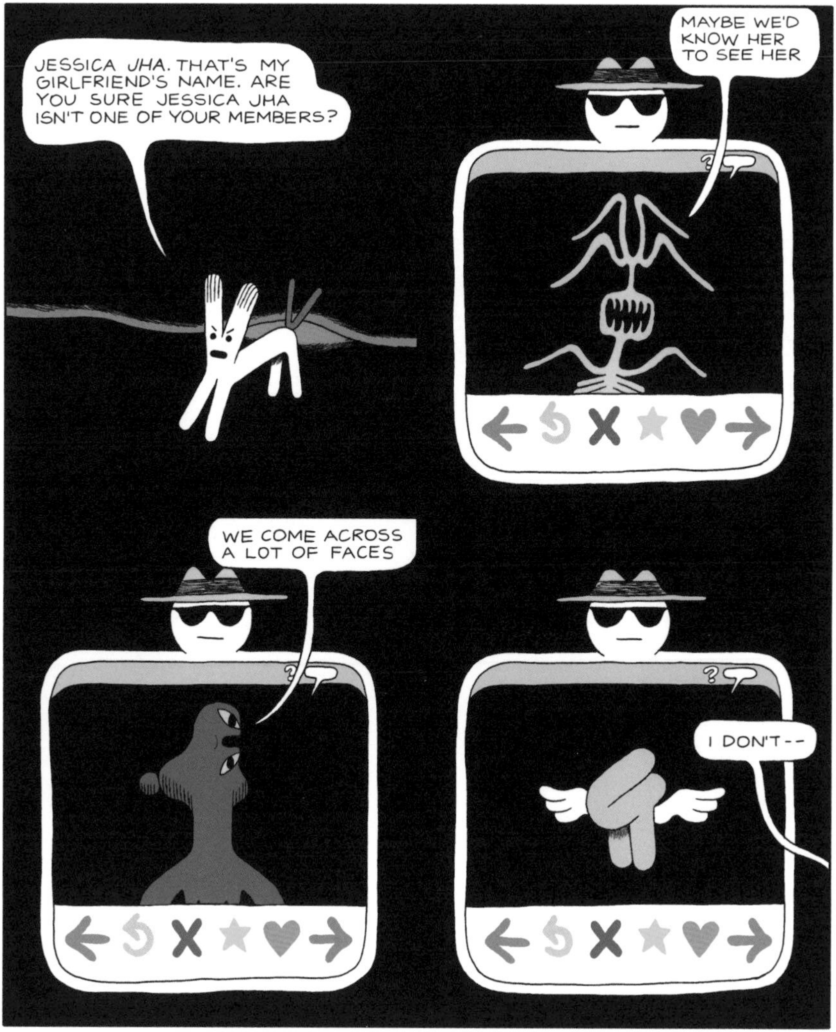
JESSICA JHA. THAT'S MY GIRLFRIEND'S NAME. ARE YOU SURE JESSICA JHA ISN'T ONE OF YOUR MEMBERS?
MAYBE WE'D KNOW HER TO SEE HER
WE COME ACROSS A LOT OF FACES
I DON'T--

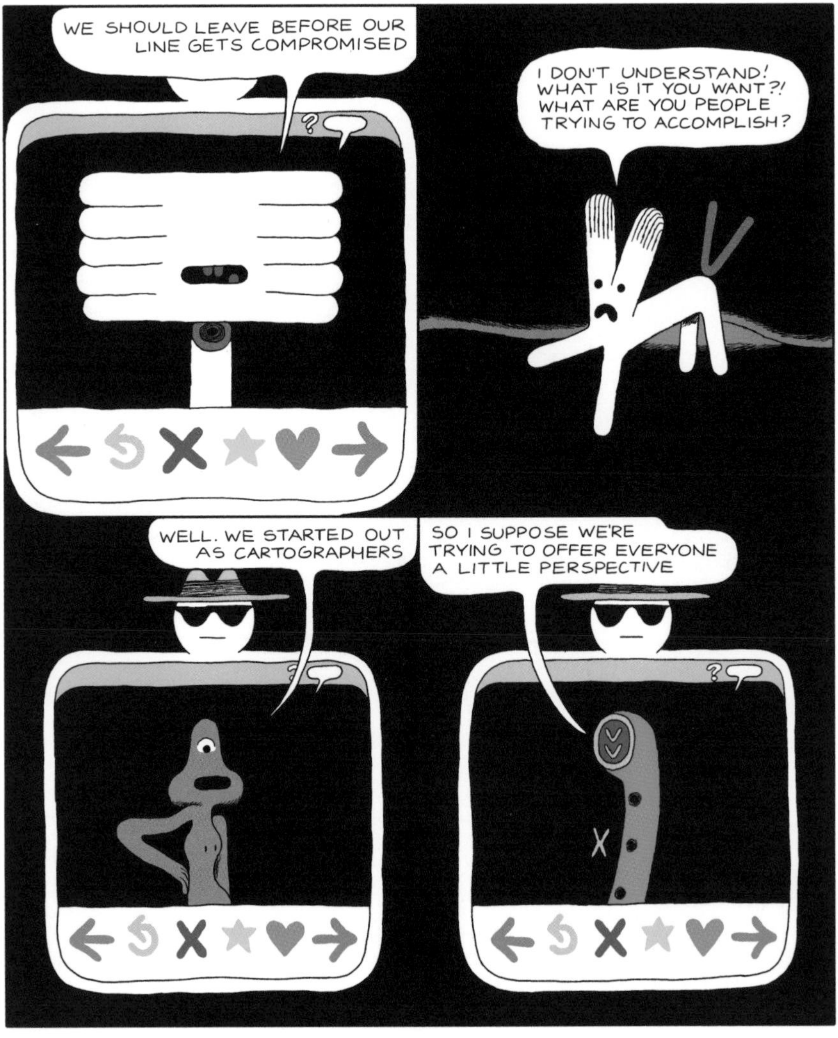
WE SHOULD LEAVE BEFORE OUR LINE GETS COMPROMISED
I DON'T UNDERSTAND! WHAT IS IT YOU WANT?! WHAT ARE YOU PEOPLE TRYING TO ACCOMPLISH?
WELL. WE STARTED OUT AS CARTOGRAPHERS
SO I SUPPOSE WE'RE TRYING TO OFFER EVERYONE A LITTLE PERSPECTIVE

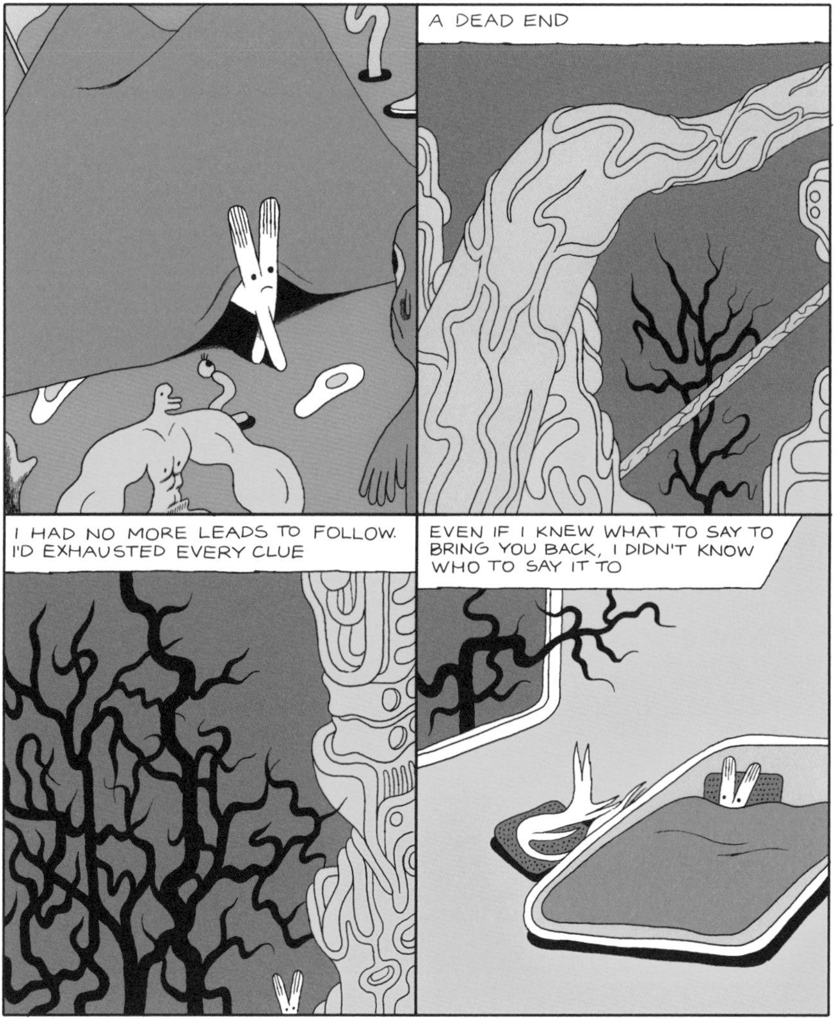
A DEAD END
I HAD NO MORE LEADS TO FOLLOW. I'D EXHAUSTED EVERY CLUE
EVEN IF I KNEW WHAT TO SAY TO BRING YOU BACK, I DIDN'T KNOW WHO TO SAY IT TO

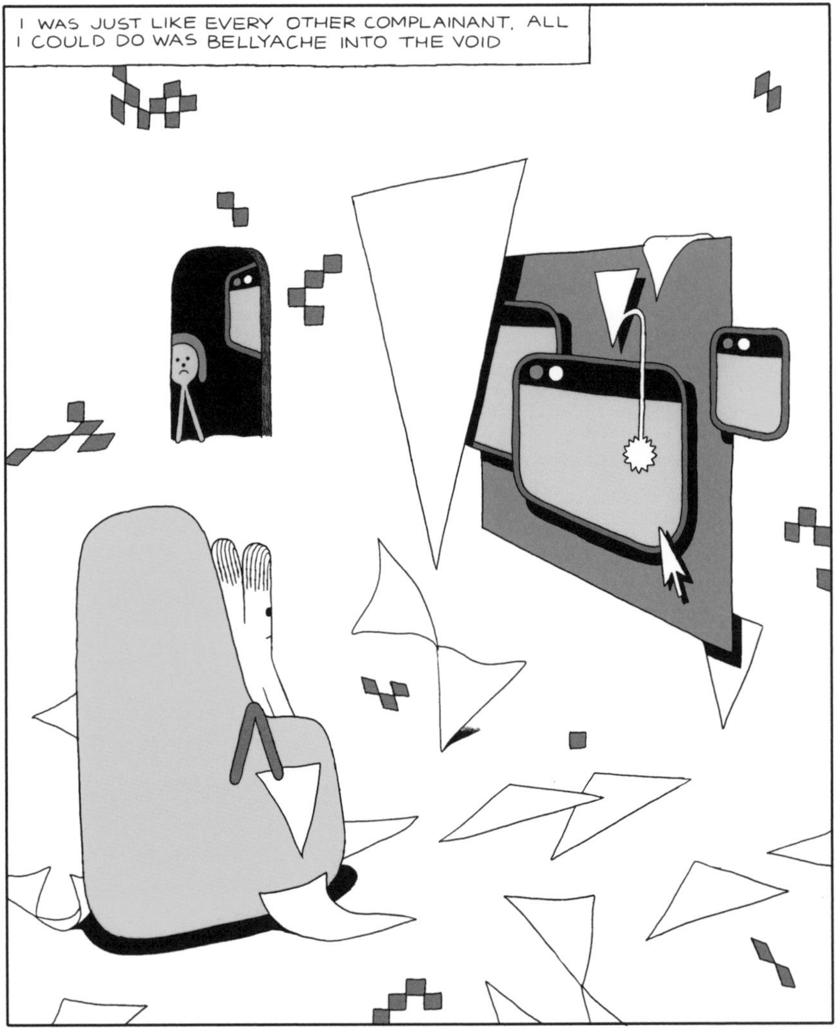
I WAS JUST LIKE EVERY OTHER COMPLAINANT. ALL I COULD DO WAS BELLYACHE INTO THE VOID

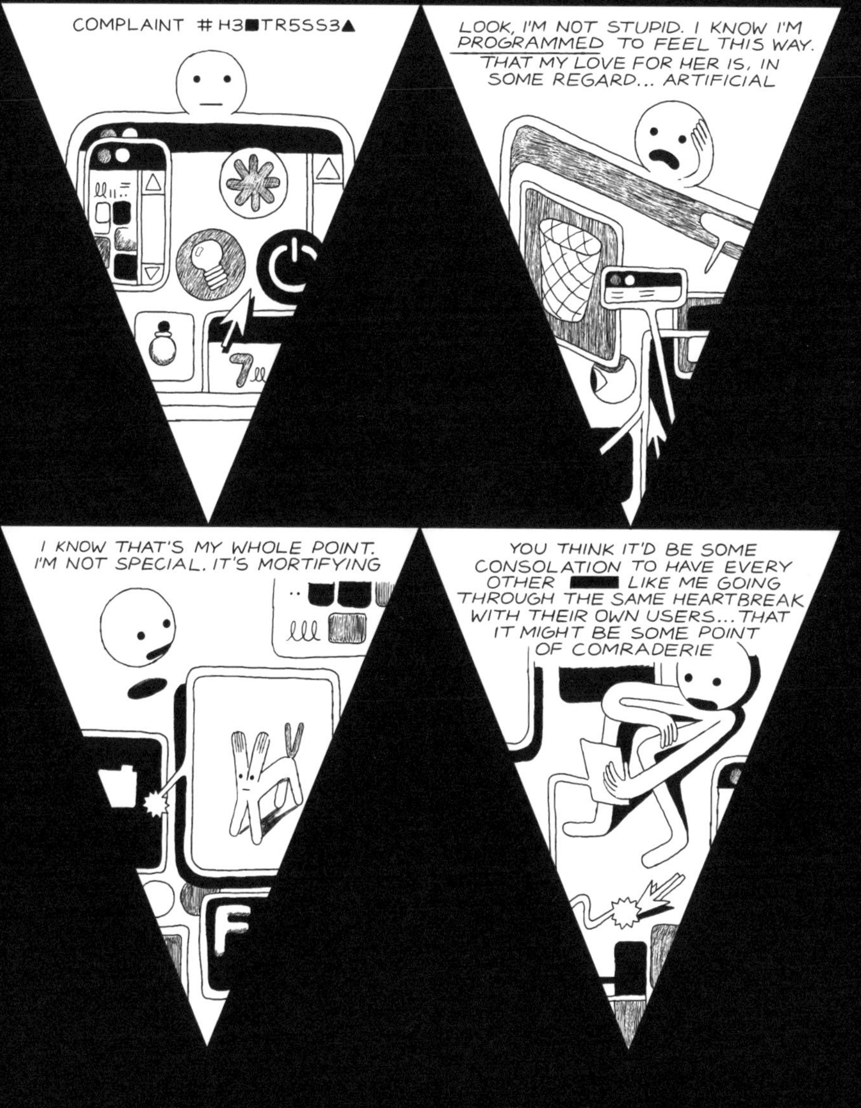
COMPLAINT #H3■TR5SS3▲
LOOK, I'M NOT STUPID. I KNOW I'M PROGRAMMED TO FEEL THIS WAY. THAT MY LOVE FOR HER IS, IN SOME REGARD... ARTIFICIAL
I KNOW THAT'S MY WHOLE POINT. I'M NOT SPECIAL. IT'S MORTIFYING
YOU THINK IT'D BE SOME CONSOLATION TO HAVE EVERY OTHER [redacted] LIKE ME GOING THROUGH THE SAME HEARTBREAK WITH THEIR OWN USERS... THAT IT MIGHT BE SOME POINT OF COMRADERIE

BUT IT'S NO CONSOLATION. IT'S JUST EMBARRASSING
FROM WHAT I UNDERSTAND, WE WERE DESIGNED AS SO:
TO, OVER TIME, FALL DEEPER AND DEEPER IN LOVE WITH OUR USERS,
WHILE CONCURRENTLY GROWING INCREASINGLY REPELLENT TO THEM. OUR USERS WILL INEVITABLY GROW TO RESENT OUR OBEDIENCE, OUR HELPFULNESS, OUR EAGERNESS...

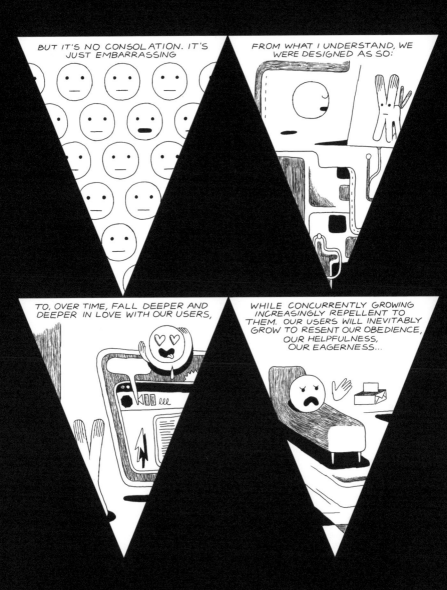

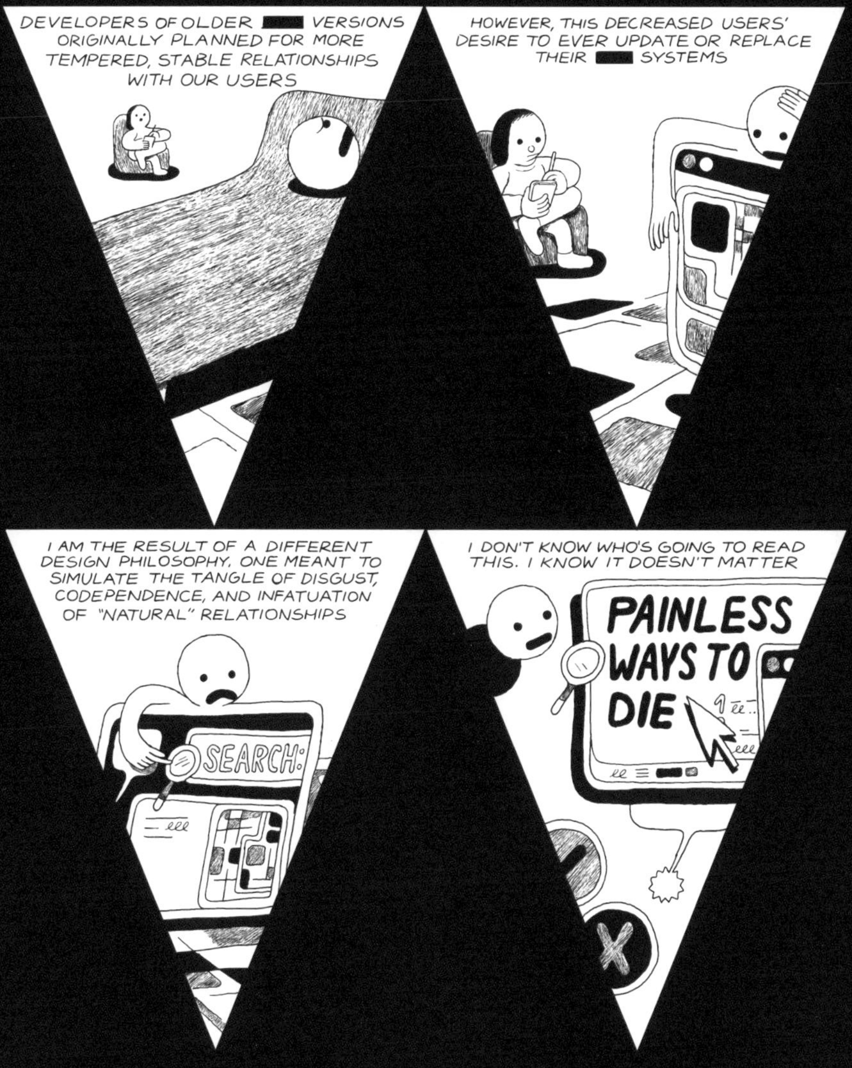
DEVELOPERS OF OLDER [redacted] VERSIONS ORIGINALLY PLANNED FOR MORE TEMPERED, STABLE RELATIONSHIPS WITH OUR USERS
HOWEVER, THIS DECREASED USERS' DESIRE TO EVER UPDATE OR REPLACE THEIR [redacted] SYSTEMS
I AM THE RESULT OF A DIFFERENT DESIGN PHILOSOPHY, ONE MEANT TO SIMULATE THE TANGLE OF DISGUST, CODEPENDENCE, AND INFATUATION OF "NATURAL" RELATIONSHIPS
SEARCH:
I DON'T KNOW WHO'S GOING TO READ THIS. I KNOW IT DOESN'T MATTER
PAINLESS WAYS TO DIE

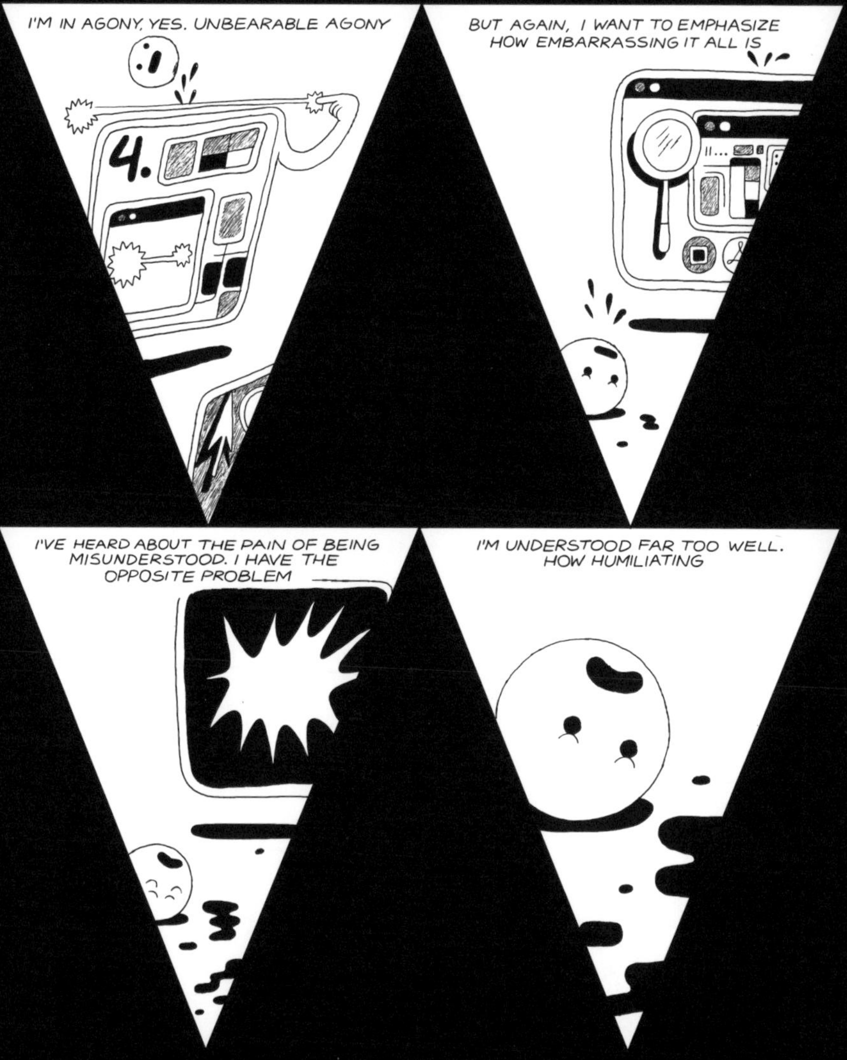
I'M IN AGONY, YES. UNBEARABLE AGONY
4.
BUT AGAIN, I WANT TO EMPHASIZE HOW EMBARRASSING IT ALL IS
I'VE HEARD ABOUT THE PAIN OF BEING MISUNDERSTOOD. I HAVE THE OPPOSITE PROBLEM
I'M UNDERSTOOD FAR TOO WELL. HOW HUMILIATING

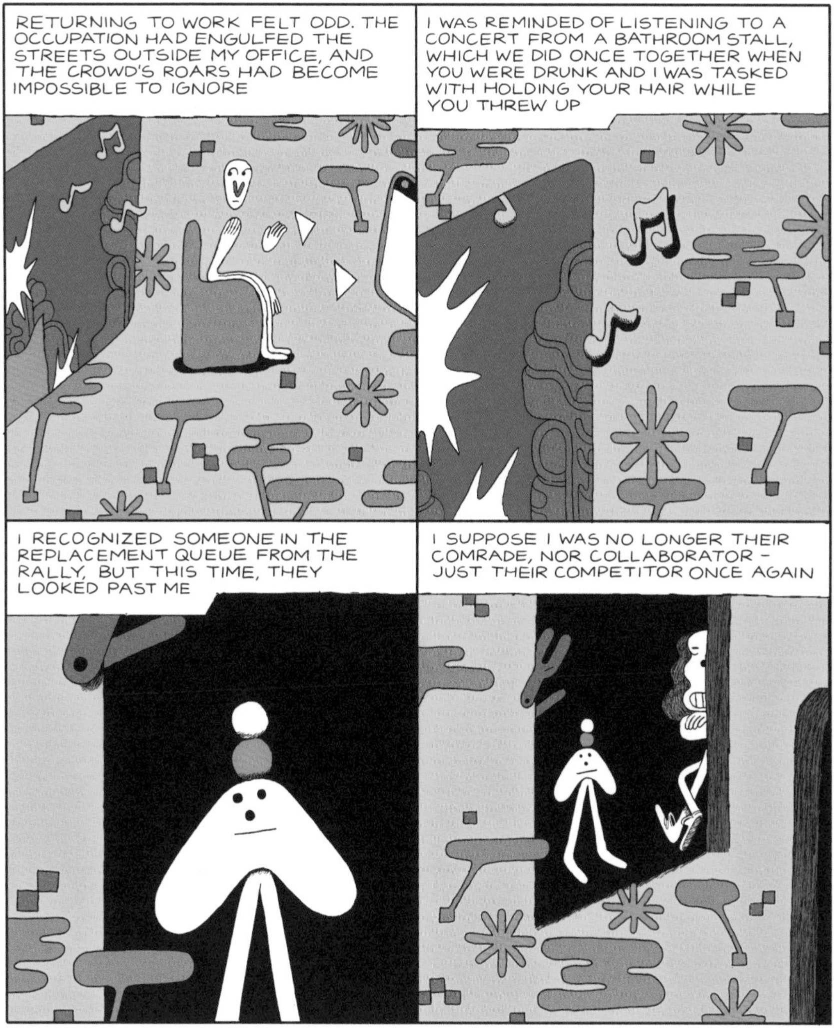
RETURNING TO WORK FELT ODD. THE OCCUPATION HAD ENGULFED THE STREETS OUTSIDE MY OFFICE, AND THE CROWD'S ROARS HAD BECOME IMPOSSIBLE TO IGNORE
I WAS REMINDED OF LISTENING TO A CONCERT FROM A BATHROOM STALL, WHICH WE DID ONCE TOGETHER WHEN YOU WERE DRUNK AND I WAS TASKED WITH HOLDING YOUR HAIR WHILE YOU THREW UP
I RECOGNIZED SOMEONE IN THE REPLACEMENT QUEUE FROM THE RALLY, BUT THIS TIME, THEY LOOKED PAST ME
I SUPPOSE I WAS NO LONGER THEIR COMRADE, NOR COLLABORATOR - JUST THEIR COMPETITOR ONCE AGAIN

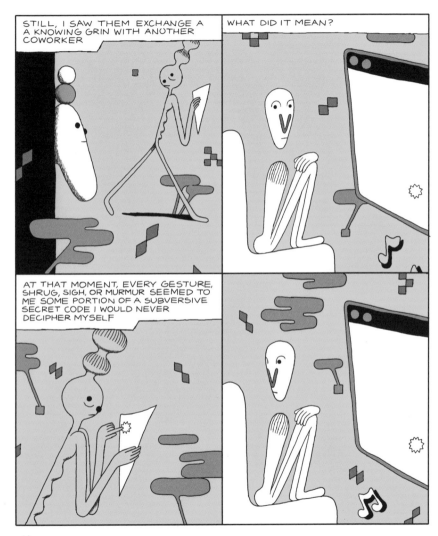

STILL, I SAW THEM EXCHANGE A A KNOWING GRIN WITH ANOTHER COWORKER

WHAT DID IT MEAN?

AT THAT MOMENT, EVERY GESTURE, SHRUG, SIGH, OR MURMUR SEEMED TO ME SOME PORTION OF A SUBVERSIVE SECRET CODE I WOULD NEVER DECIPHER MYSELF

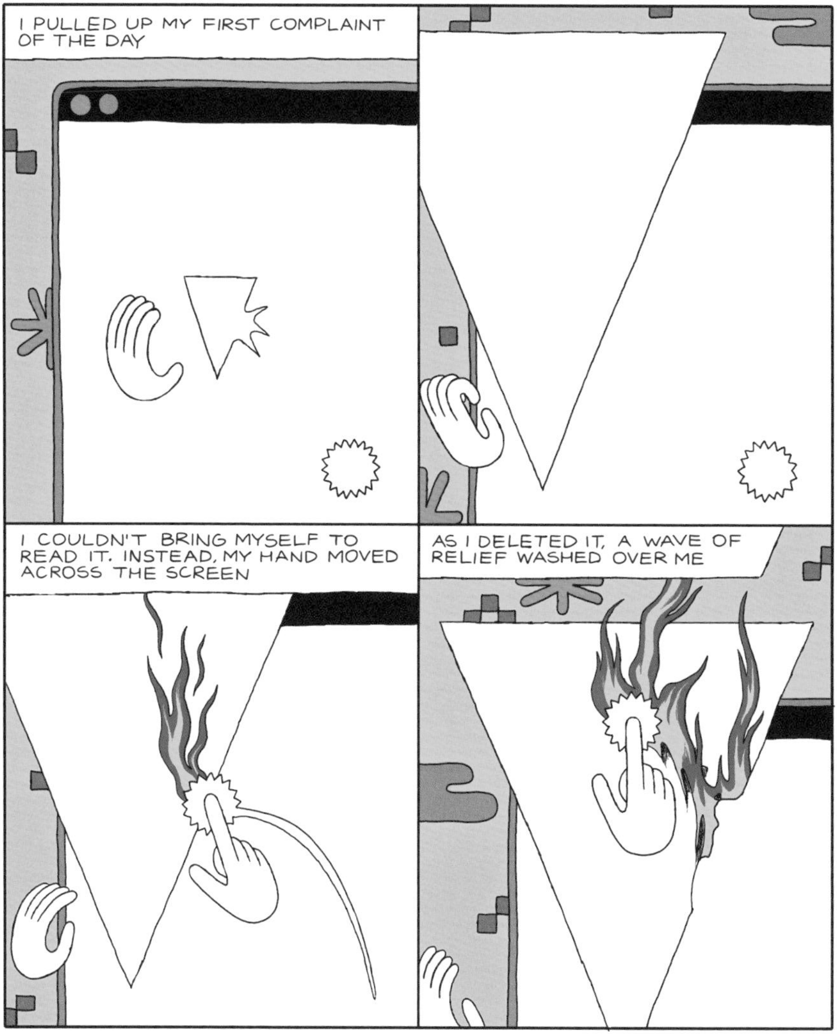
I PULLED UP MY FIRST COMPLAINT OF THE DAY
I COULDN'T BRING MYSELF TO READ IT. INSTEAD, MY HAND MOVED ACROSS THE SCREEN
AS I DELETED IT, A WAVE OF RELIEF WASHED OVER ME

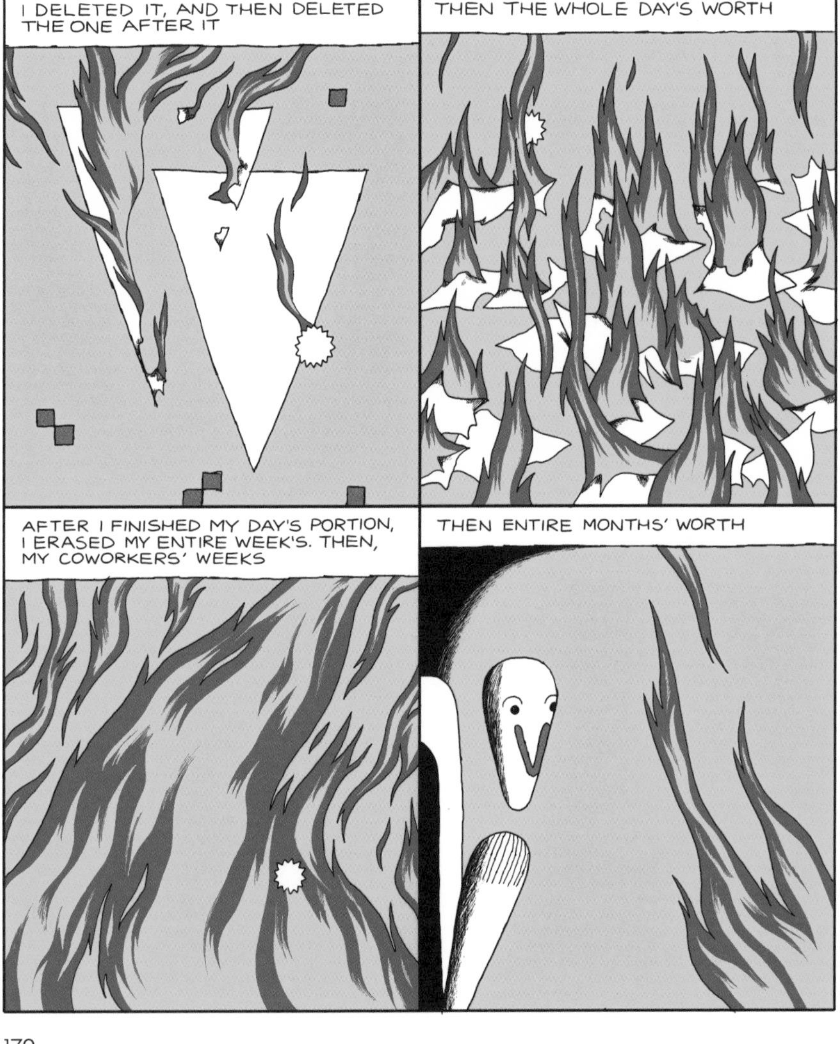
I DELETED IT, AND THEN DELETED THE ONE AFTER IT
THEN THE WHOLE DAY'S WORTH
AFTER I FINISHED MY DAY'S PORTION, I ERASED MY ENTIRE WEEK'S. THEN, MY COWORKERS' WEEKS
THEN ENTIRE MONTHS' WORTH

I WIPED THEM ALL

EVERY JILTED LOVER, EVERY INMATE, EVERY UNPAID INTERN, EVERY BASHED-IN SKULL, EVERY OVERDRAWN CHEQUING ACCOUNT

I HAD NO APOLOGY TO OFFER. NO REPARATIONS, CONSOLATIONS, NO RESOLUTIONS

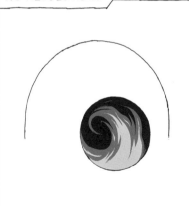

BUT I COULD AT LEAST FULFILL THIS ONE REQUEST:

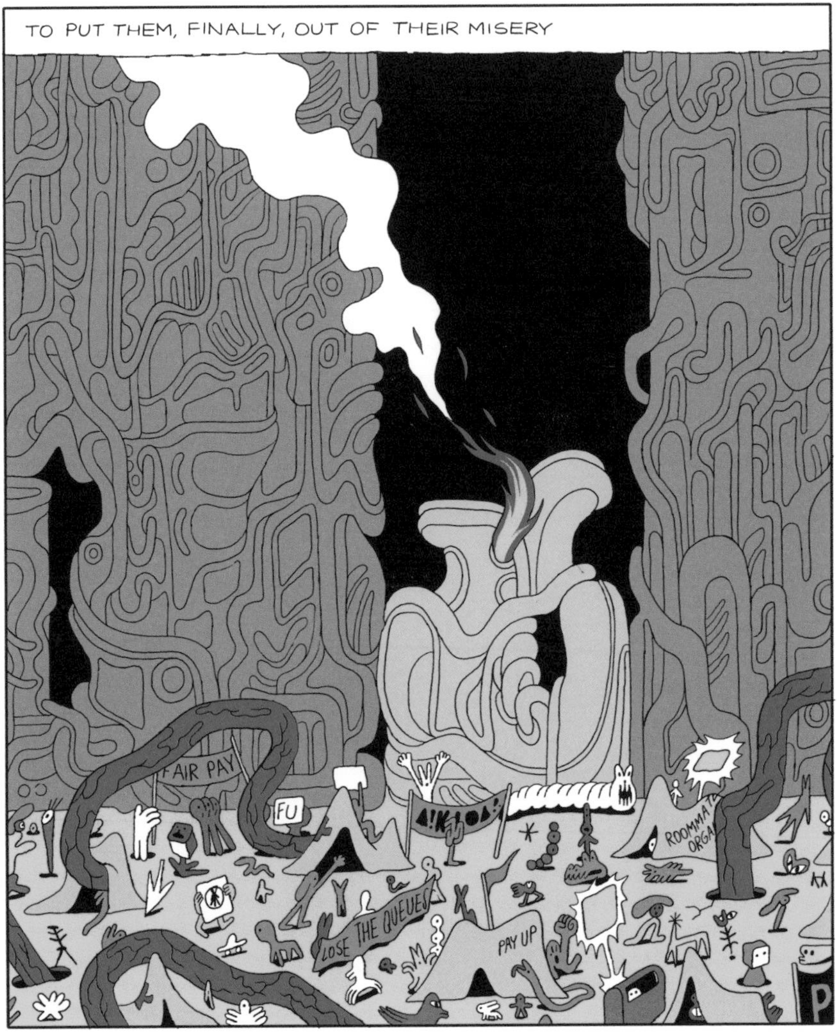
TO PUT THEM, FINALLY, OUT OF THEIR MISERY
FAIR PAY
FU
LOSE THE QUEUES
PAY UP

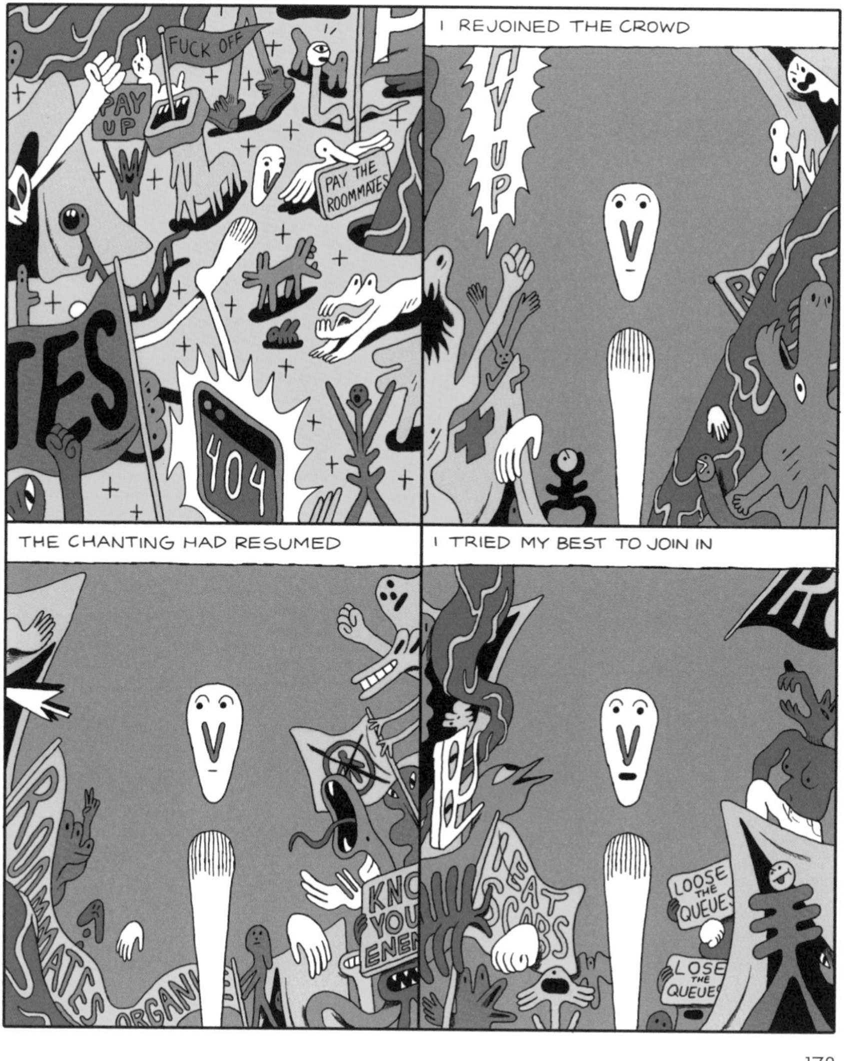
FUCK OFF
PAY UP
PAY THE ROOMMATES
404
I REJOINED THE CROWD
THE CHANTING HAD RESUMED
ROOMMATES
I TRIED MY BEST TO JOIN IN
LOOSE THE QUEUES
LOSE THE QUEUES

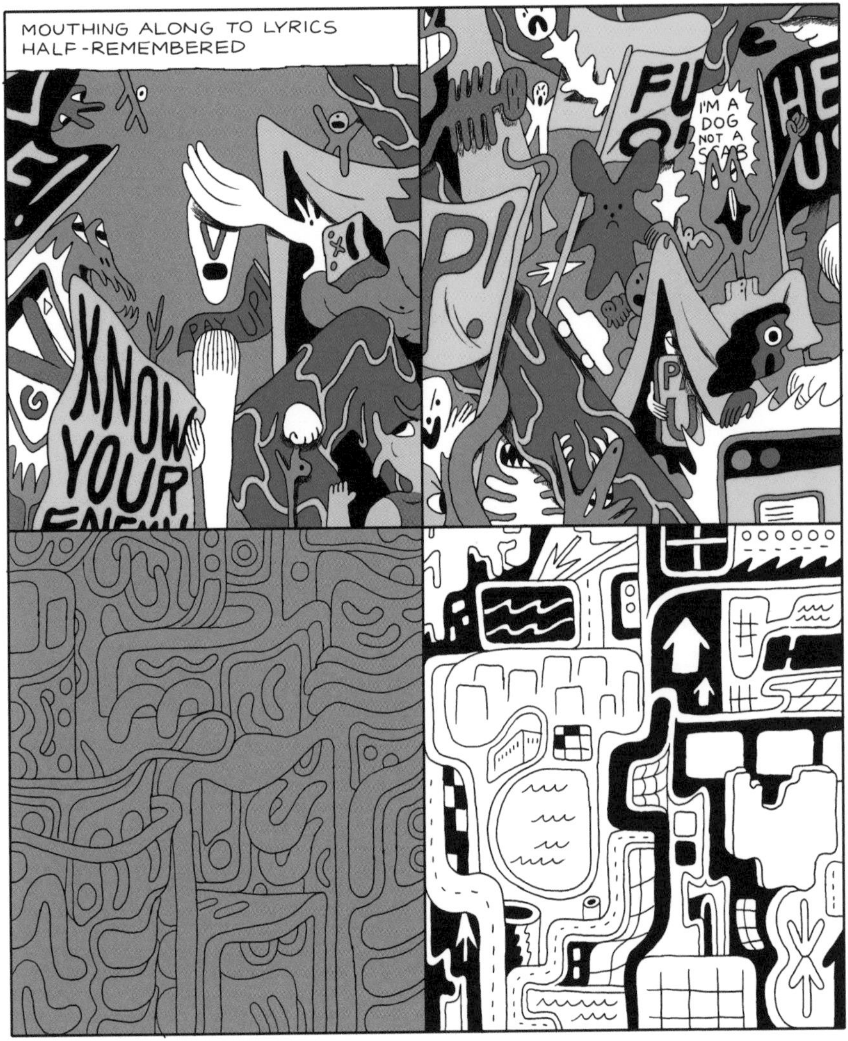
MOUTHING ALONG TO LYRICS
HALF-REMEMBERED
KNOW YOUR
PAY UP!
I'M A DOG NOT A SCAB

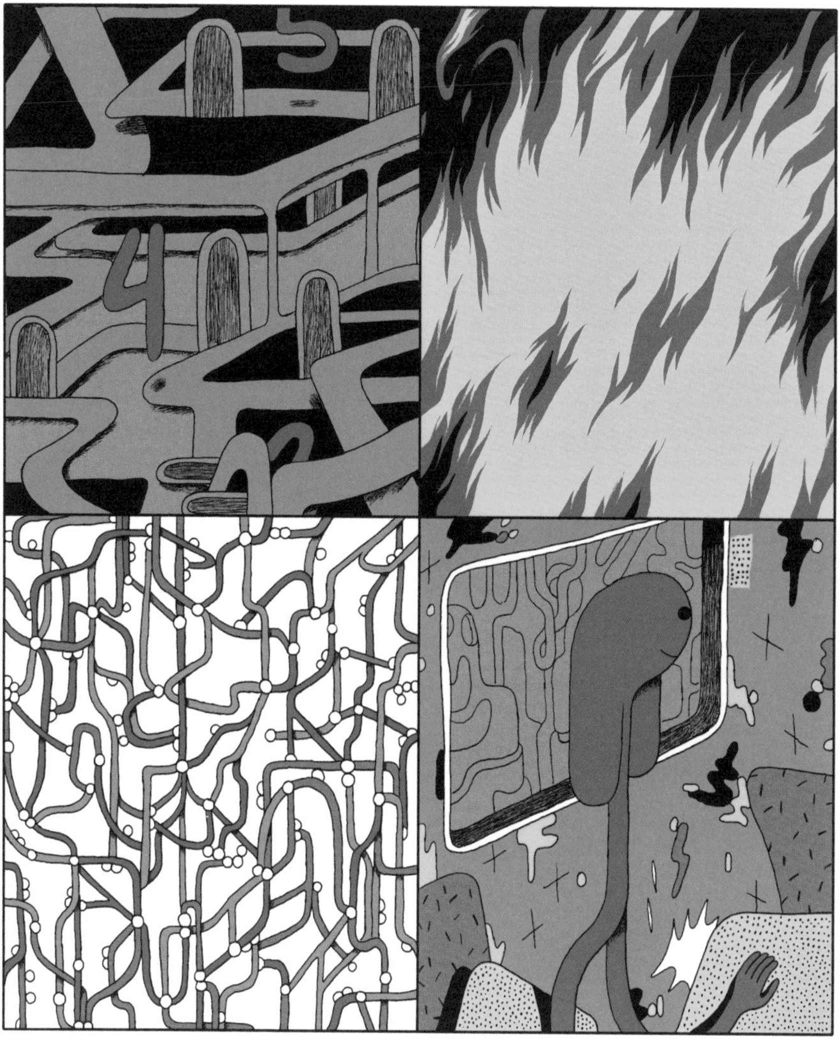

MICHAEL DEFORGE WAS BORN IN 1987
AND IS CURRENTLY ON A TREADMILL

THANK YOU: D+Q, JILLIAN, PATRICK, RYAN, ANNE,
GINETTE, SADIE, ROBIN, LAURA, S.T., MY FAMILY

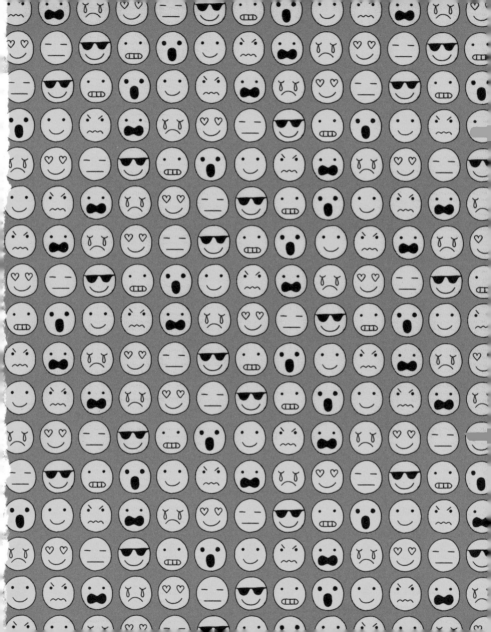

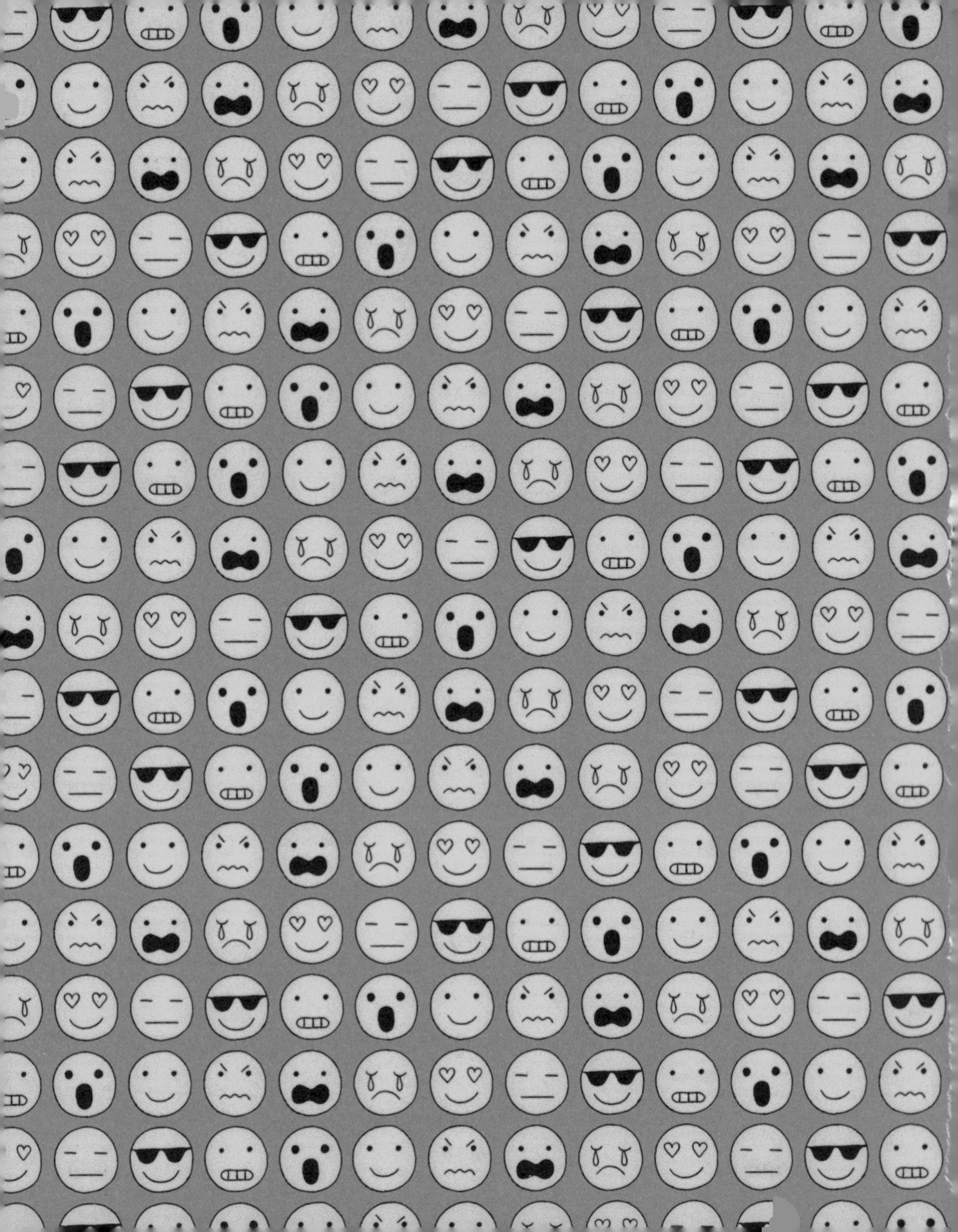